IN THE
SHADOW
OF
SALEM

IN THE SHADOW

OF

SALEM

THE ANDOVER WITCH HUNT

OF

1692

RICHARD HITE

WESTHOLME
Yardley

First Westholme paperback 2024

© 2018 Richard Hite
Maps by Paul Dangel
Maps © 2018 Westholme Publishing

The Fell typefaces used for display are digitally reproduced by Igino Marini.
www.iginomarini.com

Westholme Publishing, LLC
904 Edgewood Road
Yardley, Pennsylvania 19067
Visit our Web site at www.westholmepublishing.com

ISBN: 978-1-59416-437-8
Also available as an eBook.

Printed in the United States of America.

CONTENTS

List of Maps   *vii*

Introduction   *ix*

1. The Evil Hand is Upon Them   1

2. A Cruel Day in April   15

3. A Shadow Over Andover   34

4. Prelude to Witchcraft   45

5. Rumors and Nightmares   67

6. The Andover Witch Hunt   83

7. Look with an Evil Eye   99

8. The Touch Test   116

9. The Tribulations of Job (and Moses)   127

10. The Resistance Grows   148

11. The Trials Resume   171

12. Aftermath   178

Appendix A. Accused Witches   *199*

Appendix B. Accusers and Afflicted   *214*

Appendix C. Other Significant Personages   *220*

Appendix D. The Resisters and Their Families   *222*

Appendix E. Defenders Who Acted to Make Amends   *239*

Appendix F. Suspects with No Kin or Local Supporters   *246*

Notes   *253*

Bibliography   *266*

Acknowledgments   *271*

Index   *273*

List of Maps

First Map of New England, 1677   *xii–xiii*

Essex County, Massachusetts, c. 1692   27

Andover, Massachusetts, during the Witch Hunt   38–39

Andover Village Center in 1692   41

INTRODUCTION

FOR YEARS, historians studying the Salem, Massachusetts, witchcraft trials have described Essex County, Massachusetts, as a powder keg in 1692, the year the trials took place. It is true that a variety of issues, at home and abroad, adversely affected the British population of the entire region at that time. The colony had labored without a real centralized government since the 1689 overthrow of Edmund Andros, royal governor of the short-lived Dominion of New England—a revolt that followed in the wake of the deposition of England's reigning monarch, the Catholic king James II. Though the vast majority of the colony's residents rejoiced at Andros's ouster, they were still without a charter or any sort of governing entity recognized by the British Crown. This created difficulties in settling town boundary disputes, conflicts over ministers, and numerous other issues that had tended to arise in all of the New England colonies throughout the seventeenth century.

Compounding the lack of an "official" government was that once again, beginning in 1689, northern New England settlers had fallen victim to attacks by the some of the tribes of the Wabanaki Confederacy (primarily the Abenakis). In the years prior to the witchcraft trials, the fighting in this war was confined primarily to the frontier areas of modern-day Maine and New Hampshire. Nonetheless, the Wabanaki raids terrified the residents of Essex County, most of whom remembered all too well the devastation of King Philip's War that had ended barely ten years earlier. The entire Massachusetts Bay colony theoretically faced the danger, but Essex County's location, closer to the northern frontier and nearer to the French-controlled areas of Canada than the rest of the colony, placed it more directly in harm's way than the areas south of Boston. Although King Philip's War remains, to this day, the most devastating war per capita in American history, the fighting that broke out in 1689 may have frightened New Englanders even more initially because of the still-raw memories of the earlier war and also because, unlike King Philip's War, the later conflict was a carryover of warfare in Europe. The New Englanders had reason to fear not only Indians, but also French invaders from Canada, the latter of which were likely to supply the Wabanakis even if they did not participate directly in raids on English settlements. Historian Mary Beth Norton expertly illustrates the connections between the witch trials and the Indian wars.[1] The white residents of northern New England, primarily children and grandchildren of the so-called "Great Migration" British immigrants who had arrived in the Bay colony between 1620 and the early 1640s, generally associated all Native Americans with Satan, since the latter were not Christians. The French residents of Canada, primarily Catholic, were hated and feared by the Puritans for related reasons—they were the "wrong kind" of Christians. It is not surprising that the threat of violence from both groups helped prompt these English colonists to fear that the devil was working to eradicate their "city upon a hill" established two generations earlier.

The lack of an official governing body and the threat of attack by the Wabanakis and French cast dark shadows over the lives of all of Essex County's residents in 1692. The county consisted of eighteen separate towns,[2] each of which faced problems unique to its own population, church (and/or minister), boundaries, proximity (or lack thereof) to the ocean, distance from the frontier areas, or relations with neighboring towns, just to name a few. For that reason, perhaps it is more appropriate to refer to Essex County in 1692 as a cluster of eighteen separate powder kegs—each one needing only the right spark, or combination of sparks, to set it off. Historians know very well the events that kindled the flames in Salem Village—the fits experienced by the daughter (Betty Parris) and niece (Abigail Williams) of the community's pastor, Samuel Parris, in January and February 1692, and the diagnosis put forth by the village's doctor, William Griggs, that "the evil hand is upon them."

Once the witchcraft accusations began in Salem Village, the conflagration sent sparks flying all over Essex County. Before the end of the year 1692, fourteen of the seventeen remaining towns in the county saw at least one resident accused of witchcraft. Altogether, 156 people were formally charged with witchcraft in Massachusetts Bay in 1692, all but eighteen of whom resided in Essex County. Eleven of the accused nonresidents lived in towns that bordered the county. One can look to the situation in Essex County itself and external events that affected the county to answer the question of why the accusations occurred at all and why they happened when they did.

To that end, numerous historians have thoroughly examined Salem Village (modern-day Danvers), where the accusations of witchcraft began in February 1692. In *Salem Possessed: The Social Origins of Witchcraft* (1974) Paul Boyer and Stephen Nissenbaum examine in great detail how the village split into two separate factions prior to

Overleaf: Published in 1677 as part of William Hubbard's narrative of King Philip's War, the first map to be printed in the British Colonies shows Massachusetts and the surrounding region. The map is oriented with west at the top, and contains a wealth of information about early New England. Above (to the west of) Cape Cod, Brantry (Braintree), Dorchester, Roxbury, Cambridge, and Charlestown (C. Town) surround Boston on a peninsula. Moving to the right (north) into Essex County are the towns of Lyn (Lynn), Marblehead, Sale (Salem), Ipswich, Rowly (Rowley), Newbury, and across the Merimack (Merrimack) River, Salisbury. Moving west (upwards) along the Merrimack, is the town of Haveril (Haverhill), and across the river is Boxford and Andover—unnamed, but indicated by the number 35. Salem Village, modern Danvers, is the unnumbered community to the left of Boxford. Billerica is just above, to the west. Further west, at the top of the map, is Deerfield, a town that would be attacked by a combined French and American Indian force during Queen Anne's War in 1704. The English settlements were, naturally, almost all along rivers and bodies of water, and it is worth noting on this map their extent and juxtaposition to American Indian polities, such as the Pequid (Pequot), Naraganset (Narragansett), and Nipmuk (Nipmuc), in the forty-five years from the first Puritan landfall in Plymouth in 1620. (*Norman B. Leventhal Map Center, Boston Public Library*)

Newhaven

Gilford

Mattabesick

Hartford Winsor

16

14

Northamton

13 To

12 Springfield

15 Hadly

Sey-brook

Newlondon

Pequid Country

9 Sqabaog

Niomuk

wajuset Hill

Stoniton

17

Naraganset

31 Malborough

Lancaster
21

Sudbury

23 Groton

19

8

Water-town

33 Concord

Chen

13.

Medfield
29

25

Dedy

Cambridge 39

Bill

Woburn

Providenc

Roxbury

Town

Mount-hop

Seaconk

Dorchester

Brintry

lyn

RHODE
ISLAND

Newport

Sale

Weymoth

Pocasset. 6

Hingom

Taueon

Plimouth

Scituat Hull

4

3

Sandwi

Martins
Vineyard

Yarmoth

Cape Cod

Nantuket

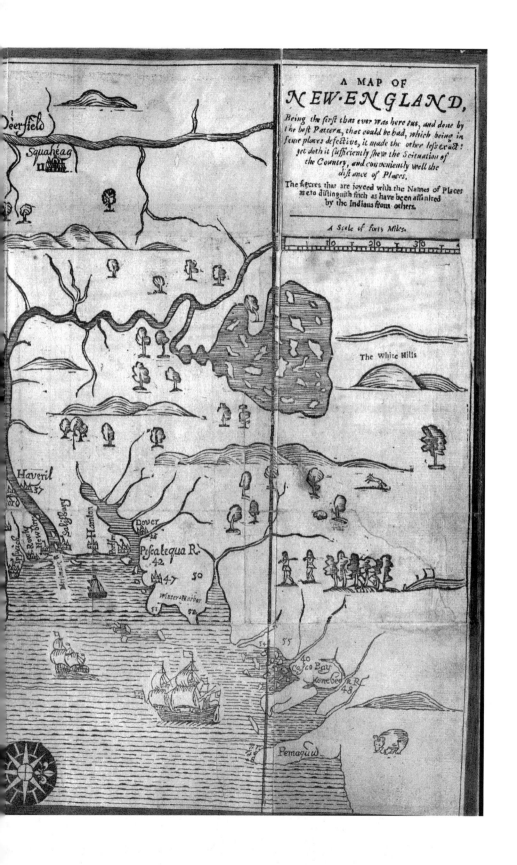

Deerfield

Squaheag

A MAP OF
NEW·ENGLAND,

Being the first that ever was here cut, and done by
the best Pattern, that could be had, which being in
some places defective, it made the other less exact:
yet doth it sufficiently shew the Scituation of
the Country, and conveniently well the
distance of Places.

The figures that are joyned with the Names of Places
are to distinguish such as have been assalted
by the Indians from others.

A Scale of forty Miles.

The White Hills

Haveril
37

Rowly Salisbury Hamton Dover
Newbery Boston Piscatequa R.
42
47 50
Winter Harbor
51 52

54 55

40
Casco Bay
Kenebeck R.
48

Pemaquid

the trials, one opposing the village's minister Samuel Parris and the other supporting him. According to the authors, these two factions generally broke down along geographic lines, with those in the eastern part of the village (the section closest to the town of Salem) more likely to oppose Parris and those in the western half (the more isolated area, more distant from the town) more likely to support him. Some in the eastern part of the village continued to attend church in the larger town of Salem and, according to Boyer and Nissenbaum, resented having to contribute to the support of the village minister. Parris's own personality did not help matters. In 1689, soon after accepting the position of pastor, he insisted that the parsonage and the two acres of land associated with it be deeded to him by the village. Such an arrangement so soon after a minister's arrival was almost unheard-of in colonial New England. Ministers did not necessarily remain in a single parish throughout their careers (although there were those that did), but for a parish's minister to own a parsonage outright that quickly was far from the norm. Nonetheless, the elected village committee accepted this arrangement, probably feeling the need to resolve the situation as quickly as possible. In the next few years, however, some in the village grew to resent Parris's demands, and the minister never hesitated to assert his right to whatever he felt he was entitled to. A frequent theme in his sermons was the betrayal of Jesus Christ by his disciple Judas Iscariot. While Parris never directly compared himself to Jesus and those who opposed him to Judas, the message would not have been lost on those who heard the sermons. The tensions between the two groups grew, and when the village doctor diagnosed the afflictions suffered by Parris's daughter and niece as witchcraft, suspicion eventually fell on some of the village's residents who had opposed the minister. Parris enjoyed the almost unqualified support of one of the two most powerful families in the village—the Putnams—and by the same token, he faced unified opposition from the other of those two families—the Porters. Both of these families held longstanding alliances with others in the village, and as the accusations mounted a clear pattern emerged. Those accused of witchcraft tended to be more closely aligned with the Porters and opposed to the minister, while the accusers were most often members of the

Putnam family itself or a family allied with the Putnams in their support of Parris. Ultimately, in 1692, twenty-six residents of Salem Village found themselves jailed on witchcraft charges.[3]

Not surprisingly, the accusations that began in Salem Village eventually spread over the entire region, They initially spilled over into the town of Salem, which saw twelve of its own citizens charged with malefic witchcraft.[4] Salem Village was not officially a separate town from the town of Salem in 1692 (even though many of its residents wished to be), a source of much of the tension within the village. Although thirteen of the other sixteen towns in Essex County had at least one accused witch in 1692, most of them did not experience the devastating effects on their entire populations that Salem Village did. All of the towns suffered from the lack of a legitimate central government and the threat of Indian raids. Salem Village was by no means the only community that labored with internal divisions over ministers and other issues. Despite all that, however, only one other town in Essex County experienced an explosion of witchcraft accusations on the level of Salem Village and the town of Salem in 1692. That town was Andover—located northwest of Salem Village.

The Andover witch hunt came about due to many contributing factors. Town resident Joseph Ballard's wife Elizabeth was gravely ill that summer. Prompted by others, he extended an invitation to the afflicted girls of Salem Village, hoping they could determine if witchcraft lay at the root of her illness. This incident stands out in existing publications as the single initiator of the witch hunt in Andover, but it was really only one step in the process. Far more so than in Salem Village, sparks that led to the explosion of accusations in Andover stemmed back to people who were themselves accused. Samuel Wardwell, who died on the gallows, put the idea of witchcraft into the head of Joseph Ballard's brother John when he expressed his concern that he was under suspicion—a prophecy that turned out to be self-fulfilling. The frail Ann Foster told of 305 witches in the region conspiring to establish the kingdom of Satan, thereby giving the witch hunters evidence that they had only identified 20 percent of the devil's disciples in the region by mid-July. Foster's granddaughter, young Mary Lacey, steered the accusations even more toward Andover by declaring its own Martha Carrier the designated "Queen in Hell." The befuddled young Elizabeth Johnson displayed her own "weapons" of affliction, showing off some of her poppets (thought to be somewhat like voodoo dolls) in the courtroom. Sarah Hooper Wardwell horrified the magistrates and others by admitting to squeezing her own infant daughter in an effort to bring physical harm to a supposed victim, Martha Sprague. For a time, the atmosphere in Andover reached the stage where confessing one's guilt seemed a reasonable strategy for avoiding the hangman's noose. Before the accusations ended, no fewer than forty-five of Andover's residents were jailed for witchcraft. Three of those were hanged and one died in prison while under a sentence of death. Andover stood alone among the other towns of Essex County in falling victim to widespread witchcraft accusations, exceeding in number those in Salem Village and Salem Town combined.

Despite this, several enlightening books on the 1692 trials mention Andover only in passing. The first book-length treatment of the trials, Charles W. Upham's 1867 work *Salem Witchcraft*, mentions Andover only once in more than six hundred pages.[5] A much later work, Marion L. Starkey's *The Devil in Massachusetts: A Modern Enquiry into the Salem Witch Trials* (1949), gives Andover more attention but oversimplifies the situation. She correctly notes that Andover resident Joseph Ballard touched off that town's spate of accusations by bringing two of the afflicted girls in to determine whether or not witchcraft was causing his wife's illness and if so, who was responsible.[6]

Some later books dedicate a few pages to the accusations in Andover, but the authors neglect to critically analyze the situation in the town. Mary Beth Norton's *In the Devil's Snare* correctly states that the vast majority of those accused in Andover confessed to dealing in the black arts, but she attributes that fact to the assumption that residents of the town (which was an autonomous community, unlike Salem Village) tended to surrender to majority opinions when pressed to do so. Her implication is that Andover was a more peaceful community, conforming to the seventeenth-century New England ideal and solving its conflicts internally.[7] Norton may be giving too much credence to the work of Enders A. Robinson, whose *Salem Witchcraft and*

Hawthorne's House of the Seven Gables (1992) is, to this point, the only book about the witch trials that focuses primarily on Andover. Robinson attributed the large number of confessions emanating from Andover to the manipulative skills of Thomas Barnard, one of the town's two ministers. Barnard, Robinson contended, convinced his parishioners that confession was the key to turning from sin and the devil to redemption and salvation. This minister, by Robinson's account, achieved this through sermons as well as individual conversations with accused witches.[8]

The reality is that these suppositions about Barnard are a drastic leap of faith. No sermon book of his is known to survive. The reasons for the large number of confessions in Andover merit more detailed study and no single factor is likely to explain all of them. Robinson's work, as its title implies, focuses heavily on the influence of Andover's witchcraft accusations on Nathaniel Hawthorne's *House of the Seven Gables*. It is true that Samuel Wardwell, one of the Andover residents hanged for witchcraft, is assumed to be the inspiration for Hawthorne's character Matthew Maule, who met a similar fate in the novel. When reading Robinson's book, it is not always easy to tell when he is citing a documented historic fact or an incident in Hawthorne's work of fiction. Even if the fictional Matthew Maule is based on Samuel Wardwell (and he probably is), one cannot assume that the fictitional character is a perfectly accurate re-creation of the convicted wizard who met his end on the gallows in 1692.

Norton also appears to overstate the role of confessors in identifying new suspects in Andover. It is true that the suspects from Andover who admitted their guilt did implicate others in their depositions—just as earlier confessors had done. But with rare exceptions, those who had confessed provided evidence only against other suspects who had already been arrested. Initial accusations that led to arrests were, as they had been in Salem Village and other communities, initiated by those claiming affliction by witches. It is true that some suspects were not interrogated until after they had been named in acknowledgments of guilt by others—but that did not mean the former were not already in jail. Sometimes confessors implicated others who were then questioned later that same day—hardly enough time for them to have been arrested based solely on testimony given just a few hours earlier. Again, Norton may be giving too much credence to Robinson's work. Robinson correctly indicates that the testimony of confessors from Andover helped to convict some of the accused witches hanged on August 19, 1692 (though only one of those hanged that day—Martha Carrier—was actually from Andover).[9] None of the initial accusations against those executed that day had come from confessors, however, and that pattern continued for the most part.

The witchcraft outbreak did begin in Salem Village, and it is unlikely that the flood of accusations in Andover would have happened without the earlier events in the neighboring village. For that reason, the events in Andover can only be understood by examining the initial accusations and confessions in the village and town of Salem.

CHAPTER ONE

The
Evil Hand
is Upon Them

Witchcraft accusations were not new in colonial New England, having occurred sporadically since the late 1630s, primarily in the colonies of Massachusetts Bay and Connecticut. Perhaps the most detailed account of the accusations prior to 1692 is historian John P. Demos's *Entertaining Satan: Witchcraft and the Culture of Early New England* (1982).[1] Demos provides a comprehensive list of the cases that preceded the Salem trials and analyzes a select few in great detail. A pattern emerges—someone (or a small group of people) in a community would fall ill or meet with some other misfortune and it would be attributed to witchcraft. This would be followed by an accusation against another individual or small group that may or may not have led to trials, convictions, and executions. In cases of acquittal of witchcraft suspects (or failure to bring them to trial), the accused and/or his or her family might file a slander suit against the accuser(s). Those accused, in most cases, were people who, for varying reasons, were regarded as disreputable in their home communities.

Prior to 1692, the largest single outbreak in New England occurred in Hartford, Connecticut, and the neighboring towns of Wethersfield and Farmington in 1662 and 1663. The accusations in the Hartford area originated with afflictions suffered by Ann Cole, a young single woman who lived in the home of her father, John Cole, and who accused other residents of afflicting her. The situation was exacerbated by an eight-year-old girl named Elizabeth Kelly, who was ill at the time (she eventually died) and who accused others of causing her illness by witchcraft. Ultimately in the Hartford area, eleven formal complaints were filed against alleged witches in 1662 and 1663. These resulted in nine formal indictments, eight trials (James Wakely, one of those indicted, fled the area), four convictions, and three or four executions.[2] Prior to 1692, this was the only real "outbreak" of witchcraft accusations in colonial New England. The other cases usually involved isolated individuals or, at most, two or three accusations (often limited to a single family if more than one person was accused).

When Dr. Griggs declared that "the evil hand is upon them" in reference to the afflictions suffered by Betty Parris and Abigail Williams, there was no reason to think that his diagnosis would lead to anything more than a single accusation (or perhaps two or three) against people in Salem Village who were already, for whatever reason, held in contempt by many in the community. Even though the number of afflicted girls increased—initially expanding to include Elizabeth Hubbard (a teenage relative of Dr. Griggs's wife who lived in their home as a servant) and Ann Putnam, the oldest daughter of Rev. Parris's most powerful supporter, Thomas Putnam—only three people were named in the first indictments, issued February 29, 1692. Two of the three initial suspects, Sarah (Solart) Good and Sarah (Warren) (Prince) Osborne, fit the pattern of those accused of witchcraft in earlier decades in New England. Good, born in neighboring Wenham as the daughter of a wealthy innkeeper, had fallen on hard times as an adult and had no fixed residence in Salem Village. She, her husband William, and daughter Dorothy were beggars in the community and Sarah had a reputation for hostility, even toward those who helped her. Osborne, a once-respected widow, had scandalized herself by marrying a much younger male servant whose indenture she had purchased and also by becoming involved in a dispute over land with her sons by her first husband. The third initial suspect was Tituba, a Native American (not an African American as she is often depicted), who was a slave of Samuel Parris. The fact that she was a slave is undoubtedly the reason she is most often depicted as African, even though documents from the witchcraft examinations specifically refer to her as an Indian. Unlike Good and Osborne, Tituba did not fit the stereotype of the New England witch from previous decades. Slaves had not previously been targets of accusations. In this instance, the fact that she was an Indian may have been the key factor—the threat of hostile actions by the Wabanaki Confederacy had driven the fear of American Indians among the white population of Essex County to unprecedented levels.

Four afflicted girls, three accused witches—the witchcraft "crisis" in Salem Village could easily have gone no further than this. The three accused may or may not have been convicted and executed. If not convicted, Good and Osborne might have sued for slander—a slave would not have been afforded that privilege. Perhaps a master could have sued on behalf of a slave—but in this case, the master, Samuel Parris, stood firmly on the side of those who accused Tituba. The day after their arrest, the three accused women were brought before two judges from the town of Salem, John Hathorne and Jonathan Corwin, in Ingersoll's Tavern in Salem Village. Good and Osborne both maintained their innocence, although Good accused Osborne in an obvious effort to shift the blame away from herself. Tituba, however, confessed to the crime—and the things she described in her confession ensured that the accusations would not end with her and the other two suspects. This is the first example of one of the most frustrating facets of the entire tragedy of 1692. A careful examination of the evidence reveals that the witch hunt appeared on the verge of running its course on several occasions, only to have the flames fanned anew.

When the magistrates interrogated Tituba on March 1, she initially denied any role in hurting the afflicted children. Under pressure from Judge Hathorne, notorious for his leading questions that implied a presumption of guilt, she quickly stated that "the devil came to me and bid me serve him." Even after admitting that, she did not initially confess to inflicting harm upon the children, but as Hathorne persisted, she eventually conceded that when threatened by others who *were* hurting them, she had followed suit. Most important, though, Tituba not only implicated Good and Osborne for afflicting the girls, but she also stated that two other women she did not know had taken part and that a man she did not recognize—a tall man of Boston— also participated and forced her to hurt the children. This testimony made it clear to the magistrates and all others concerned that they had not yet arrested all of the witches who were afflicting the minister's family members and the other two young victims. There was no question in the minds of the magistrates that Tituba had to be questioned further. The next day, Hathorne and Corwin subjected the slave to another round of interrogation. She repeated the story of the four women (including Good and Osborne) and the man, but this time, she added the further statement that she had been pressured to sign a book and that she had seen a total of nine signatures and marks already there. Again, she could name none other than her two fellow suspects, but she stated that the man told her some of those who signed were from this town (Salem Village) and some were from Boston.

The fact that Tituba went beyond confessing her own involvement and implicating Good and Osborne ensured that the hunt for witches would not stop with the initial three accusations. For those in Salem Village who thought that the case would end with the prosecution and conviction of those three women, Tituba's confession struck terror in their hearts. By Tituba's account, there were at least seven more practicing witches in the colony and at least some of them, aside from Sarah Good and Sarah Osborne, lived in their midst. Thirty years earlier, a confession by Rebecca Greensmith, one of those accused in Hartford, had played a role in expanding the witch hunt there.[3] Unlike Greensmith, though, Tituba did not name the other witches (except for Good and Osborne), thereby leaving others in the village to find different means of identifying them.

Given the significance of Tituba's confession, it is important to address the question of why she did it. English-born merchant Robert

Calef, who was residing in Boston at the time of the trials and opposed them, published his book *More Wonders of the Invisible World* in London in 1700 (the title was chosen deliberately to discredit Cotton Mather's work *Wonders of the Invisible World* that had defended the witchcraft proceedings). In his work, Calef reported that Tituba's master, Samuel Parris, had convinced her to confess by whipping her. This may very well be true, although Calef's account is at best secondhand (he was not in Salem Village at the time). However, if Parris did convince his slave to confess by means of physical abuse, then the question of *his* motive must be examined. Some writers on the subject have suggested that he and his most prominent supporter in the village, Thomas Putnam, formulated and led a conspiracy to use witchcraft accusations to rid the village of those who opposed Parris and wished to maintain the village's ties to the town of Salem. It is true that as the accusations continued, opponents of Parris and their family members were most often the targets of accusation—Martha Corey, Rebecca Nurse, Daniel Andrew, and George Jacobs, just to name a few. It is also true that the accusers usually came from the ranks of those who supported Parris, led by Putnam. But to assume that this was part of a plot contrived by the minister and his most prominent ally at this early stage stretches the bounds of credibility. The suggestion that Parris coerced Tituba to confess for the express purpose of bringing down these people and others does not withstand a thoughtful examination of the evidence. Tituba did not name any other alleged witches except Good and Osborne. Had Parris already planned to set in motion a process that would lead to the execution of at least some of those who opposed his ministry and intended to use Tituba to initiate the process, it seems logical that he would have given her names of people he wanted her to implicate. She did not name any other individuals.

If Parris did, in fact, convince Tituba to confess by physically abusing her, another motive seems far more likely. Those who assume that the witchcraft persecutions of 1692 spawned from a conspiracy discount a significant fact about the era—the average person in the Massachusetts Bay colony genuinely believed in witchcraft. Most formally educated people of the time shared this belief, although there were exceptions. Even Increase Mather, one of the great intellectuals of the era in New England, did not reject belief in witchcraft. His pamphlet that cast doubt on the use of spectral evidence to convict people of witchcraft played a major role in ending the trials, but not by refuting the existences of witches. Mather simply argued that more than spectral evidence (testimony that a suspect's shape had inflicted harm on an afflicted person) was needed to convict. He did not discount the idea that a specter resembling a suspect could harm another person—he merely argued that it was impossible to know that the devil could not take on the appearance of an innocent person to attack his victims. There is no reason to think that Parris did not truly believe his daughter and niece were bewitched, and that his parishioner, Thomas Putnam, believed the same about his own daughter Ann. The minister's whipping of Tituba (if it happened) was probably intended to speed up the process of bringing her and her fellow witches to justice so that the afflicted girls in the village would be cured as soon as possible. Parris may have been as shocked as anyone else when his slave claimed that there were other witches besides herself, Sarah Good, and Sarah Osborne—and just as frightened.

None of this is intended to absolve Samuel Parris of the major role he played in promoting the witchcraft accusations. Indeed, it is hard to find anyone who deserves more of the blame for setting the whole process in motion. Less than a month after Tituba's confession, Parris faced the necessity of dealing with the fact that two respected church members, Martha Corey and Rebecca Towne Nurse, had been jailed on suspicion of practicing malefic witchcraft. On March 27, he preached a sermon in which he declared, "There are devils as well as saints . . . here in Christ's little Church."[4] His thematic text from the Bible for the sermon was the quote from Jesus found in the Gospel of John 6:70—"Have I not chosen you twelve, and one of you is a devil?"[5] Parris knew that some members of his congregation had doubts about the validity of the charges against Corey and Nurse who, unlike Good and Osborne, were far from fitting the pattern of accused witches in New England in that era. Parris himself believed the charges and used his pulpit in his efforts to put those doubts to rest. He never renounced his beliefs, and in fact, throughout the following spring, summer, and fall, exacerbated the fears of witchcraft in his sermons. The only thing attributed to Parris that seems doubtful is the idea that when he coerced Tituba into confessing (if he did), he already planned, along with Thomas Putnam and others, to promote the accusation, conviction, and eventual execution of people like Martha Corey and Rebecca Nurse.

The wording of Tituba's first confession, as recorded by Magistrate Jonathan Corwin (and also in less detail by Joseph Putnam, younger half-brother of Thomas), suggests that Tituba may have stumbled into a confession while attempting to exonerate herself at the expense of Good and Osborne. John Hathorne, as would become his pattern, phrased his questions in a manner that presumed guilt. The first few lines of Corwin's transcription of the examination at the hearing of March 1 bear this out (spelling modernized to facilitate understanding).

HATHORNE: Why do you hurt these children? What harm have they done to you?
TITUBA: They do no harm to me, I no hurt them at all.
HATHORNE: Why have you done it?
TITUBA: I have done nothing, I can't tell when the devil works.

Now Hathorne seizes on this statement as evidence that Tituba knows that the devil has something to do with afflicting the children.

HATHORNE: What, doth the Devil tell you he hurts them?
TITUBA: No, he tells me nothing.
HATHORNE: Do you never see something appear in some shape?
TITUBA: No, never see anything.
HATHORNE: What familiarity have you with the Devil or what is it that you converse with all? Tell the truth. Who it is that hurts them?
TITUBA: The Devil for ought I know.
HATHORNE: What appearance or how doth he appear when he hurts them, with what shape or what is he like that hurts them?

At this point, Tituba may have realized that she had given Hathorne the impression she somehow knew of the devil's workings and felt there was no way of turning back from that. After this, she first admits having been approached by the devil, possibly thinking she would not be regarded as guilty of anything if she claimed to have resisted him. Her response becomes rambling. (At this point, Corwin is varying between quoting Tituba directly and writing in third person.)

> TITUBA: Like a man, I think yesterday being in a leanto chamber I saw a thing like a man, that told me serve him and I told him no I would not do such thing. She charges Goody Osborne and Sarah Good as those that hurt the children and would have had her done it, she saith she hath seen four, two of which she knew not, she saw them last night as she was washing the room, they told me hurt the children and would have had me gone to Boston, there was 5 of the them with the man, they told me if I would not go and hurt them they would do so to me, at first I did agree with them but afterward I told them I do so no more.

In this response, Tituba shifts her stance twice—first, she admits to encountering a man (presumably the devil) who bids her to serve him, but she says at first that she refused. Then she shifts her stance again, admitting to have harmed the children under threat from the devil and others (Good, Osborne, and two other women she does not know). She may have thought that if she claimed to have been forced to hurt the children by others, she would not be held responsible. Ultimately, it is difficult to know her thoughts, especially considering she was being grilled by Hathorne and listening to the screams of the wailing girls.

Hathorne now sees an opening and continues his leading questions:

> HATHORNE: Would they have had you hurt the children the last night?
> TITUBA: Yes, but I was sorry and I said I would do so no more, but told I would fear God.
> HATHORNE: But why did you not do so before?

Tituba may now realize that acknowledging hurting the children only under pressure from others may not be an adequate defense.

TITUBA: Why they tell me I had done so before and therefore I must go on, these were the four women and the man, but she knew none but Osborne and Good only, the others were of Boston.

HATHORNE: At first being with them, what then appeared to you what was it like that got you to do it?

TITUBA: One like a man just as I was going to sleep came to me, this was when the children were first hurt, he said he would kill the children and she would never be well, and he said if I would not serve him, he would do so to me.

Tituba may have felt she had said too much and could not talk her way out of the situation. She began describing such incidents as riding on a pole with Good and Osborne and seeing numerous animals (familiars) associated with the other witches such as birds and wolves. Already, she had all but ensured that this outbreak of witchcraft accusations would not end with herself, Good, and Osborne. Instead, it was already on course to, at the very least, approach the numbers from the Hartford persecutions thirty years earlier.

It is noteworthy that at this stage, Tituba identified those she did not know as being from Boston. She did *not* say that there were others from Salem Village involved (aside from Good and Osborne). That being the case, it appears that if she did confess as a result of abuse by her master Samuel Parris, the latter's motivation was not (at least at that point) to eliminate his opponents in the village by having them charged with witchcraft. It was in her second examination the next day that Tituba talked of seeing nine signatures or marks in the book the man brought her to sign. Only then did she say that some of the signers were from Salem Village. Parris would not have had the opportunity to whip her and tell her what to say during the night that passed between her first and second examinations because she was in jail.

Another important fact that casts doubt on the idea of any sort of conspiracy at this early stage is the identity of the other man who took notes on Tituba's testimony and the examinations of the other two accused witches. Joseph Putnam, the younger half-brother of Thomas Putnam, was not on good terms with Thomas—they had disputed the terms of the will of their father, Thomas Putnam, Sr. who had died six years earlier.[6] Joseph, who unlike the rest of the Putnams, opposed the minister (undoubtedly influenced by the fact that he had married into the Porter family who led the opposition), later became an outspoken opponent of the witch trials when they expanded to include others in the village and the town who also opposed Parris. Nothing Joseph wrote in his notes of these first examinations, though, gives any hint that he doubted the guilt of the first three women accused of witchcraft. The fact that he opposed the trials later is not evidence that he did not believe in witchcraft at all. If he was typical of his time, he probably did.

The fact that the average person in seventeenth-century Massachusetts Bay did believe in witchcraft is examined in Chadwick Hansen's *Witchcraft at Salem* (1969). Hansen also gives detailed attention to the effects of that belief: "We must bear in mind that in a society that believes in witchcraft, it works. If you believe in witchcraft and you discover that someone has been melting your wax image over a slow fire or muttering charms over your nail parings, the probability is that you will get extremely sick. To be sure, your symptoms will be psychosomatic rather than organic."[7] The symptoms would be the same even if the alleged perpetrator was not actually melting the waxen image as long as the "victim" genuinely believed he or she was doing it. Hansen's analysis does not explain what caused the initial fits experienced by the children in Samuel Parris's household. While it is possible that they actually were, at least initially, suffering from some type of physical illness, it is more likely that they were merely reacting to the general tension in the Parris household that was created by the sudden uncertainty of the minister's situation in the village.[8] Once witchcraft was diagnosed as the cause, however, their terror would only have exacerbated their symptoms. It is not surprising that as word of the diagnosis spread through the community, the fear that spread along with it would have caused others to have similar reactions. The teenage Elizabeth Hubbard, who lived in Dr. Griggs's household, was a natural candidate, having heard of the diagnosis firsthand. Twelve-year-old Ann Putnam, as the daughter of the minister's leading supporter and a contemporary (and likely playmate) of his niece Abigail

Williams, would have also learned quickly of the alleged bewitchment. Stricken by fear, it is not at all surprising that she began to experience similar symptoms. The terror would only have spread further with Tituba's revelation of more witches in the community, and, again, the next people to begin experiencing bewitchment after that incident were intimately acquainted with some of those already suffering. Ann Putnam's mother, Ann (Carr) Putnam, referred to in documents as Ann Putnam, Sr., began falling victim to fits soon after Tituba's testimony and the Putnams' servant Mercy Lewis (an orphan whose parents had died in the Indian fighting in Maine) followed suit. The affliction soon spread beyond the Putnams' immediate household. Seventeen-year-old Mary Walcott, a step-cousin of Ann Putnam and her siblings (Thomas Putnam's sister Deliverance had married Mary's father, Jonathan Walcott, after the death of Walcott's first wife), fell victim by late March as well. Mary might also have been influenced by the fact that the Walcotts were some of the minister's nearest neighbors, and she would have seen the symptoms experienced by the girls in his household. In all of these cases and the others, Hansen's view that their symptoms were psychosomatic reactions to a genuine belief in witchcraft seems more viable than the idea that they were, from the very beginning, part of a concocted scheme to bring down members of a rival faction.

The idea that terror-induced fits, rather than a plot by the minister's opponents, initiated the witch hunt in Salem Village begs the question of why the accusations broke down along factional lines. That is not a hard question to answer. In any society, in the past as well as the present, it is all too easy for people to believe the worst of others who oppose them in some way. Conversations about members of rival factions, voicing all kinds of suspicions, would have occurred in households in seventeenth-century New England just as they do today—whether it involved personal acquaintances or political leaders known only by reputation. The first two afflicted girls happened to reside in the household of the minister himself. Parris and his family would, of course, have interacted more with his supporters than his opponents, so it is only natural that a fear-induced psychosis that originated in his home would spread more readily to the homes of his allies. In a society that believes in witchcraft and also believes anyone could make a pact with the devil, families that experienced what they perceived as demonic attacks would naturally first suspect those they were already in conflict with for other reasons. Martha Corey, her husband Giles, Rebecca Nurse, and her husband Francis had cast their lot with the opposition to the village's minister. That made them prime candidates for suspicion. It is easy to imagine a terrified parent, standing over a daughter who was writhing on a bed and screaming for some unseen specter to leave her alone, pleading with the child to say who it was that tormented her. If the child could not name anyone, it is also easy to envision the parent thinking back over any disagreements he or she may have had with other villagers, remembering someone, and thinking "Is it her?" or "Is it him?" Samuel and Elizabeth Parris and Thomas and Ann Putnam spent countless days and nights witnessing the girls in their households in the throes of such fits, whether it was their own daughters or otherwise. Any of them might have thought of Martha Corey or Rebecca Nurse, women generally highly regarded in the community, but whose families identified with an opposing faction in village politics (Rebecca's husband Francis, after all, was a member of the anti-Parris village committee). An afflicted child hearing her mother or father ask, "Is it Goody Corey?" or "Is it Goody Nurse?" could easily have seen a previously unidentifiable face morph into a familiar one. The power of suggestion is high for those in the grip of fear for their lives.

There were, of course, cases in which accusers named people whom they may have genuinely disliked or feared for legitimate reasons. Two young women who claimed bewitchment lived in households headed by men who did not take their afflictions seriously. Both of these women were servants—Mary Warren in the home of John Procter and Sarah Churchill (or Churchwell) in the house of George Jacobs. Procter and Jacobs reacted far differently to the hysterical symptoms of their servants than the Putnams and Parrises did to the symptoms of their daughters and other women in their households. These two masters both assumed their servants were playacting in order to escape their household chores. In Procter's case, in particular, he may have actually stopped his servant's fits by standing over her with a whip and forcing her to work at the spinning wheel. Neither man called in a doctor to examine the young woman in his household or asked who was hurting her. In a sense, the reactions of Procter and Jacobs are not altogether surprising—these women were their servants, not their family. It is true that Thomas Putnam took the fits of his own servant, Mercy Lewis, seriously, but his situation was different—his daughter and wife were also afflicted. By dismissing their maids' fits as playacting, rather than encouraging them to name those that were tormenting them, Procter and Jacobs ultimately turned the youthful "victims" against themselves. The two men ultimately paid for their reactions with their lives as both were among the group of five hanged on August 19, 1692. Procter's wife, Elizabeth (Bassett) Procter, was also tried and convicted, but was spared due to the fact that she was pregnant. The afflicted servants, Warren and Churchill, both accused their own masters of afflicting them and in the process, fell into the same pattern of accusations of the other girls from the Parris and Putnam families who started the whole process and received a crucial boost from Tituba's confession.

Tituba herself vanished from the pages of history after the trials were over. She was not executed—anyone who confessed and never recanted the confession was not put to death in 1692 though, contrary to popular belief, that was not the intention of the magistrates. Confessors in earlier trials, including the aforementioned Rebecca Greensmith of Hartford, had been hanged. Tituba, however, simply remained in jail throughout the trials and was sold to another owner afterward in order to pay her jail fees. Her confession was her single most significant action during the whole process—contrary to legend, she did not spark the girls' fear by teaching them ways of fortune telling that she had learned in her native West Indies.[9] She did incite further accusations because she indicated that she had seen more witches than just the two who were initially accused along with her. Tituba's statements to the magistrates ensured that the witchcraft crisis of 1692 would not end with the first three accused. At the very least, this outbreak would compare with events in Hartford thirty years earlier. Tituba may have been violently coerced into confessing by her master, Samuel Parris. It is equally possible that she simply yielded under the intense questioning by Magistrate John Hathorne. She might have stumbled into a confession while attempting to exonerate herself. Regardless of the reason for her actions, she played a major role in launching the accusations in the Salem witch trials.

Chapter Two

A
Cruel Day
in April

APRIL 19 IS BEST KNOWN in the United States as the anniversary of the battle of Lexington and Concord, which launched the War of American Independence in 1775. In Massachusetts, it is observed as a state holiday—Patriots' Day. It is doubtful, though, that many Americans—even residents of Massachusetts—know that not one, but three major events in the witch trials occurred on that same date in 1692.[1] On that day, three of the most significant witchcraft suspects of the entire year came to court for their first examinations—Bridget Bishop of the town of Salem, Abigail Hobbs of the neighboring town of Topsfield, and Mary Warren of Salem Village. Of the three, Bishop is arguably the most famous (though Warren is also well known due to the significance of her character in Arthur Miller's play *The Crucible*). Though not one of the first accused, Bishop was the first one to be convicted and hanged for witchcraft in 1692—unquestionably because, of all the suspects, the evidence against her was the strongest. As previously noted, the average person in Massachusetts Bay in the

1690s believed in witchcraft—a nonbeliever would have been quite an anomaly at the time. In a society that believes in witchcraft, it would be naïve to think that no one actually practiced it. Chadwick Hansen, whose aforementioned work on the trials stresses that intense belief in witchcraft can cause those who believe themselves under a spell to suffer very real symptoms of bewitchment, argues that Bishop was a practicing witch—one who performed her craft with the intent of bringing harm to others.[2]

Bridget Bishop's story indicates that her neighbors believed she was capable of practicing witchcraft. She had been accused of witchcraft once before—in 1680, while she was married to an earlier husband, Thomas Oliver (she had married Edward Bishop after Oliver's death some years earlier). Much of the testimony against her resembled statements made against others—that is, statements by the afflicted girls and others who complained of her that her "shape" or "apparition" appeared to them and pinched them or harmed them in other ways. Some of the evidence against Bishop differed from that against other suspects, however; John Bly and William Bly (father and son), who had been employed by her in the 1680s to take down a wall in her cellar, testified to having found "poppits" made of rags and bristles with pins in them. This evidence that Bishop used these items with the intent to inflict injury upon others made it easier to convict her earlier than others against whom the evidence was less obvious. She was the first to be brought to trial once the newly arrived governor, Sir William Phips (who reached Boston from England bearing a new charter on May 14), established a special court to try the cases—the Court of Oyer and Terminer (meaning "to hear and determine"). Bishop was hastily convicted and was hanged in the town of Salem on June 10—the first suspect to be convicted and executed. Her significance can hardly be understated. The fact that evidence against her hinted that she did, in fact, practice malefic witchcraft, gave credence to the proceedings of the newly formed court and inflamed the fervor of those who were most strongly pushing the accusations.

It is no accident that Bridget Bishop is the accused witch who is depicted in the theatrical production in twenty-first-century Salem entitled *Cry Innocent*. Actors portray Bishop, some of the judges, and the witnesses against her at reenactments of her examination, using actual testimony from the records. Tourists from all over the world who visit Salem act as jurors. They do not decide guilt or innocence, but instead they determine whether or not evidence against Bishop is sufficient to warrant prosecution. At some of these performances, a majority decides that the evidence is indeed adequate to warrant a trial.

While the case against Bishop may have, in the eyes of some, legitimized the trials, the confession of Abigail Hobbs may have spurred the accusations to new levels. A total of ten people had been examined prior to April 19, when Bishop, Hobbs, and Warren were interrogated along with a man who had just been arrested (Giles Corey, husband of Martha). Though Hobbs is perhaps the least famous of these, her examination may ultimately have provided the next major spark to the persecutions. With the exception of Dorothy Good (a four-year-old daughter of Sarah Good), no one had confessed since Tituba seven weeks earlier. The potential was there for the accusations to wind down at that point. Mary Beth Norton points to Hobbs's confession as a major cause of what she terms an "explosion" of accusations over the seven weeks that followed—fifty-four as opposed to the ten that had been arrested on suspicion prior to the group of four that included Hobbs.[3] The nineteenth of April did, indeed, change everything.

This is not to suggest that without Abigail Hobbs's confession, she and the other three examined on April 19 would have been the last ones charged, or even among the last few. Part of the problem was that until the new governor arrived with the charter, there was no legal means to try the accused, and even after their preliminary examinations, they were just languishing in jail. Those in the forefront of the accusations in Salem Village (Samuel Parris, Thomas Putnam, Thomas's brother Edward Putnam, and the Putnams' brother-in-law Jonathan Walcott) had unquestionably gone beyond believing the girls' torments were the work of just a handful of "handmaidens of Satan" by mid-April. As already noted, the idea that these four men and a few others in the village had launched the witch hunt for the sole purpose of bring down their adversaries in local politics is dubious at best. By this point, though, it is realistic to think that the accusations leveled against people identified with the opposition to Reverend Parris—Martha Corey, Giles Corey, Rebecca Nurse, Sarah (Towne) Cloyce (Rebecca's sister), Elizabeth Procter, and John Procter[4]—motivated these men to keep pressing for more rather than concluding, after a certain point, that all of the guilty parties were in jail and to simply wait until a mechanism was in place to prosecute. Parris, with his own inflammatory sermons, contributed the most to keeping the accusations going, perhaps secretly hoping to see more of his opponents jailed. The minister, more than anyone else in the village, must have felt vindicated by the pattern the accusations were taking. He had successfully, to that point, identified his opposition with the devil.

Nonetheless, the hostile feelings between the opposing factions cannot be realistically viewed as the sole force driving the witch hunt, and the arrest of Abigail Hobbs, in and of itself, serves as evidence for that. Hobbs resided in the neighboring town of Topsfield with her father, William Hobbs, her stepmother Deliverance, and some siblings, but until about three years earlier, she and her family had lived on the Maine frontier in the Casco Bay area. The leaders of the efforts to root out witches in Salem Village had no political motive to attack the Hobbs family. Abigail Hobbs was only the second nonresident of Salem Village or the town of Salem to fall under suspicion.[5] The fact that she was arrested in the first place demonstrates that political considerations alone did not control the process. Despite her youth—she was only fourteen at the time of her arrest—this adolescent girl was exactly the kind of person who could have been expected to draw the attention of those who not only believed in witchcraft, but thought themselves to be under attack by witches. For reasons no one understood, Abigail Hobbs deliberately cultivated a reputation for witchcraft. Testimony against her by people who knew her in Topsfield revealed as much. Priscilla Chubb of Topsfield noted in her testimony that she had confronted Abigail about her "wicked carriages and disobedience to her father and mother" and that Abigail had responded by saying that she "did not care what anybody said to her for she had seen the Devil and had made a covenant or Bargain with him." The testimony of two teenage sisters, Lydia and Elizabeth Nichols, revealed that Abigail was in the habit of sleeping in the woods overnight alone. They asked her why she was not afraid and her response was that she was not afraid of anything because she had "sold herself body and soul to the old boy."[6] The elder of the two Nichols girls (Lydia) also claimed that Hobbs had threatened her with raising "all the folks thereabouts" (presumably others who had contracted with the devil) when Lydia criticized her for her rude behavior.

The possible explanations for Abigail Hobbs's claims are many. She may have been traumatized by the threat posed by the Wabanakis a few years earlier, which was the probable reason for her family's return to Topsfield (she had been born there before the move to Maine). She might have enjoyed the notoriety of making such claims. It is also possible that she was a child who was in some ways "different" and suffered abuse at the hands of her peers. Concocting a story of having made a contract with the devil might have been a means of scaring bullies away. Regardless of her reasons, stories about her outlandish claims must have spread beyond Topsfield even before the witch hunt began. The afflicted girls of Salem Village could easily have heard about her and only naturally assumed that she was one of the ones who attacked them. John Putnam, Jr., a cousin of Thomas and Edward, was among those who swore out a warrant against Abigail Hobbs. When examined by John Hathorne and Jonathan Corwin on April 19, the teenage girl shocked the entire assembly by confessing. The content of her admissions revealed things to the magistrates and others that had probably never occurred to them.

In discussing Abigail Hobbs's confession, Mary Beth Norton stresses the fact that it was crucial in linking witchcraft to the Indian war on the Maine frontier. Hobbs was explicit in noting that her first encounter with the devil had taken place three or four years earlier in Casco Bay, an area of Maine that had seen significant warfare. The fact that Hobbs claimed to have encountered the devil there also provided the first indication that he was active in recruiting potential converts not only in the Salem Village and its immediate environs, but also throughout northern New England. This, according to Norton, sparked the explosion of witchcraft accusations all over Essex County and some areas beyond, including Casco Bay where George

Burroughs (a predecessor of Samuel Parris in Salem Village who was, by that time, minister in the town of Wells, Maine) resided.[7] One eventual result was the arrest of Burroughs himself who came to be stereotyped as the ringleader of the entire witchcraft conspiracy that had, in the minds of many of the residents, fallen over northeastern Massachusetts Bay and its outlying frontier areas. Four months to the day after a disturbed adolescent's ramblings struck heightened terror into the hearts of the witch hunters, the minister met his fate on the gallows in the town of Salem.

Norton's work, however, did not highlight everything new that Abigail Hobbs introduced into the situation with her confession. The geographic expansion was crucial, of course, but Hobbs also widened the time frame. Tituba acknowledged having made a covenant only six weeks before her confession in early March, specifically the night before Abigail Williams first became ill. By contrast, Hobbs indicated that her pact with the devil had occurred three or four years previously while she was still residing with her family in Casco Bay—probably not coincidentally the amount of time that had elapsed since the outbreak of the frontier hostilities. This statement suggested that the devil had been actively seeking recruits for an attack on the colony for several years by the spring of 1692—not just a few weeks. That gave the leaders of the persecution reason to believe that there had been far more time for people to have made such pacts with Satan than originally thought. This implication could have been just as crucial in the rapid growth of accusations as the geographic expansion. There was also a third component to Hobbs's testimony—differing from that of Tituba—that took on added significance as the actual trials began in early June. After first saying without elaboration that she pinched two of the afflicted girls of Salem Village (Ann Putnam and Mercy Lewis), she restated that comment to specify that the devil had been the one who did the actual pinching in her (Hobbs's) shape. She further acknowledged that the devil did so with her consent.

This aspect of Hobbs's confession gave credibility to the single most controversial type of evidence that was allowed at the witchcraft trials that followed in the summer of 1692—spectral evidence. From the very beginning of the examinations, the afflicted had been testifying that the "apparitions" or "shapes" of those accused had been pinching them or hurting them in various other ways. Tituba, however, had said nothing in her own confession about allowing the devil to take her shape to harm anyone. By stating that she had given the devil this permission, Abigail Hobbs implied that her approval was necessary for him to appear as her when inflicting harm on others. This was precisely what those who advocated the use of spectral evidence believed—that the devil lacked the power to take the shape of an innocent person when attacking and injuring those who were afflicted. Abigail Hobbs's confession was never cited as evidence to prove this—but that does not mean that the judges of the Court of Oyer and Terminer did not take it into account when the trials began.

From April 19 until the beginning of the witchcraft trials in early June, the number of people jailed on suspicion of witchcraft more than quadrupled. To attribute that solely to the confession of Abigail Hobbs would be a drastic oversimplification, but there is no denying that her testimony took the witch hunters along new paths that they had not followed before. Hobbs's examination and that of Bridget Bishop were enough, in and of themselves, to cement the nineteenth of April as the most significant date of the witchcraft crisis since the day of Tituba's confession. But a third examination conducted that same day—that of Mary Warren—was also crucial for much different reasons.

As previously noted, Warren was a servant in the home of John and Elizabeth (Bassett) Procter. On April 8, the warrant for the arrest of Elizabeth Procter and Sarah Cloyce included instructions to George Herrick (Marshall of Essex County) to summon Mary Warren (along with Elizabeth Hubbard) to give evidence against the suspects. This is the first mention of Warren in any surviving records of the witch hunt—Hubbard was already well-established as an "afflicted" girl. Warren had apparently complained of supernatural attacks by her mistress. However, when Procter was examined on April 11 (along with her husband John Procter, for whom no arrest warrant survives), her servant was not among those who testified against her. Nor did Warren testify against John Procter that day. It is quite likely that this three-day period (a weekend) was the time frame in which John Procter scared his servant "out of her fits," so to speak, by standing over her with a whip and forcing her to labor at the spinning wheel. If that story is true, then whatever it was that had frightened the young woman into accusing Elizabeth Procter of witchcraft must have been overridden by the imminent threat of a thrashing by her master.

Poor Mary Warren, however, found herself trapped between two equally dangerous alternatives. Having failed to testify against the Procters, she found herself arrested on witchcraft charges on April 18. The other afflicted girls had turned against her when she defected from their ranks. Upon being brought before Judges Hathorne and Corwin the following day (the same day that Bishop and Hobbs were first examined), she first accused the other girls of "dissembling," meaning they were distorting the truth. This could, theoretically, have been a turning point in the witchcraft crisis—one of the afflicted girls had, from all appearances, exposed them as perpetrators of fraud. As would be expected, the other long-established victims of malefic magic fell into their usual fits, accusing Warren of tormenting them. Others (including Tituba's husband, John Indian, who had recently become a "victim" of witchcraft) joined in the chorus of accusations. Unfortunately but not surprisingly, Warren—now safe from John Procter's whip—failed to stand her ground. She first offered a brief confession to the crime of witchcraft but then fell into her own fit and began screaming of being tormented by her mistress and by Martha Corey. She quickly backpedaled in her confession, denying that she signed or put a mark in the devil's book. But the other afflicted individuals had fallen silent. Mary Warren had rejoined their ranks. She was now safe from the threat of physical punishment by John Procter, who was in jail. Her safest course of action was to cooperate with the other accusers. It may be, of course, that she believed herself tormented by witches all along and that her brief defection from the ranks of the afflicted was instigated only by the more immediate threat of a lashing from John Procter. This incident, dramatized in *The Crucible*, is one of the most historically accurate scenes in the entire play, though that is not saying much. When looking at the entire witchcraft episode, however, Warren's turnabout, though important, was not quite as significant as Abigail Hobbs's confession or Bridget Bishop's examination.

Even if Mary Warren had just held her ground and continued to denounce the other afflicted girls as frauds, the proceedings would not have ground to a halt. After all, Warren was merely a servant in the home of a resident of Salem Village. The idea that someone of her station could have discredited the testimony of the likes of Ann Putnam, the daughter of one of the village's most prominent residents, or Abigail Williams, the niece of the village minister, strains credulity. Warren's return to the ranks of the afflicted did strengthen their credibility, and it led to her exoneration of any suspicion of witchcraft. This was to resonate in Andover the following summer when some of the accused there not only confessed but also joined the ranks of the afflicted accusers. Warren herself testified against some of the Andover suspects.

Mary Warren's statement that the other afflicted girls "did but dissemble" to a degree undermines Chadwick Hansen's contention that the "victims" of witchcraft in 1692 suffered from psychosomatic trauma. Other writers, before and since Hansen, have contended that the accusers merely perpetrated fraud. One of the post-Hansen authors to make the case for playacting is Bernard Rosenthal, who argued in *Salem Story: Reading the Witch Trials of 1692* (1993) that the core group of youthful accusers deliberately falsified from the beginning and continued to fabricate throughout the proceedings. Specifically, he identified young Ann Putnam and Elizabeth Hubbard as the two most active liars, noting that each of them testified against seventeen of the twenty suspects who died by judicial hands in 1692.[8] Rosenthal also noted that the group increased in number throughout the year and that the experience of Mary Warren demonstrated to others in the group that there would be consequences for walking away from the participants once one joined the chorus.

Nonetheless, it takes a major leap of faith to assume that this group of girls and young women callously sent people they knew to be innocent to their deaths. The accusers, like nearly all their contemporaries and elders, genuinely believed in witchcraft, and in that terrible year, they truly believed themselves to be under supernatural siege. The courtroom transcripts, in most cases, are not thorough enough to determine whether or not they were turning their torments on and off on cue. To assume that they acted only out of desire to bring about the deaths of people they knew to be innocent attributes to them a willingness to engage in what amounted to cold-blooded murder. It is hard to fathom that level of malice on the part of such a large group of people. Regardless of the girls' behavior in the daytime (away from the courtroom), they may very well have experienced real symptoms of what was considered bewitchment at home —especially at night, in their "world lit only by fire."[9] As darkness fell and the clarity of the day grew dim, the mind could wander. Sights imagined while awake (some of which could lead to fits in cases of extreme anxiety) could turn into very real nightmares during sleep. In the courtroom, when seeing the very people who had starred in their dreams, the "victims" may easily have lapsed back into the symptoms they endured at home after dark. They had other reasons to be afraid. They may have feared the wrath of their parents if they publicly denied the torments they had displayed (whether willingly or not) at home. The fear of falling victim to accusation as Mary Warren did (however temporarily) would have added to the pressure. Aside from that, the adulation they were receiving, not only from their parents but also from adults in positions of power, would have strengthened the idea in their minds that they were doing the right thing. In a society that believed that the fate of one's soul in the afterlife was foreordained, people would constantly be searching for signs of God's favor. They would also be looking for any possible clues pointing to actions that God wished them to take. For the afflicted girls of 1692, the chance to bring these "witches" to justice may have been just the ticket they sought to their own salvation. The torments they endured, in the darkness of their own homes and in the courtroom, were the sufferings they had to bear as part of their purification process.

Regardless of how real the sufferings of the afflicted were, the events of the nineteenth of April fed a frenzy that did not abate in Essex County for months. One of those examined that fateful day had less than two months to live. The others lived to see the effects of that day's testimony play themselves out to the end.[10]

The spread of the witch hunt beyond the boundaries of Salem Village, Salem Town, and the immediate vicinity resulted in several "one-witch towns"—towns that saw only one resident, usually someone disreputable in some way, arrested on witchcraft charges. Some of them were people who had been previously accused of witchcraft in their home communities. The afflicted girls of Salem Village came to know their names by reputation, even if they were not personally acquainted with them. One of those was Susanna North Martin of the town of Amesbury, which borders New Hampshire. Martin, a widow, was one of six suspects named in a complaint filed by Thomas Putnam and Jonathan Walcott on April 30, 1692. By that time, Martin was over seventy years old. Her late husband, George Martin, had been one of the original proprietors of Amesbury. Among the other original proprietors was William Sargent, whose two sons William, Jr. and Thomas, accused Susanna Martin of witchcraft in 1669. The two young men also accused Martin, then in her late forties, of several immoralities according to slander charges filed by her husband. William supposedly said that Susanna had given birth to an illegitimate child prior to her marriage and then wrung its neck. Thomas allegedly claimed that the Martins' son George was illegitimate and that another of their sons, Richard, was his mother's "imp."[11] William Sargent, Jr. was convicted of slander for the charges of immorality, but the court records say nothing about the witchcraft charge (the charges against Thomas were dropped). Susanna, on the other hand, was presumably tried and acquitted of witchcraft at that time, but the records of that trial do not exist.

These earlier allegations made Susanna Martin a logical candidate for suspicion nearly a quarter century later—especially once Abigail Hobbs's confession gave the impression that the devil had been actively recruiting for several years in northern New England. On the same day Putnam and Walcott filed a complaint against her, a warrant was issued for her arrest and the constable of Amesbury immediately complied, delivering her to Salem two days later. Coincidentally the constable, Orlando Bagley, was married to Mary Sargent, a sister of the two men who had accused Martin of witchcraft more than twenty years earlier. Testimony against Martin demonstrates that the reputation for witchcraft had persisted since the earlier accusation, despite the fact that she was not convicted at that time. The afflicted girls of Salem Village, of course, testified to tortures at the hands of Martin's "shape," but she also faced condemnation by other residents of Amesbury and the neighboring town of Salisbury. John Kimball of Amesbury told of being harassed by a spectral puppy in the woods after having decided against buying a puppy from Martin. Sarah Atkinson, also of Amesbury, related how Martin arrived at her home with her clothes clean and dry despite wet and muddy conditions outdoors. Perhaps the most bizarre accusation directed at Martin was the claim of John Allen of Amesbury that after having refused her a favor because his oxen were too tired to complete the task she requested, some of the oxen had drowned themselves. When she came to trial, Martin was convicted and was one of five hanged on July 19.

The neighboring town of Salisbury also had its own witch, Mary (Perkins) Bradbury. Unlike Susanna Martin, Bradbury had never faced formal charges of witchcraft—perhaps because she and her husband Thomas were more prominent in Salisbury than the Martins were in Amesbury. Nonetheless she carried the reputation, and the fact that she lived in Salisbury may have added to her misfortune. Salisbury happened to be the childhood home of Ann (Carr) Putnam, the wife of Thomas Putnam of Salem Village, and the mother of Ann Putnam, who had risen to a position of leadership among the afflicted girls. The elder Ann Putnam had testified to suffering from attacks by witches herself. On May 26, the younger Ann Putnam and her step-cousin Mary Walcott complained of spectral assaults by Bradbury. The warrant for Bradbury's arrest has not survived, but she was brought to trial in September. As in the other cases, the afflicted girls accused her of the usual supernatural attacks, but her reputation for witchcraft followed her to Salem as well. Two fellow residents of Salisbury who testified against her were none other than Ann Carr Put-

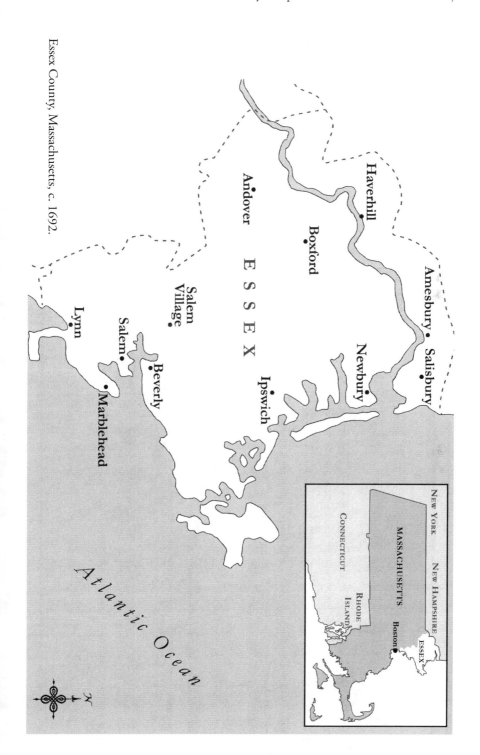

Essex County, Massachusetts, c. 1692.

nam's brothers James and Richard Carr. James had apparently competed for the affections of a young widow, Rebecca Wheelwright Maverick, with Bradbury's son, William Bradbury, about 1672. Soon after the widow treated James with more kindness than William one evening, James noted that he developed a strange illness that gave him a feeling as if "living creatures did run about every part of my body ready to tear me to pieces and so I continued for about three quarters of a year." James further testified that he eventually saw a doctor (Anthony Crosby) who concluded that he was bewitched. The doctor, he said, suggested Mary Bradbury as the culprit, saying he believed her to be "a great deal worse than Goody Martin" (an obvious reference to Susanna Martin, further evidence of *her* reputation). The incident James's brother Richard described supposedly happened about seven years later, when he was riding past the Bradbury home with his father George Carr and a teenage boy named Zerubbabel Endicott, who resided with the Carr family at the time. Richard claimed that a blue boar came from the Bradbury house just after Mary Bradbury went inside and charged the horses, causing George Carr's horse to stumble. Endicott corroborated the story and said that all of them concluded that Bradbury herself had taken the shape of the blue boar.

Mary Bradbury, however, appears not to have been as widely disliked in Salisbury as Susanna Martin was in Amesbury. No fewer than 113 residents of Salisbury and neighboring towns signed a petition on her behalf that was filed by her husband Thomas on July 22. Mary was seventy-seven years old by this time and Thomas was four years older. They had resided in Salisbury for fifty-two years by 1692, and even the Carr family did not unite in believing Mary guilty of witchcraft. William Carr, a brother of the aforementioned James and Richard Carr, signed the petition along with his wife Elizabeth Pike Carr. A few families came together in large numbers to support their neighbor, most prolifically that of Roger and Sarah Eastman, contemporaries of the Bradburys who had settled in Salisbury the same year the latter couple had arrived there. The elderly Eastman couple signed the petition along with four of their sons, the sons' wives, and one of their daughters—a total of eleven people. Despite all of this support, Mary Bradbury was tried in September and condemned to hang.

Somehow, she escaped from jail before the appointed date of her execution—September 22, a day that saw more hangings than any previous date (eight). How she escaped remains a mystery—given her age at the time she must have had help. The process may have included the bribery of a jailer.

No comparable support came to Wilmot Redd of Marblehead, one of eleven suspects named in a complaint filed by Salem Village residents John Walcott (son of Jonathan Walcott) and Joseph Houlton on May 28. Warrants for the arrest of all of those named were issued the same day, and Redd was brought to the tavern of Nathaniel Ingersoll of Salem Village three days later by Marblehead's constable James Smith. At her first examination, Redd, like the others, was implicated by the same group of afflicted girls from Salem Village who had testified against all of the others. Later testimony against Redd, however, referenced the curse that she had pronounced on Mrs. Simms (first name not given) who had accused Redd's maid of stealing laundry from her. Marblehead resident Sarah Dodd stated flatly that she heard Redd wish that Simms have no "ease of nature" while in Marblehead, and Ambrose Gale, another resident, testified that Simms did suffer accordingly until leaving town. A neighbor, Charity Pitman, was more explicit, claiming that Redd had expressed the wish that Simms might not *mingere* (urinate) nor *cacare* (defecate) if she did not leave town. Pitman further testified that Simms was then afflicted with the "distemper of the dry bellyache" (constipation). If Mrs. Simms did, in fact, believe Redd to be a witch, she might very well have suffered the symptoms described. Not surprisingly, Redd went to the gallows on September 22. Unlike Mary Bradbury, Redd did not inspire anyone in her home community to present a petition on her behalf. She was not well-liked there and apparently had an existing reputation for witchcraft.

Despite the convictions of Susanna Martin, Mary Bradbury, and Wilmot Redd, however, their respective hometowns (Amesbury, Salisbury, and Marblehead) did not see widespread outbreaks of accusations. Those three communities were "one-witch towns" in 1692 that saw their sole long-suspected practitioner of the black arts convicted and sentenced to death (though Bradbury escaped). Another suspect, listed in the same complaint of May 28 that included Wilmot Redd, was Martha Allen Carrier of Andover. Like Redd, Bradbury, and Martin, Carrier was the first person arrested from her town of residence. A warrant for her arrest was sent to John Ballard, the constable of the South End of Andover (the growing town had, since 1676, been in the habit of designating two constables, one each for the northern and southern sections of the community).[12] Ballard acted immediately, bringing Carrier in to be examined by the magistrates. Carrier, like the previously mentioned suspects, inspired loathing in her hometown. She had never been previously accused of witchcraft, at least not in any way that made it into a public document, but she had been blamed for bringing smallpox to Andover two years earlier when she and some of her children came down with it shortly after relocating from neighboring Billerica. Carrier had been born in Andover, a daughter of Andrew and Faith (Ingalls) Allen, who were among the first settlers in the town when it was founded, but she had met her husband Thomas Carrier while living with her older sister, Mary, and Mary's husband Roger Toothaker in Billerica. The Carriers had spent the early years of their married life in Billerica but had come to Martha's birthplace after falling into difficult financial circumstances. That alone made them less than welcome in Andover, but when they all survived the smallpox epidemic, even though it began in their household, they met with even more hostility. Martha's father and both of her brothers (Andrew and John) died in the epidemic, along with two of her nephews, the wife of one brother, and the husband of a sister (James Holt). Six other Andover residents also fell victim to the dreaded disease for a total of thirteen deaths in the town.[13] Clearly, the afflicted girls of Salem knew Carrier by reputation, as several of them cried out that she had killed thirteen people during their examinations. Mary Walcott spoke of a vision of thirteen ghosts.

As with other witchcraft suspects from outside Salem Village, Carrier also faced accusations from neighbors. Some of the testimony suggests that Carrier, like Wilmot Redd, hurled curses at people in anger. Soon after moving back to Andover, she got into a dispute over a property boundary with her neighbor Benjamin Abbot, who testified that Carrier angrily threatened him, saying she "would stick as close to Benjamin Abbot as the bark stuck to the tree and that I should repent of it afore seven years came to an end and that Dr. Prescott [presumably a doctor in Andover] could never cure me." Abbot went on to describe how he suffered from swelling in his feet and sores in his side and groin that did not heal until Carrier's arrest. Abbot's wife Sarah Farnum Abbot corroborated his testimony and also mentioned mysterious deaths of several of their cattle after Carrier's threats. The Abbots' testimony was echoed by Carrier's own nephew, Allen Toothaker, who not only supported their statements but also claimed to have experienced similar sores that had only healed after the arrest of his aunt. Toothaker also lost some cattle in ways he described as inexplicable, all of which he attributed to the occult powers of Martha Carrier who, he believed, had turned her magic against him after he had a physical altercation with her son, Richard Carrier.

Evidence such as this demonstrates that Martha Carrier pronounced "curses" on people. It is not evidence that she actually practiced witchcraft, as Hansen's thesis would suggest. Hansen does not directly cite Carrier as one guilty of witchcraft in his 1969 monograph, but he does do so in a later essay, stating that she probably regarded her own words as dangerous weapons and deliberately used them as such.[14] That is a questionable point. She could just as easily have only been expressing frustration at those she swore at, but if they believed strongly enough that her words had real power, that alone could have worsened their ailments. Benjamin Abbot and Allen Toothaker fell victim not to Martha Carrier or to the occult, but to their own faith in her ability to inflict harm by the spoken word. Their symptoms, if real, were at least partly psychosomatic. Toothaker had actually been wounded in a battle with the Indians, but the wound had taken longer than he expected to heal and he held his aunt responsible for that. His own fears of her supposed witchcraft may have been the actual culprit.

Coincidentally, it was Allen Toothaker's own father, Roger Toothaker, who first drew the attention of the witch hunters to the family, and it may have been at least partly because of her association with her brother-in-law that Martha Carrier herself first fell under suspicion. Roger Toothaker, a physician, made the mistake of boasting that he had taught his daughter how to kill a witch and that she had done so by taking the urine of someone who was afflicted by a specific witch (who was not named), putting it into an earthen pot, and leaving the pot in a hot oven overnight. The next morning, Toothaker claimed, the witch was dead. Though a resident of Billerica, Toothaker had related this story to at least two residents of Beverly, a town very close to Salem Village.[15] Not surprisingly, it eventually reached the ears of the afflicted children there and they complained of him. He was arrested on May 18, ten days before his sister-in-law, Martha Carrier, and it is noteworthy that his own wife Mary (Martha's sister) and nine-year-old daughter Margaret were also included in the same complaint as Martha. Toothaker never came to trial—he died in the Boston prison on June 16, less than a month after his arrest. His own loose tongue had gotten him into trouble and had dragged his wife, daughter, and sister-in-law into the fray with him. Toothaker was not the only one to arouse suspicion against himself and his family by being overly talkative. Martha, however, had established enough of an unsavory reputation on her own that she might have eventually been accused anyway. Like the aforementioned suspects from the "one-witch towns," Martha Carrier was convicted and sentenced to hang. She was one of five executed on August 19.

Unlike Amesbury, Salisbury, and Marblehead, though, Andover was not a "one-witch town." Before the year 1692 ended, Andover saw more of its residents arrested for witchcraft than any other community. It is noteworthy, however, that after Martha Carrier's arrest prior to May 31 (the day she was examined), no other Andover resident was charged for more than six weeks. That fact alone indicates that Martha Carrier's arrest did not, in and of itself, cause the later outbreak of accusations in Andover. Carrier may have done some things to arouse suspicions against herself (though the smallpox outbreak cannot realistically be blamed on her), but it was subsequent events that brought about accusations against other Andover residents. Carrier's name was frequently invoked during examinations of the later

Andover suspects, but without the actions of others later in the year Andover could easily have been just another "one-witch town." It faced many of the same problems Salem Village faced at the time—the lack of a real colony government and the threats posed by the French and Native Americans to the north and west. Andover also faced its own specific issues relating to its church and ministers, just as Salem Village did. Other issues had caused disputes within the town's borders. The same could be said of nearly all of the towns in Essex County and the surrounding area at the time. None of the towns in the county, or anywhere in the colony for that matter, still fit John Winthrop's vision of a "city upon a hill" (of course, the idea that any of them ever did is questionable at best). Despite this, aside from Salem Village, only in Andover did a full-fledged witch hunt explode in 1692. For it to happen there and only there, a combination of circumstances had to come together to ignite the flames.

CHAPTER THREE

A Shadow
Over
Andover

I N 1692, FORTY-FIVE of the total number of people arrested on witchcraft charges resided in Andover. Twenty-three residents of Andover can be shown to have formally accused someone of witchcraft, complained of affliction by witchcraft, or testified against a witchcraft suspect. This does not include those accusers who had been accused of witchcraft themselves and had confessed. With two possible exceptions (to be identified later), confessors only implicated others who had already been arrested.

Very few formal complaints survive for the accusations of Andover residents. Aside from Martha Carrier, formal accusations survive for only seven of the accused witches of Andover. In numerous cases, it is possible to make educated guesses about who filed the complaints based on who testified against the suspect and who his or her alleged victims were. The data that does survive on alleged victims of witchcraft and on those who testified against suspects provides adequate evidence to characterize accusers in Andover to some degree.

A broader look is necessary when considering the witchcraft accusations associated with Andover. The town had been semi-officially separated into a South End and North End for more than a decade by 1692, with separate tax listings being created from each region and a constable designated for each area at the annual town meetings. Of the forty-five residents accused of witchcraft, twenty-four lived in the North End while twenty-one resided in the South End—a clear piece of evidence that there was no regional distinction in Andover like the one Boyer and Nissenbaum described in Salem Village. The so-called "Andover phase" of the witch hunt spilled over into five neighboring towns, each of which can be associated with one of the two regions of Andover. The towns of Billerica and Reading can be lumped together with Andover's South End, and Haverhill, Boxford, and Rowley are more appropriately identified with the North End. Altogether, eighteen people from these five additional towns were formally indicted for witchcraft in 1692—bringing the total number of accused witches from the Andover region to sixty-three. Of these, thirty-seven resided in northern Andover or one of its associated communities while twenty-six lived in the South End or one of its "satellite" towns. The other five towns also produced eight additional accusers and/or afflicted in 1692, including the single most active afflicted girl, the teenage Martha Sprague of Boxford. These numbers brought the total number of identifiable accusers to thirty-one. Seventeen of those resided in the North End or one of the towns associated with it while fourteen lived in the South End or one of its adjoining communities.

To address the question of what (if anything) distinguished Andover from other Essex County towns in 1692, one needs to go back to the history of the town from its founding in 1646.[1] The Faulkner list, a document that dates from sometime prior to 1662, includes the names of twenty-three men known to be the first freeholders (property owners) in Andover, in the chronological order of their arrival in the town. The list (named for the first town clerk, Edmund Faulkner, who prepared it) arranges the men in the approximate (though not exact) order of their economic status, measured in the initial acreage each obtained upon arriving in the newly formed town. The first name on the list is that of Simon Bradstreet (born 1603 in

Horbling, Lincolnshire, England) who was later to serve as acting governor of the Massachusetts Bay colony after the overthrow of Edmund Andros. Bradstreet's initial allotment in Andover was twenty acres, which was matched only by that of John Osgood, whose name appeared second on the Faulkner list. Prior to moving to Andover, Osgood had established himself as a person of some substance in the coastal town of Newbury—not coincidentally, the previous home of thirteen of the twenty-three original Andover freeholders. By the same token, the last eight men on the list each received only four or five acres, the lowest amount of land obtained by any original settler.

The hierarchical nature of the list is exemplified by the previous relationship between John Stevens (fifth on the list; eight acres) and John Lovejoy (seventeenth; five acres). Stevens and Lovejoy had arrived in the colony together on the ship *Confidence* in 1638 with the sixteen-year-old Lovejoy as a servant to Stevens, who was already a married father. Like John Osgood, these two men had resided in Newbury before moving to Andover. Lovejoy's sister Grace, two years older than her brother, also came to Massachusetts Bay as a servant to the Stevens family. Grace is now believed to have been the wife of William Ballard, another former Newbury resident whose name appears just before John Lovejoy's on the Faulkner list.[2]

Of the twenty-three resident nonsuspects involved in accusations, twelve resided in Andover's North End while eleven lived in the South End—again, no discernible regional distinction. This number does include a caveat though—of the twenty-three involved in accusations, eight of them (six South Enders and two North Enders) accused *only* Martha (Allen) Carrier. When those accusers are removed from the analysis, ten North Enders and five South Enders remain—a statistic that does suggest a regional imbalance. The significance of that statistic is minimized, however, when examining who accused who. Accusers from both sections of Andover were just as likely to complain of their neighbors in their own section of the town as they were to cry out on those in the opposite end of the community—a contrast to the situation in Salem Village as described by Boyer and Nissenbaum. Also, while the fact that eight of the accusers only testified against Martha Carrier is worth mentioning, its significance may ultimately be minimal. She *was* accused six weeks before any other Andover suspect was and the initial complaint against her *did* originate in Salem Village, but by the time she came to trial in early August, the Andover witch hunt was well under way and she had been fully engulfed in it, having been associated with several other suspects from the town. Her notoriety had come to exceed that of most of the other suspects—Cotton Mather was to identify her as the designated "Queen in Hell" in his writings later in the year, an appellation initially bestowed upon her by another Andover resident. The testimony against her by neighbors occurred at that time, not when she was initially arrested, so the events in her native town undeniably influenced those depositions. Carrier's imagined rise to a leadership position among the witches in the minds of the persecutors was one of the factors stoking the fire in Andover anyway.

Boyer and Nissenbaum looked at another group in their analysis of the accusations in Salem Village—those who defended various suspects. In the village, the data usually consisted of petitions declaring belief in the innocence of specific suspects. For Andover, four such petitions exist, all of which defend groups of suspects if not all of them. Overall, seventy-two residents of Andover signed at least one of the petitions. Of those, forty-one resided in the South End of town while thirty-one resided in the North End. While the discrepancy there is noticeable (57 percent of defenders from the South End and 43 percent from the North End), it is not significant enough to draw any conclusions about a regional dichotomy. It is also worth noting that these petitioners resided in forty-six different households in Andover. Of the homes represented in the petitions, twenty-three were located in the North End and twenty-three in the South End—further evidence that no geographical division in Andover determined the course the witch hunt took.

Aside from being divided into two distinct regions, Andover shared other commonalities with Salem Village in 1692. Andover had its own issues with its minister (or ministers in Andover's case). The similarity ends there, though, because Andover's conflict differed drastically from that of Salem Village. By 1692, the Andover dispute was

The village of Andover in 1692.
1. John Barker and his daughter
Mary. 2. Timothy Osgood.
3. Ephraim and Hannah Eames Foster and daughter Rose. 4. Robert
and Rebecca Blake Eames. 5. John
and Mary Osgood Marston.
6. William Barker. 7. Daniel and
Hannah Chandler Bixby. 8. Thomas
Chandler. 9. Walter Wright and
stepson John Sadie. 10. Andrew Peters. 11. Francis Johnson. 12. Joseph
and Sarah Lord Wilson and daughter Sarah. 13. Samuel Phelps and
daughter Sarah. 14. Samuel Wardwell and family. 15. Henry Ingalls.
16. Samuel Ingalls. 17. Henry Ingalls, Jr. 18. Edward Farrington.
19. Francis Dane, Jr. 20. Benjamin
and Sarah Farnum Abbot.
21. George Abbot. 22. John Abbot.
23. William Ballard. 24. Joseph and
Phebe Dane Robinson. 25. Mary
Lacey and daughter Mary. 26. Constable John Ballard. 27. William and
Phebe Chandler. 28. Joseph and
Elizabeth Phelps Ballard.
29. Martha Carrier and children.
30. Samuel Preston. 31. Samuel
Holt. 32. Henry Holt. 33. Ann Foster and son Andrew. 34. Robert and
Mary Marshall Russell and son
James. Note: some of the accusers
and/or their family members eventually switched sides and defended
the accused. See Appendix B.
(This map is based with permission
on one produced by the Historical
Societies of Andover and North Andover, copyright 1992.)

🏠 Households that accused others of witchcraft
🏠 Households that defended those accused of witchcraft
🏠 Households with family members accused of witchcraft

BILLERICA

WOBU

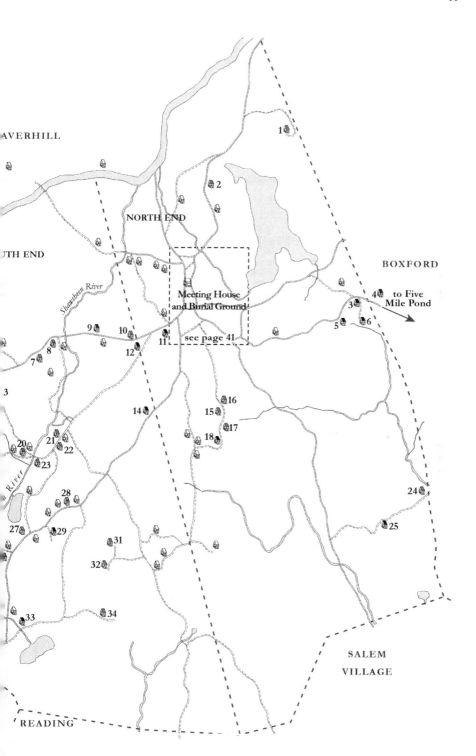

more than ten years old and though it had officially been resolved, some tensions over it may have lingered. The issue involved the aging Francis Dane (seventy-six years old at the beginning of 1692), who had served as the town's minister since 1649, and Thomas Barnard, a much younger man, who had accepted the town's invitation to serve as a second minister in 1682. Such an arrangement was not unusual in Puritan New England. As a town's long-established minister aged, the selectmen of the town would often hire a younger clergyman to serve essentially as an apprentice to the older man, with the idea that the young preacher would succeed his mentor when the latter died or became too infirm to carry out his duties. In a sense, Andover waited longer than it should have to take this action. A year prior to hiring Barnard, the selectmen of Andover petitioned the court in Boston for permission to engage a new minister since, as they noted, Dane had not preached regularly in the previous few years due to infirmities incident to his age (he was sixty-five at the beginning of 1681).[3] Dane apparently did not object to the hiring of Barnard. The controversy arose when the town's selectmen asked to be relieved of paying their elderly minister any longer because, as they noted, he was in "comfortable circumstances."[4] Dane objected to this and so in a town meeting of October 10, 1681, a committee of seven prominent town residents, some of them sitting selectmen, accepted the responsibility of acting on Dane's salary.[5] This same committee also extended the invitation to Barnard early the next year after a unanimous supporting vote at a town meeting on January 2, 1682. The salary decision evidently satisfied Dane, though the court in Boston had to get involved again.[6] Dane was to receive an annual salary of thirty pounds. Though Barnard was to receive more—fifty pounds a year—he may not have been as pleased with the settlement as his mentor-to-be was. The younger man did have the assurance that once Dane died or ceased

Andover Village Center in 1692. 1. Rebecca Aslebee Johnson and daughter, Rebecca. 2. Abigail Dane Faulkner. 3. John and Mary Clements Osgood. 4. Rev. Thomas Barnard. 5. Rev. Francis Dane. 6. Justice of the Peace Dudley Bradstreet. 7. John and Eunice Potter Frye. 8. John Aslebee. 9. Samuel Martin and daughter Abigail. 10. Mary Ayer Parker and son John. 11. John and Mary Tyler Bridges and daughters. 12. Nathaniel and Deliverance Haseltine Dane. 13. Ralph Farnum, Sr. (This map is based with permission on one produced by the Historical Societies of Andover and North Andover, copyright 1992.)

Households that accused others of witchcraft
Households that defended those accused of witchcraft
Households with family members accused of witchcraft

to play any role in the ministry at all, he would receive the full eighty pounds per year. Given Dane's obviously less-than-ideal health at the time, Barnard probably never envisioned that the aging minister would live another fifteen years. As time went on, Barnard may have increasingly chafed at the continued influence of the older man.

As the years passed and the town continued to pay Dane a salary, others in Andover may have come to resent their aging minister as a drain on the town's finances. That feeling, if it existed, is not likely to have been universal though. After all, Dane had served as the town's minister for more than three decades and for a large percentage of the population, he had been the only spiritual leader they had ever known. To some of the adults, particularly those whose parents were dead, he might have been a father figure of sorts. Any who felt that way could have seen Barnard as a usurper of sorts, though none of them could deny the reality that Dane would not be there forever and that the town had to be prepared for that eventuality.

Unfortunately for historians of Andover, there are no surviving pro- or anti-Dane petitions (or pro- or anti-Barnard petitions), so if separate factions formed behind each of the ministers, no records exist to identify which townspeople supported which one. The lack of such records could simply indicate that no such factionalism existed. Neither minister left a sermon book that survives, so much of the type of evidence that exists for the conflict over Samuel Parris in Salem Village simply is not there for Andover. Dane was a native of Hertfordshire, the same English home as that of two of the earliest settlers of the South End, Thomas Chandler and George Abbot. Dane himself resided in the North End because that is where the church was—as did the younger pastor, Thomas Barnard. Dane's immediate family concentrated mostly in the North End as well—by 1692, all six of his children were married and four resided there (his son Francis lived in the South End and Hannah had married William Goodhue of Ipswich and moved there). As will be shown, though, he also had strong ties to the South End through the family of his late first wife Elizabeth Ingalls, who was the mother of all of his children. In addition, the aforementioned Thomas Chandler, his brother William, and their sister Hannah (widow of George Abbot) were Dane's stepsiblings, their widowed mother Annis having married the minister's widowed father,

John Dane, in 1643. The twice-widowed Francis Dane further cemented this connection in 1690 by marrying his stepsister Hannah.

Thomas Barnard, who had only resided in Andover for ten years by the time of the witchcraft trials, lacked the extensive family connections in Andover that his older counterpart had. There is no evidence that he was related to Stephen Barnard (a son of original Andover proprietor Robert Barnard) who resided in the South End in 1692 (Robert Barnard had long since left for Nantucket). Thomas Barnard had been born in Hartford, Connecticut, in 1657, a son of Francis Barnard and Hannah Merrill who married in Hartford in 1644. In 1659, Thomas's parents took him and his older siblings to the newly created town of Hadley, Massachusetts—a town established by a group of conservative Puritans from Hartford (including the Barnards) who opposed the teachings of Hartford minister Samuel Stone, who embraced the new idea of a halfway covenant. The young Thomas Barnard grew to adolescence in this frontier town. Ironically, had it not been for this move, he would have retained some memories from his early childhood of the witchcraft outbreak that took place in Hartford in 1662 and 1663. He probably did hear about it because the settlers of Hadley retained ties to Hartford, and his parents must have learned of the trials there. He undoubtedly remembered the trial of Robert Williams, prosecuted for witchcraft in Hadley in 1669. Williams was acquitted of witchcraft but was convicted of lying, for which he was whipped and fined.

Thomas Barnard enrolled at Harvard in the 1670s to train for the ministry, completing his course of study in 1679. While there, he probably made the acquaintance of Cotton Mather who, though six years his junior, had begun his studies at an extraordinarily early age. It is not certain how Barnard came to the attention of the selectmen of Andover but, it is not surprising that the town's leaders would consider recent Harvard graduates in looking for a new minister. Still a bachelor when he began his duties in Andover, Barnard soon married Elizabeth Price of Salem, meaning that he did not establish marital ties to his newly adopted community.

Because Dane had family connections to both sections of Andover and Barnard lacked ties to either, kinship gives no reason to think either area would have favored one minister over the other. None of this proves whether tensions existed among the residents of Andover because of the ministers in 1692. Such conflicts were hardly an aberration at that time in Essex County and, as can easily be demonstrated, controversies over clergy (and/or churches) alone did not ensure outbreaks of witchcraft arrests in specific towns. A town comparable to Andover in that regard is Newbury. The latter town, though only a decade older than Andover, was the previous home of more than half of the former's original proprietors and there were still numerous family ties between the two towns in 1692. Differences are notable—Newbury was on the sea and Andover was not, though the Merrimack River gave it a direct link to the ocean. Andover was also more exposed to Native American hostilities due to its frontier location. Newbury had its own history of controversies over ministers and churches. The town's original minister, Thomas Parker (uncle of Andover founders Joseph and Nathan Parker), was still active in the 1660s. As would be the case in Andover nearly two decades later, the town had also engaged a younger minister, John Woodbridge (Thomas Parker's own nephew, who had actually been Francis Dane's predecessor in Andover). Despite the familial relationship between the two ministers, division in the town began immediately, with factions forming around each of the two men.[7] The tension was further exacerbated when Edward Woodman, one of the town's prominent early settlers, publicly attacked both men and drew the support of a significant portion of the congregation.[8] The controversy in Newbury's church raged for nearly a decade. Though that schism was resolved by 1692, another had flared up by that time, with residents in the west end of town petitioning for permission to form their own parish.[9] That question begs for comparison with Salem Village. Despite the ongoing controversy, however, not a single resident of Newbury was accused of witchcraft in 1692. Clearly, religious disputes alone did not lead to suspicions of practicing black arts in a specific town. Newbury, like Salem Village and Andover, was a powder keg— but no spark set it off in that crucial year. So, the key question remains unanswered—why did so many witchcraft accusations occur in Andover in 1692?

CHAPTER FOUR

Prelude
to
Witchcraft

I N A LEGAL DOCUMENT with very dark portents, dated March 5, 1650, Job Tyler, recorded as a resident of Andover, acknowledged a debt of sixteen pounds to John Godfrey, then of Newbury, and bound himself to pay the debt in wheat and rye over the next two years, mortgaging his dwelling house (located in Andover), land, and three cows. The document was witnessed by Richard Barker, an original proprietor, and his wife Joanne.[1] How Job Tyler came to be indebted to John Godfrey is not known, but by the end of the decade, Godfrey had taken up residence in Andover and it is highly unlikely that very many of the town's residents were pleased by that. John Godfrey was a lifelong bachelor who spent his adult life drifting from town to town in Essex County, working as a herdsman. By all accounts, Godfrey was a difficult man to get along with. He had been recorded as a resident of Andover two years before the mortgage and if that, in any way, induced him to return to the town, it probably did not endear Job Tyler to the residents. Nearly a decade later, while once again residing in Andover (1659), John Godfrey found himself charged with witchcraft—the town's first resident to face such a charge and the only one prior to 1692. Members of the Tyler family testified against Godfrey in his trial—claiming that while Godfrey worked for them, he came into their home accompanied by a large bird which he then tried to catch until it disappeared through a chink in a board. When Job Tyler asked Godfrey why the bird had come, Godfrey had told him that it came to "suck your wife."[2] Job and his wife Mary's two oldest children, Moses and Mary, both confirmed their father's account. Despite their testimony, however, Godfrey was acquitted (convictions for witchcraft were much harder to obtain in New England prior to 1692 than in that notorious year). Twice more (in 1662 and 1665), John Godfrey faced charges of engaging in diabolical arts and in the latter year, Job and Moses Tyler attested to the truth of their 1659 depositions as did Mary. Nonetheless, Godfrey was never convicted.

John Godfrey was not the only source of problems for Job Tyler during his time in Andover. If he had been, Tyler's reputation in the town might not have suffered as it did, because Godfrey was regarded as a troublemaker himself. In fact, despite the conflicts between Godfrey and the Tylers, there were times that Godfrey collaborated with them, which could not have helped the reputation of either party. In 1658, Job Tyler apprenticed his second son, Hopestill (aged about thirteen), to Thomas Chandler who, though only in his early thirties, had already established himself as a prominent citizen of Andover. Four years later, Job wished to break the indenture for unknown reasons and resorted to extralegal methods for doing so. On June 23, 1662, a search warrant was issued to the constables of the towns of Ipswich and Wenham for the apprehension of Hopestill (called Hope in the records), noting that he had run away from his master, Thomas Chandler.[3] Nathan Parker (an Andover founder and prominent resident whose wife Mary was to die on the gallows in 1692) testified that he had personally written the apprenticeship document four years earlier at the request of Chandler and the elder Tyler, which he had then shown to Simon Bradstreet (Andover's most prominent resident), who had approved of the wording. The agreement, according to Parker, was that Hope was to serve Chandler for nine and a half years during which time Chandler would teach him the trade of blacksmith and also to teach him to read the Bible and to write well enough to maintain a needed book for his trade. In addition, Chandler was to provide the boy with "meat, drink, washing, lodging, and clothes."[4] Parker also testified that at the time he prepared the document, Job Tyler and Thomas Chandler had asked him to keep it for them. Later, Tyler had changed his mind and asked for it on numerous occasions, but he (Parker) refused to give it to him because he felt compelled to honor the original request. Parker had kept the paper for more than three years until one day when Moses Tyler, Hope's older brother (accompanied by none other than John Godfrey) had come to Parker's home while he (Parker) and his wife were not there and retrieved it. Parker's children and his maid had told him who had taken the document.[5]

Children and maids might not have been regarded as the most credible sources available, but at that point, not surprisingly, John Godfrey turned on the Tylers. He described how Moses took the indenture from Parker's house, accompanied not only by him (Godfrey), but also by Job Tyler's wife (Moses's mother). Godfrey further testified that as he was walking with Moses back to the Tyler farm, Moses had boasted that "I have got my brother's indenture and now let Chandler do what he can, we will take Hope away from him."[6] Godfrey went on to say that Moses had burned the document in the presence of his father and assured the elder Tyler that he could take Hope when he wished because Chandler could not prove anything in writing.[7] Despite the lack of documentation of the apprenticeship, Thomas Chandler won the case—assisted by the testimony of the double-dealing John Godfrey, although Nathan Parker's statement was undoubtedly more crucial. Chandler's growing prominence (he had been appointed constable of Andover earlier in the year) could not have hurt him, either.

Losing this case was not the only setback Job Tyler's family suffered in 1662, however. About six weeks prior to the court case, their home had burned. This event was referenced during the court case by William Ballard, one of the town's original proprietors, who had taken Mary Tyler and her children into his home after the fire. They were still there when the apprenticeship case came before the court.[8] This may explain why Job Tyler wanted to extricate his son Hopestill from the indenture to Thomas Chandler—he needed his help in rebuilding the house. By that time, Hopestill was about seventeen years old and except for Moses (who was about twenty-one), Job had no other son older than nine. But Job did not succeed in breaking his contract with Thomas Chandler, and before the end of the year, he and his family left Andover for Roxbury, probably never intending to return. In October of that year, they conveyed their last tract of land in town to their old nemesis, John Godfrey, noting that it included their dwelling house (presumably recently rebuilt). The deed does not mention any compensation to them by Godfrey so it may be that they were simply paying off debts Job owed to him.

The relocation did not end the Tylers' troubles with Andover, much to their undoubted chagrin. Job had filed a suit against Godfrey, which was decided in Godfrey's favor in 1665 (the year the latter last faced witchcraft charges). In the meantime, Job had apparently been freely voicing his opinion of Thomas Chandler to anyone who would listen in the three years that had elapsed since he failed in his quest to free his son Hopestill from the indenture to Chandler. Hopestill's master sued the elder Tyler for slander and once again prevailed. The courts ruled that because Job Tyler was poor, he should not be fined more than six pounds, but they forced him to submit to the humiliation of publicly posting an apology to Chandler in the meeting houses of Andover and Roxbury, confessing, among other things, that he had called Chandler a "cheating, lying, whoring knave fit for all manner of bawdery" and that he had thus "wickedly slandered" Chandler "without any just ground."[9] Job ended the apology by appealing to Chandler (and God) to forgive him.

By 1668, Job Tyler and most of his family had relocated to the newly incorporated town of Mendon, more than fifty miles southwest of Andover, out of the boundaries of Essex County. Moses, who had married Prudence Blake on July 16, 1666, remained near Andover, settling in Rowley Village. The eldest daughter Mary, married since November 18, 1662, to Richard Post of Woburn, eventually joined her parents in this new community with her husband. Their conflicts with Thomas Chandler were not over though. On March 31, 1668, Job Tyler complained to the Court of Essex County that on August 20 of the previous year, Chandler and John Stevens (also of Andover) had seized two oxen and two cows from his son-in-law Richard Post, who was delivering the animals to Tyler at the time. Tyler was undoubtedly hoping to see Chandler subjected to a humiliation similar to the one he had endured three years earlier. Chandler, however, was not poor. He offered Tyler twenty pounds to settle and also offered to remit his son's bond of one hundred pounds.[10] Chandler also suggested the court allow Tyler whatever they deemed appropriate "provided he might be quiet."[11] Tyler undoubtedly needed money, but it is doubtful that this settlement satisfied him. His desire for revenge remained unfulfilled and he may have realized by then that it always would be. Nonetheless, the move may have given the family more hope for a settled, peaceful life than they had ever experienced. Two more of Job and Mary's children (Hannah and Chandler's former apprentice Hopestill) married on January 20, 1668, in Mendon to another pair of siblings (James and Mary Lovett, respectively, children of Daniel Lovett). None of the family anticipated the coming of King Philip's War. Mendon, unfortunately, was on the edge of the frontier and when the fighting broke out, the warring tribes quickly swept in. Among the first casualties was Richard Post, killed in Mendon on July 14, 1675, leaving Mary with three children of her own and two stepchildren. Then, early in 1676, the Indians burned almost the entire town. Once again, Job Tyler and his family had lost a home to fire. They fled back in the direction they had come, settling near Moses in what was then Rowley Village (to become the town of Boxford in 1685).

The term sex offender is a late twentieth-century creation. It does not appear in any documents from earlier times, certainly none from as long ago as the late seventeenth century. Such people did exist in the past though and while the general disdain of them was not as public as it is today (there was no offender registry at that time), their neighbors would have known who they were once they had been exposed. Undoubtedly, those who knew of their transgressions often avoided them or treated them with contempt. In 1692, a twenty-nine-year-old bachelor with just such a reputation resided in the North End of Andover with a married brother and his family. His name was Timothy Swan.

Timothy Swan had been born not in Andover but in the neighboring town of Haverhill on March 12, 1663, the fifth of twelve children of Robert and Elizabeth (Acie) Swan.[12] Robert Swan was among those summoned to testify against John Godfrey when he was prosecuted for witchcraft in 1665. Swan was also a prominent citizen of Haverhill, serving as a selectman in 1669 and holding other offices and serving on various committees until his death on February 11, 1698.[13] However, his reputation was not spotless. On April 29, 1680, Swan acknowledged that

> upon the Towne meeting day at Haverhil in February last past, I did behave myself in a tumultuous & seditious manner, openly opposing them that then pleaded for the law of the country to be observed & abetting them that did oppose & act contrary to the law, which was the just greif of many yet present; publique affairs being carried on, what wee could by a faction: At which time I also did speak reproachfully of the lawes or law of the country: Saying that men were led about by the lawes like a company of puppy dogs; with other taunting & reproachful words & expressions toward some men in pticular.[14]

Robert went on to express the hope that he "may be kept from a railing spirit & tongue which I have heretofore too much & often made use of to the abuseing of my Neighbours."[15] His full statement was read in the public congregation in May 1680. In all probability, the pastor read the confession aloud while Robert Swan stood in his pew with his head bowed, as was the practice of the time.

Among the Swan family's neighbors in Haverhill was Michael Emerson, born in 1627 in Cadney Parish, Lincoinshire, England, who had arrived in the Massachusetts Bay colony by 1651, apparently as a single man. He was married in Haverhill April 1, 1657, to Hannah

Webster, a daughter of John and Mary (Shatswell) Webster who had lived in the town of Ipswich and then later in Newbury, the town noted earlier as the previous residence of thirteen of the twenty-three original proprietors of Andover. The Emersons had fifteen children, though only eight lived to adulthood. Michael and his brother Robert Emerson bought land from Timothy Swan's father in 1663 and there was no hint of any hostility between the two families at the time.[16] Michael Emerson was also rising to prominence, even though he was the first generation of his family to live in the colony and had not had his father to help pave the way for him as Robert Swan had. In 1659, Emerson served as constable in Haverhill, a position that often helped launch young men into positions of greater importance later. In 1676, however, he ran into legal problems. The Essex County Court fined him and bound him to good behavior in May 1676 for "cruel and excessive beating of his daughter with a flail swingle and for kicking her."[17] This abuse must have been especially severe for a father in that era to have been summoned to court. The records do not indicate which of Michael Emerson's daughters he was accused of abusing. He had five of them by that time, ranging in age from eighteen months to eighteen years. His oldest daughter Hannah was later to go down in history as Hannah Dustin who, at age thirty-nine in 1697, was taken prisoner by Native Americans in a raid on Haverhill only to escape later after tomahawking her captors to death and scalping them with the help of two fellow captives. But the most likely candidate for the mistreatment is Elizabeth Emerson, then eleven years old, having been born January 26, 1665, in Haverhill. Elizabeth's subsequent behavior, more than that of Hannah, suggests that she could have been a survivor of abuse.

Elizabeth Emerson and Timothy Swan, less than two years apart in age, grew up as close neighbors. Any good will that might have existed between the two (if there ever had been any) ended by the latter half of the year 1685, when Elizabeth and her father filed rape charges against Swan, claiming that the young man had tricked her by asking to see her parents' new bedchamber.[18] At that point, the complaint stated, Swan had forced himself upon her, holding her down with one arm pressed against her throat to keep her quiet as he did so.[19] This charge was apparently not taken seriously by the courts for what seems, in the twenty-first century, a very odd reason. Elizabeth Emerson was pregnant. Seventeenth-century Puritans generally believed that conception could only occur during consensual intercourse so the judges generally assumed Elizabeth willingly participated.[20]

Still single, Elizabeth Emerson gave birth to a daughter on April 10, 1686. While in labor, she named Timothy Swan as the father. Such identification by a woman in the process of giving birth carried huge significance at that time. Elizabeth was not the first Emerson daughter to conceive a child out of wedlock—her older sister Mary (born in 1660) had done so a few years earlier, but her child's father (Hugh Matthews) had married her before her child was born. Timothy Swan, however, denied the charges and he was supported in his evasion of responsibility by his father Robert, who claimed that he had "charged him (Timothy) not to go into that wicked house (the Emerson home) and that his son had obeyed and furthermore his son could not abide the jade (Elizabeth). He further declared that he should stand by his son."[21] The rape charge went nowhere, based largely on statements attributed to women present at the birth of Elizabeth's daughter (named Dorothy after Timothy Swan's sister). These women questioned why there was no evidence at the time of the alleged rape that Elizabeth had fought back, such as telltale scratches on Swan's face.[22] The court did order Swan to pay for the maintenance of the child, but he proved a neglectful father, often late with payments and frequently paying in worthless goods such as rusty hardware.[23]

The scandal marked both Elizabeth Emerson and Timothy Swan for the rest of their lives, and neither lived to celebrate a thirtieth birthday. Five years later, in 1691, the still-unmarried Elizabeth gave birth to twins, who apparently died the day of their birth (possibly stillborn but if not, they could have died for any number of reasons). No one had been certain Elizabeth was pregnant prior to the birth (perhaps she was significantly overweight by that time), and she delivered the babies alone, with no assistance from her parents or a midwife. After they died, she sewed the bodies in a bag and buried them in her parents' garden. Ultimately, she was convicted of murdering the twins and went to the gallows for the crime on June 8, 1693.

Nonetheless, she outlived Timothy Swan, the alleged father of her first child, by four months.

After dodging his responsibilities as the father of Elizabeth Emerson's daughter, Timothy Swan left his childhood home in Haverhill for the neighboring town of Andover, where he apparently resided with his older married brother, Robert Swan, Jr. He probably maintained as little contact with the Emersons as possible and probably was unaware that Elizabeth's cousin Joseph Emerson (born in 1669) married Martha Toothaker, the daughter of Roger and Mary (Allen) Toothaker in 1690. That connection gained more significance in 1692, however, when Swan and the Toothaker family became embroiled in the witchcraft accusations. Like his alleged victim of six years earlier, Timothy Swan remained single in 1692 at twenty-nine years old. Unmarried men of that age in Andover were far from unusual, as historian Philip Greven's work has demonstrated. But Timothy Swan had the added burden of the accusation of rape and the dodging of his responsibility to his child to diminish his prospects. It is true that from a legal perspective in colonial New England, rape of a single woman was not treated as harshly as the rape of a married or engaged woman. This was because the latter was viewed as an offense against the woman's husband or fiancé.[24] Even though Timothy Swan never suffered legal repercussions for his mistreatment of Elizabeth Emerson, it would be naïve to think that he went entirely unpunished. Though Timothy Swan's transgressions occurred in Haverhill, news of the kind of person he was (or was assumed to be) would have followed him to Andover. As such, he was not a man any young woman in Andover would have been likely to want as a husband. No genuinely loving father would have wished a daughter to marry a man with Swan's history. Some young women may very well have hurled angry words at him if he approached them in an amorous manner. If the objects of his desire did not react that way themselves, their mothers or other older female relatives may have. Whatever antagonisms Timothy Swan may have felt from the feminine gender in general turned into fear in that fateful summer of 1692.

There is little doubt that Timothy Swan suffered from some type of serious physical malady by the time the witchcraft accusations burst onto the scene in Andover—he was to die that following winter on February 2, 1693. Just when he became convinced that his illness had diabolical origins is not clear—only one of the surviving formal complaints against witchcraft suspects was filed by him and that was a month after accused witches began confessing to attacking him. There is no record that he ever appeared in court to testify—probably because he was not well enough. Some of those who admitted to hurting him may very well have spoken angrily to him in the past. Others may have openly expressed a wish that some misfortune would befall him, whether in speaking directly to him or expressing their desire to others. When he actually did fall ill, those who had heard curses directed his way might have believed that his antagonists were attacking him by supernatural means. Some of the confessors may have come to believe in, and fear, their own previously unknown occult powers and that might have motivated them to admit their presumed guilt. Considering Swan's reputation, his sickness might have been ignored at other times. It is certainly possible that some of his neighbors secretly hoped that witches would carry the disreputable young man to an early grave. But in the charged atmosphere of 1692, a general fear of witchcraft could have overwhelmed any ill will the residents of Andover might have harbored toward young Swan. If this previously healthy youth could fall victim to the diabolical arts, so could they. Some of the other accusers may not have cared if the witches were stopped in time to save Swan's life or not—but they would have wanted to bring his presumed tormentors to justice before they claimed any more victims.

Even if Timothy Swan was as widely loathed in Andover as events in 1692 suggest, he was not the most hated man in town—at least not for the nine-month period from April 1689 until January 1690. That dishonor belonged to Hugh Stone, a longtime resident of the town who had married Hannah Foster there on October 15, 1667. The question of Stone's own origins remains unresolved, although his first name Hugh suggests a Scottish background. He was not a native of

Andover but his wife Hannah, a daughter of Andrew and Ann Foster, had lived her entire life in the town. Andrew Foster had been one of the original proprietors of Andover and one of the first settlers of the South End. This particular Foster family has long been thought to be of Scottish or English borderlands origin based on the membership of Andrew and Ann's grandson in the Boston-based Scots Charitable Association. The given name Andrew and the fact that they lived in an area known as the "Old Briton" neighborhood in Andover's South End gives credence to that identification, though no genealogists have ever satisfactorily determined Ann's maiden name, much less her origin in the British Isles.[25] If Hugh Stone and Hannah Foster did, indeed, both have Scottish roots, that could help explain their marriage. Andrew Foster died in 1685, aged 100 or 106 years (the number is a bit difficult to read) according to the town's death records—though that age could easily be a bit exaggerated. Five adult children, including Hannah Stone, survived Andrew at the time of his death in 1685, a small family by the standards of the era, but Andrew's unusually advanced age at the time he and Ann started their married life may account for that.[26]

At first glance in the town's vital records, the lives of Hugh and Hannah (Foster) Stone seem rather conventional. Their first child, John Stone, was born November 24, 1668, slightly more than a year after their marriage, and afterward they continued to have children every two to three years until the birth of their seventh child, Kezia, recorded as having occurred April 22, 1686. But the records of the quarterly courts of Essex County show that the Stones' married life was anything but idyllic.

Between 1680 and 1686, the courts fined Hugh Stone for drunkenness on three separate occasions. In September 1680, the Quarterly Court of Essex County fined him ten shillings for being drunk.[27] In April 1683, the same court levied a fine of twelve shillings and sixpence against Stone after he admitted to being drunk in public.[28] In November 1685 Stone acknowledged that he was "distempered with drink at his own house" the previous September 24.[29] Someone cited that frequently in the courts for drinking undoubtedly had a problem with alcohol consumption. Drinking at taverns was a common pastime for men of that era, and someone who overindulged enough (even if just occasionally) to find himself in legal trouble can only be assumed to have been an alcoholic. Whether or not this also led Hugh Stone into frequent physical and verbal abuse of his wife and children can only be speculated on, but it appears likely. Such mistreatment would have had to be extreme in that era to have drawn the attention of legal authorities. Hannah's parents and siblings must have known about it and been concerned, but they may have felt helpless to intervene. Other residents of the town may have also known and disdained Hugh Stone for his actions. Much like Timothy Swan (though for different reasons), Stone must not have been popular in Andover, especially not in the South End where he lived. It is doubtful, though, that anyone was prepared for the stunning incident that occurred in the spring of 1689.

On April 20, a drunken Stone murdered his wife Hannah by slashing her throat with a knife. She was pregnant with their eighth child at the time. The murder was the first in Andover in the four decades since its founding. The killing sent shock waves through the community, but no one was more devastated than Hannah's widowed mother. Ann Foster's grief could not have been alleviated the following January when Stone went to the gallows. In his final words to the onlookers, he noted that contention in his family, possibly including his mother-in-law (though he apparently did not specifically name anyone), had contributed to his act, although he also acknowledged having been under the influence of alcohol.[30] Regardless of how vague her son-in-law's final words had been, they must have added a burden of guilt to an already bereaved mother. Stone himself had no known relatives in Andover, so it does appear he referred to his wife's family in his statement. The Foster family's grim mood could only have worsened later in 1690 when the Stones' second son Simon was gravely wounded in a fight with Indians while serving in the militia in a garrison in Exeter, New Hampshire. Simon Stone did survive, despite nine bullet wounds, but his health may have been permanently affected. Aged nineteen at the time, he did not marry until 1716, when he was forty-five. The whole situation could only have added to his already stricken grandmother's heartbreak.

Lost in her own sorrows, Ann Foster may have eventually pondered the role of witchcraft in her misfortunes. Other family members, also devastated, could have entertained similar thoughts. The widow's eldest son, Andrew Foster, Jr., was among those who testified against Martha Carrier when she was tried for witchcraft in 1692. The youngest Foster daughter Mary (born in 1652) who, like her sister Hannah had married a non-native of Andover (Lawrence Lacey), experienced family problems of her own. Mary's oldest daughter (born in 1674), also named Mary, ran away from home briefly two years after the murder of her aunt Hannah. Such actions were probably no more unusual on the part of teenagers then than they are now, but when a family endures the trauma of a murder, any such transgression magnifies in significance. In 1692, the aforementioned three generations—widow Ann Foster, daughter Mary (Foster) Lacey, and granddaughter Mary Lacey—all found themselves charged with witchcraft. The witch hunters of 1692 showed a propensity to attack those already suffering adversity. Once arrested, all three, wittingly or not, transformed themselves into leading actors in the drama that unfolded in Andover. The roles played by the bereaved grandmother and her troubled granddaughter stand out as especially significant.

Martha Allen Carrier (born about 1653) spent her childhood in Andover's South End as a daughter of original town proprietor Andrew Allen and his wife Faith Ingalls Allen. She eventually followed her older married sister Mary Allen Toothaker to the neighboring town of Billerica, where she met and married Thomas Carrier, a man apparently more than twenty years her senior (though his age, like that of Andrew Foster, could have been exaggerated late in his life). Sometime between 1684 (when their daughter Sarah was born in Billerica) and 1689 (the year of birth of their daughter Hannah), the Carriers and their children relocated to Andover. From all indications, they lacked adequate means of self-support and were thus not welcomed by the town's leaders, who feared the financial burden of providing for them. Late in 1690, the selectmen grew concerned with the family's presence in town for another reason. They issued this notice to Martha's two brothers and two of her brothers-in-law on October 14, 1690:

> To Samuel Holt, James Holt, Andrew Allen, and John Allen, Neighbors and Friends—We the subscribers of Andover have been informed that your sister Carrier and some of her children are smitten with that contagious disease the smallpox and some have been soe inconsiderate as to think that the care of them belongs to the selectmen of Andover which does not, for they took care when first they came to town to warn them out again and have attended the law therein: and shall only take care that they doe not spread the distemper with wicked carelessness which we are afrayd they have already done: you had best take what care you can about them, nature and religion requiring of it. We hope we have done faithfully in this information and we are your friends and servants.[31]

Nearly a month later, the selectmen took further action against the Carriers, issuing the following warrant to the South End's constable Walter Wright on November 9: "Whereas it has pleased God to visit those of the Widdow Allen's family which she hath taken into her house with that contagious disease the smallpox, it being as we think part of our duty to prevent the spreading of said distemper we therefore require you in their Majesties' names to warn said family not to goe near any house soe as to endanger them by said infection nor to come to the public meeting till they may come with safety to others: but what they want let them acquaint you with: which provide for them out of their own estates."[32]

By the time this warrant was issued, Martha Carrier's father, the elder Andrew Allen, had been dead for two weeks, having died October 24, apparently of smallpox. Seven other residents of Andover died from the same disease before the end of the year, all of them relatives of the Carriers. The dead were Martha's brothers, Andrew, Jr. and John (ages 33 and 28 respectively, both of whom died November 26), John's wife Mercy Peters Allen (died December 25), James Holt (age 39, husband of Hannah Allen Holt, a sister of Martha, died December 14), James Holt, Jr. (an infant son of James and Hannah, died December 13), Francis Ingalls (age 27, bachelor son of Henry and Mary Osgood Ingalls, died December 9), and Sarah Holt Marks (wife of Roger Marks and sister of James Holt, died December 22). Five other deaths occurred in that same time frame, but the town records do not note the cause of death. The other dead included John Lovejoy (aged about 68, former Stevens family servant and original town proprietor, died November 7), George Abbot (aged 3, son of William and Elizabeth, died November 16), Stephen Johnson (aged about 50, husband of Elizabeth Dane Johnson, died November 30), Thomas Allen (age 3, son of Andrew, Jr. and wife Elizabeth Richardson Allen, died December 22), and John Poor (age 32, bachelor son of Daniel and Mary Poor, died December 24). The total number of deaths in Andover over the last three months of 1690 totaled thirteen. At her preliminary examination on May 31, three of the afflicted girls of Salem Village—Susannah Sheldon, Elizabeth Hubbard, and Ann Putnam—directly accused Martha Carrier of murdering thirteen people. A fourth, Mary Walcott, claimed to have seen thirteen ghosts.[33]

To assume that Martha Carrier was accused of witchcraft entirely because she and her family were held responsible for the 1690 outbreak of smallpox in Andover drastically oversimplifies the situation. If anything, the blaming of the Carriers for the epidemic may stem back to their already questionable reputation. In 1676 (two years after the Carriers' marriage), the selectmen of Billerica had Thomas Carrier "warned out" of town. The warrant referred to "Thomas Carrier, alias Morgan, Welchman."[34] Such "warnings out," as they were called in that era, were not actual orders to leave a town. Towns issued them primarily to protect themselves from financial responsibility for families they feared might become indigent. Thomas and Martha Carrier's oldest son Richard was born in July 1674, just two months after their wedding. This taint could very well have followed them throughout their married lives, although they had done the proper thing and wed before the birth. Martha's choice of a landless laborer for a husband may not have been popular with her family; there are many legends about Thomas Carrier that are unlikely to be true but the fact that people in the area did believe them affected his life and that of his family. He was described as a very large and strong man—over seven feet tall in some accounts. One of the stories about him was that he had served as a bodyguard to King Charles I (deposed during the English Revolution of the 1640s), only to turn traitor and join the revolutionaries. The most extreme legend identified Carrier as the actual executioner of the king in 1649. With all of the wild tales surrounding him, it is no surprise that his family was regarded with suspicion. To some degree, it is surprising that his wife, rather than he, fell victim to witchcraft charges in 1692. The simple fact that women were targeted for accusation far more often than men can never be overlooked. In general, residents of Billerica and Andover disliked the entire Carrier household, and Martha's unpleasant disposition (evidenced by testimony against her at her examinations and trial) obviously did little to help matters. Once her brother-in-law in Billerica and his wife (Martha's sister) came under suspicion, Martha's own eventual arrest would not have shocked anyone who knew her.

One reason often cited for the accusations against Martha Carrier is her relationship to Andover's senior minister Francis Dane. She was his niece by marriage, her mother Faith (Ingalls) Allen having been a sister to the preacher's first wife Elizabeth (who had died in 1676). It is true that Dane may have had his enemies in Andover, and he had a history of skepticism about witchcraft (having defended John Godfrey in the 1660s), but ultimately, this idea does not withstand careful scrutiny. Carrier established a negative reputation in her own right, not only because of the smallpox epidemic, but also because of her tendency to quarrel with neighbors. In fact, one of her accusers (Benjamin Abbott) was Dane's stepson, his widowed mother Hannah (Chandler) Abbot having married the aging minister two years before the trials. The same suggestion has also been advanced concerning Elizabeth (Jackson) Howe of Topsfield, who was arrested the same day as Martha Carrier, and was married to Dane's nephew, James Howe. Elizabeth Howe, like Martha Carrier, eventually went to the gallows. In Howe's case, no one who testified against her lived in Andover or had any reason for a vendetta against Francis Dane. It is true that two of Dane's own daughters and five of his grandchildren eventually went to jail on charges of sorcery, but their relationship to

Martha Carrier was probably more important than their connection to Andover's senior pastor.

Despite Martha Carrier's significance to the Andover accusations, she could easily have been the only suspect from the town to be formally charged. It took not only the negativity surrounding her and her family but also the events described in the preceding chapters to create a general atmosphere of mistrust among a significant number of the town's residents. The memory of the witchcraft accusations against John Godfrey thirty years earlier was still alive and well, despite the fact that Godfrey himself had been dead for more than a decade. Andover was not unique in facing such internal disputes, and numerous neighboring towns had also faced sorrows such as murder and epidemic diseases but managed to emerge from 1692 virtually unscathed from witchcraft accusations. In Andover, though, the fact that the accusations involved residents already affected by contentiousness and tragedy demonstrates that the earlier incidents helped dictate the path the persecutions took once they started.

Although conditions in Andover were ripe for an explosion in 1692, just as they were in Salem Village and numerous other communities in Essex County, they still needed sparks. The first of those sparks came from one man without direct family ties to any of the town's earliest settlers. He had lived in the town only since the early 1670s, but by 1692 everyone in Andover knew who he was—and some had come to fear him.

In June 1692, Samuel Wardwell had ample reason to be worried. For nearly two decades, he had entertained and sometimes mystified his neighbors in Andover by telling their fortunes and revealing their private secrets. Ephraim Foster, who served as constable for the North End of Andover in 1692,[35] recalled that Wardwell had predicted his (Foster's) wife would give birth to five daughters before bearing a son.[36] According to James Bridges, a man in his early twenties, Wardwell had embarrassed him by revealing his infatuation with a fourteen-year-old girl in town, something Bridges, by his own account, had never admitted to anyone before.[37] Bridges acknowledged the truth of Wardwell's revelation, and the town records nearly bear out Foster's claim. The first four children listed for Ephraim Foster and his wife Hannah (Eames) Foster in Andover were, indeed, girls. The fifth child listed for the couple had been a son, but it is certainly possible that, prior to the birth of this son, a stillborn girl had been left unlisted. Thomas Chandler, the prominent original proprietor and longtime antagonist of the Tyler family, recalled that Wardwell often told young people their fortunes and described him as being "much addicted to it."[38]

Prior to 1692, a pastime such as fortune telling might have seemed like harmless fun to Wardwell's neighbors in Andover. It did not, after all, compare to pronouncing curses on people or sticking pins in poppets, as some of those accused of witchcraft in the spring of that year had done. As the fear of witchcraft ran rampant in Essex County during that fateful spring, however, people who habitually indulged in pastimes that evoked the supernatural in any way had reason to fear that their neighbors might grow suspicious of them. Wardwell must have grown increasingly nervous when the accusations reached Andover in late May with the arrest of Martha Carrier, a native of the town.

Samuel Wardwell was not born in Andover, nor did he grow up there. He was christened in the First Church of Boston May 16, 1643, though he was probably born in Exeter, New Hampshire, where his parents (Thomas and Elizabeth) had resided until shortly before his baptism. Thomas Wardwell died only three years later, leaving Elizabeth with four children of which Samuel was the youngest. Records of the family after that time are scant for several years, until Samuel's oldest brother Eliakim and his wife Lydia (Perkins) Wardwell (some records of them spell the surname as Wardell) took up residence in the town of Hampton, New Hampshire. It may be that Eliakim's mother and his fatherless younger siblings lived with him and Lydia for a time there. The young couple drew the attention of the authorities, though, for drifting toward the Quaker faith and habitually skipping the weekly Puritan church services. In April 1663, Lydia took the shocking step of protesting by walking into the church in Newbury during a Sunday morning service and stripping naked before the congregation.[39] She was publicly flogged for this offense, and the following year she and Eliakim left New England for new lands that had opened for settlement in New Jersey.

Samuel Wardwell was barely beyond adolescence at this point, and his sentiments on the matter are not recorded. Some researchers of the witch trials contend that his connection to his Quaker brother and sister-in-law contributed to his eventual arrest for witchcraft nearly thirty years later. There is, however, no noticeable correlation between family connections to Quakers in the 1660s (when persecution of Quakers was at its peak in Massachusetts Bay) and suspicion of witchcraft in 1692. The same is true of those still living (and their families) who had faced legal reprisals for hospitality to Quakers three decades earlier. In Samuel Wardwell's case, aspects of his later life seem to have played a far greater role in drawing attention to him. He apparently was married for the first time in the late 1660s to a woman whose identity remains a mystery, by whom he had a son, named Thomas (for Samuel's father, no doubt, even though he barely remembered him). This first wife died after only a brief time, perhaps in childbirth. The first record of Samuel Wardwell in Andover is his marriage there on January 9, 1673, to a young widow, Sarah (Hooper) Hawkes, who also had one small child, a daughter named Sarah Hawkes. The widow's first husband, Adam Hawkes, had been more than forty years her senior, and while his children by his first marriage had inherited the largest portion of his estate, the young mother and her daughter had been provided for. Her father, William Hooper, was also a prosperous weaver in the town of Reading, Massachusetts, where Sarah had been born. Obtaining the hand of this young woman was perhaps a step up the economic ladder for Samuel Wardwell, and some students of the witchcraft accusations had focused on his upward mobility as a reason that suspicion fell on him in 1692. But it is not certain that Wardwell was necessarily impoverished at that time. The early death of his father limits the existence of records that would have shed light on the financial situation he grew up in, but it is noteworthy that in 1664, one of his cousins, Elihu Wardwell, married Elizabeth Wade in Ipswich in 1665. Elizabeth was a daughter of

Jonathan Wade, one of the most prominent citizens of the community. Elizabeth Wade's brother Nathaniel later married Mercy Bradstreet, a daughter of Andover's leading citizen Simon Bradstreet. This family connection (though not a really close one) may have played a role in Samuel's decision to settle in Andover. Again, Samuel's personal habits appear to have contributed more to the accusations against him than any financial gain he may have experienced.

In Wardwell's time, a belief in the ability to foretell the future was commonplace. In the modern world, such beliefs are often regarded as superstitious nonsense. So how can a modern researcher reconcile Wardwell's apparent success in his craft—assuming that it was not made up from whole cloth by a few malicious neighbors whose sole purpose was to send him to the gallows (a highly unlikely scenario)? The prediction that Hannah (Eames) Foster would give birth to five girls before having a son defies any logical explanation and may have simply been an imagined memory of her husband Ephraim, who knew of Wardwell's reputation for clairvoyance and found himself in the grip of the terror of witchcraft endemic in 1692. Some of the reputed wizard's predictions are not so farfetched, though. Samuel Wardwell might have possessed an unusually keen sense of observation. He may have realized James Bridges's attraction to the fourteen-year-old girl he spoke of by watching how the young man behaved in her presence or by the expression on his face when he spoke to her or talked of her. Another of Wardwell's supposed predictions involved a young man named John Farnum who, according to the deposition of the teenager Abigail Martin, asked Wardwell to tell him his fortune. Among Wardwell's predictions was that Farnum would soon fall from a horse which, according to Martin, came true. This type of prediction could have been a self-fulfilling prophecy for Farnum if he believed it strongly enough. For Wardwell, having a prediction like this come to fruition might have been particularly dangerous. It could have led Farnum and others to believe that Wardwell had actually caused the accident by occult means.

Samuel Wardwell's major mistake came sometime in the summer of 1692. Perhaps he was seeking assurance that he was not under suspicion of witchcraft. His marriage to Sarah (Hooper) Hawkes had drawn others of her family to Andover, with two of her sisters, Rebecca and Hannah, marrying two brothers who were natives of the town, John and William Ballard, respectively. John Ballard, as previously noted, was serving as the constable of the South End of Andover in 1692 and it was he who had arrested Martha Carrier and taken her to Salem for examination in late May of that year. Samuel and Sarah also lived in the South End of the town, and their interactions with the Ballards were undoubtedly frequent. The husbands of Sarah (Hooper) Wardwell's sisters had a third brother, Joseph Ballard. By that fateful summer, Joseph's wife, Elizabeth (Phelps) Ballard, had been dangerously ill for some time. With the entire region in the grip of the fear of witchcraft, any illness or misfortune could have led residents of the area to blame the occult. Samuel Wardwell feared that suspicion would fall on him.

John Ballard was a man Samuel Wardwell undoubtedly trusted. The two men had been brothers-in-law for more than a decade by 1692, Ballard's marriage to Rebecca Hooper having occurred in 1681. Wardwell knew that Ballard had been to Salem when he took Martha Carrier there to face justice. If anyone could tell him how serious the threat he faced was, John Ballard was the man. Perhaps Wardwell had heard rumors that Elizabeth (Phelps) Ballard's illness resulted from witchcraft. Perhaps some in the town had whispered rumors that Wardwell was the culprit. Whatever prompted him to raise the issue, Wardwell asked his brother-in-law if it was true that Joseph Ballard believed his wife to be bewitched and suspected him (Wardwell) of being responsible.[40]

John Ballard was completely taken aback by his brother-in-law's question. To his knowledge, Joseph had never voiced any suspicion of Wardwell or, for that matter, even raised the suggestion that Elizabeth's sickness had anything to do with witchcraft. According to Joseph's later deposition, he had never thought Wardwell was responsible for his wife's illness until John told him of the question Wardwell raised. Once the subject of witchcraft was broached, however, Joseph Ballard could not get it out of his mind. As time passed and his wife failed to improve, he pondered the question even more. Eventually, Joseph took steps that brought a series of accusations to Andover and among those accused was Samuel Wardwell (surprisingly, he was not among the first arrested). Not so surprisingly, the suspicion that befell Wardwell also led to the arrest of his wife, his stepdaughter Sarah Hawkes, and his own oldest daughter Mercy Wardwell. In trying to reassure himself, Samuel Wardwell had inadvertently sparked a chain reaction that bought many to grief in Andover, including himself and some of his own family.

CHAPTER FIVE

Rumors
and
Nightmares

U NLIKE THE ACCUSED wizard Samuel Wardwell, Joseph and John
Ballard were lifelong residents of Andover. The exact birthdate
of Joseph, the elder of the two, is not known, but if he was not born
in Andover he must have arrived there as a very young child with his
parents, who were among the first proprietors of the town when it
was founded in 1646. John, nearly a decade younger than Joseph, was
born in Andover in 1653. The third Ballard brother, William, must
have been born in the late 1640s. Their father, also named William
Ballard, did not deed any land to his sons during his lifetime, which
limited their marriage prospects.[1] The two younger Ballards had
ample reason for gratitude to Sarah and Samuel Wardwell for their
marriages to Sarah's sisters, but John did not show much appreciation
in that fateful year of 1692. William Ballard, Jr. dissented from his
two brothers in his actions regarding the witchcraft accusations, but
his role was a minor one.[2] Joseph and John Ballard played major roles
in bringing the persecutions to Andover, with tragic consequences.

Although the wives of John and William Ballard were sisters and William was closer to John's age than Joseph was, it appears that John may have interacted with Joseph more frequently. In 1682, Andover's selectmen offered twenty acres along with the full privileges of townsmen to any residents who were willing to build and operate a gristmill, fulling mill, or sawmill along the Shawsheen River in the growing south end of town. With their aging father showing no signs of relinquishing any of his land, Joseph and John Ballard took advantage of this offer in 1688, constructing a system of mills that would remain in operation for two centuries in a then-isolated section of Andover still known as Ballardvale.[3] Samuel Wardwell, a carpenter, may very well have assisted in the building of these mills. In addition to the economic opportunity these mills offered, Joseph Ballard may also have seen this as a means of expanding his own growing influence in the town. His father William, though among Andover's original proprietors, had never served as a selectman, at least not according to the surviving town meeting minutes, which date from 1656. Neither had his presumed maternal uncle, John Lovejoy, who was also among Andover's founders. But Joseph had been named a selectman in 1687, one of a few residents who were starting to break the longtime stranglehold that a small group (Dudley Bradstreet, John Osgood, John Frye, and Richard Barker) had held on the position for more than a decade. The office of selectman was the highest office one could hold in a Massachusetts Bay town during the colonial era—the selectmen made all of the town's major decisions. Prior to that time, Joseph had served two stints as constable of the South End of Andover—in 1680 and 1682. The job of constable often served as a springboard to positions of greater responsibility later in life. It was showing signs of doing that for Joseph Ballard by the time he embarked on his venture as a miller, and perhaps his younger brother John saw partnering with Joseph in this enterprise as a means of elevating his own stature in the town. John also needed the financial benefits—his wife, Rebecca, had given birth to their fourth child, Sherebiah, in 1688, and with Rebecca still only thirty-two years old, they had every reason to expect the arrival of several more children before the end of the century. As it turned out, the elder William Ballard died in 1689, a year after John and Joseph began their new enterprise, and these two younger Ballards divided their father's property with their third brother William and gave their widowed mother Grace a room in her late husband's house for as long as she lived (it is likely that John and his family lived in this house also).[4] This further raised the economic status of all three Ballard brothers, and it may have played a role in the naming of John as constable of the South End in early March 1692. John, thirty-nine years old at the time, undoubtedly welcomed the appointment at first, having seen what it had helped lead to for Joseph.

John's initial involvement in the witchcraft accusations had come in late May 1692, when he arrested Andover resident Martha Carrier for witchcraft after she had been complained against by residents of Salem Village. Soon after that time, however, new accusations ground to a halt as trials for those already charged began in earnest. At that point, John Ballard may have felt he would have no further involvement in the drama playing out in neighboring Salem, except for possibly escorting witnesses there to testify against Carrier. He was probably more worried at that point about the illness of his sister-in-law Elizabeth, the wife of his brother Joseph. John's concern must have been significant, but Joseph would have been beside himself. Aside from his love for his wife, Joseph had at least five children still at home to worry about, the youngest an eight-year-old son named Uriah. But Joseph Ballard's situation was hardly unusual in an era in which any number of fevers or epidemic diseases could cut short the lives of those who seemed vigorous only days before. Whatever Elizabeth Ballard's illness was, it seems that her husband never gave a remote thought to the idea that witchcraft might be involved—until he heard a rumor to that effect passed on to him by his brother, the constable. For John Ballard, the seed had been planted in his mind by the loose tongue of his brother-in-law Samuel Wardwell—a man who seemed to expect the witchcraft suspicion to fall on him at any time. This fear became a self-fulfilling prophecy.

Having taken Martha Carrier to Salem to await her trial, John Ballard may have had more exposure to what was happening in Salem than anyone else in Andover. Going there may also have reawakened some childhood memories. The Ballards were not without exposure to the accusations against John Godfrey thirty years earlier. In 1662 their parents, William and Grace, had taken in Job Tyler's wife Mary and their children for a time after their home had burned. That was three years after the first suspicions of Godfrey, in which the Tylers had been at the forefront, with the two oldest children (Moses and Mary) having testified against the suspected wizard. Some of the Tyler children were contemporaries of the three Ballard brothers and their six sisters, and young John Ballard, aged nine at the time, would have been particularly impressionable if the Tyler children shared their suspicions of Godfrey with him. All of the Ballard children would have heard of the various misfortunes that had befallen the Tyler family, and they probably never forgot it. Belief in witchcraft was the norm, and the Ballards probably suspected just as strongly as their house-guests did that sorcery played a role in their hardships.

In any event, there is no reason to believe that John Ballard questioned the reality of witchcraft, and once the thought that witches could be responsible for his sister-in-law's ailment was suggested to him, he could not have considered keeping the idea from Joseph. The record does not show how long Joseph agonized over the possibility that witches had sickened his wife before he took action. He could have simply accused Samuel Wardwell, whose previous activities and loose tongue made him an easy target. But once Joseph Ballard had witchcraft on his mind, he felt the need to consult the "experts," so to speak. Despite the fact that witchcraft suspicions had fallen on people all over Essex County and beyond, no one outside Salem Village had yet taken the step of asking some of the afflicted girls residing in that community to travel to their own town and determine whether or not the black arts were responsible for an illness or other misfortune. Joseph Ballard issued that unprecedented invitation, and two of the girls of Salem Village (their identities are unknown, but subsequent events suggest Mary Warren was one of them) came to Andover, a town they may never have visited before. Surprisingly enough, they did not concentrate on Samuel Wardwell at that time. Instead, they focused first on the most melancholy widow in Andover as the source of the danger Joseph's wife, Elizabeth (Phelps) Ballard, faced.

In July 1692, the widow Ann Foster was probably in her mid-seventies and was apparently quite frail physically. Her adverse circumstances recall a statement attributed to Rebecca Nurse at the time of her own arrest for witchcraft: "What sin hath God found out in me unrepented of that He should lay such an affliction on me in my old age?" Nurse, of course, was implying not that she was guilty of witchcraft (if she actually said this), but that she was being punished for some other sin when she fell under suspicion. In the case of Ann Foster, the murder of her daughter and the harm suffered by her grandson could easily have occasioned similar thoughts before the witchcraft accusations even began. Perhaps she was not entirely surprised when the afflicted girls from Salem Village focused on her as their first suspect in the town when they came to identify witches there in July 1692.

The complaint against Ann Foster does not survive, but it is generally thought to have been filed by Joseph Ballard. One cannot rule out Timothy Swan, who was also sick, and, as previously noted, was hardly likely to have been popular among women of any age in Andover. He was specifically named as a victim of Ann Foster in the record of her examination, whereas Elizabeth (Phelps) Ballard was not. The initial documentation associated with Ann Foster does indicate that she was accused of hurting others, even though they are not named; therefore, Joseph Ballard could have been her initial formal accuser.

Ultimately though, the question of who filed the official complaint against Ann Foster is unimportant. Of far greater significance is what her arrest led to. Between the infirmities of her advanced age and the emotional devastation she had endured, she may have been the most frail person to be arrested on suspicion of witchcraft throughout the entire notorious year of 1692. As such, she was particularly vulnerable to the interrogations that she and all of the other suspects were subjected to after their arrests. Examination records show that the judges questioned her at least four times over a period of seven days beginning July 15. Regrettably, these records do not contain the specific questions and answers, such as were given in Tituba's confession four months earlier, but they provide enough details to illustrate their significance. Ann Foster became the eighth suspect to confess to witchcraft—notably the second adult of European background, though it is not clear whether that made her statements any more credible in such a fear-driven environment.[5] Notes from her first deposition, dated July 15, indicated that the devil had appeared to her three times, always in the shape of a bird, and had given her the power to strike down the afflicted with her eyes. She also mentioned that the already imprisoned Martha Carrier—perhaps the only suspect she was personally acquainted with—had "persuaded her to hurt these people."[6] The next day, Foster was more specific, saying that Carrier had made her a witch about six years earlier and had incited her to bewitch a few specific people (including two children of Carrier's brother Andrew Allen). She also mentioned that she and Carrier had ridden on sticks to a meeting at Salem Village where she saw, among others, George Burroughs, the minister of Wells. She said that while there, she had "tied a knot in a rag and threw it into the fire to hurt Timothy Swan,"[7] and that she had hurt others who were complaining against her by squeezing poppets.

To this point, there was nothing new in Ann Foster's statements, although any confession was noteworthy at that point because there had been so few of them. The two other suspects she named (Martha Carrier and George Burroughs) had already been jailed on suspicion of witchcraft. The judges were not satisfied, though, and interrogated her again on July 18. Aspects of Foster's testimony that day went far beyond anything any confessor or accuser had previously stated. One oddly specific item Foster mentioned was that she and Carrier had ridden together to the meeting in Salem Village and that the pole had broken. They had fallen, she said, but she had held on to Carrier's neck until they arrived even though she had badly injured her leg. The most significant new item in the confession of July 18, though, involved the number of witches mentioned. Foster claimed that others at the meeting told her that a total of 305 witches were in the country. Three days later, she confirmed everything she had said in all of the previous confessions and put her mark to it, further stating the intention of the group was to set up the devil's kingdom.

The next two suspects arrested were inextricably intertwined with Foster. On July 19, the day after Foster first spoke of 305 witches in the region (and also the same day five convicted witches went to the gallows in Salem), Joseph Ballard filed another complaint against two suspects: Mary Foster Lacey (age forty) and her eighteen-year-old daughter (also named Mary Lacey); respectively, the daughter and granddaughter of Ann Foster. Their identities echoed a pattern long-established in Salem Village and surrounding communities earlier that year. This familial connection between suspects was not surprising. Already, Martha Corey and her husband Giles were languishing in jail awaiting trial by the summer of 1692. John and Elizabeth Bassett Procter were another married couple who had been arrested, and they had been joined by their son William. Two sisters of the aforementioned Rebecca Nurse, Sarah Towne Cloyce and Mary Towne Esty (or Easty), had also fallen under suspicion after the arrest of Rebecca. The arrest and confession of the teenage Abigail Hobbs had been followed by indictments against her stepmother Deliverance and her father William. It was not unexpected that the same cloud of suspicion over Ann Foster would also envelop her daughter and granddaughter.

Although the Lacey family resided in the North End, Mary Foster Lacey was a native of the South End, having only moved to the North End when married. (As previously noted her husband was Lawrence Lacey, a relative newcomer to the town at the time of their wedding in 1673.) They were the parents of five children, the oldest of whom (who was accused along with her mother) was Mary, born in 1674. The murder of Mary Foster Lacey's sister Hannah in 1689 must have devastated her as well as her mother Ann Foster. If the tragic event incapacitated Mary Foster Lacey in any way, her eldest daughter might have had to take on more even household responsibilities than she would have under normal circumstances (her burden would have been heavy anyway). The younger Mary mentioned in the course of her confession that she had previously run away from her parents' home for two days, blaming the devil for enticing her to do so. She mentioned having obtained food at the home of her cousin John Stone (the eldest son of her murdered aunt) during her absence.[8] In reality, it was probably a simple act of adolescent rebellion, common at that age. An added workload in a household wracked by grief would only have served as added motivation. In 1692, the eighteen-year-old Mary Lacey was obviously a troubled young woman—one whose emotions helped to wreak havoc in her native community.

The warrant for the arrest of the two Lacey women was issued on July 20, and they were apprehended on July 21 by the North End's constable Ephraim Foster (not a close relative). Upon delivering them to jail, Foster noted that he and others had searched the Lacey home for poppets and had found a parcel of rags, yarn, and tape, along with another parcel of quills. No one in the family, according to the constable, knew what they were for.[9] But this physical evidence of the practice of witchcraft proved unnecessary when the Laceys came before four of the judges of the court for examination, along with Ann Foster, who was being grilled for the fourth time. Ann Foster did not deny anything she had previously confessed, but she refused to incriminate her daughter and granddaughter. The two younger women, however, both freely confessed. The elder Lacey even admitted to riding on the broom with her mother and Martha Carrier to the meeting of witches in Salem Village and also disclosed that she had been "baptized" as a witch three to four years earlier—the first confessor to mention baptism. The teenage daughter followed suit, though she initially claimed to have been a witch for only about a week, having been made one by her mother. The court proceedings note that as the younger Lacey testified, Mary Warren fell into a violent fit—a hint that Warren may have been one of the afflicted girls who came to Andover at Joseph Ballard's request. In a test that would play a major role later in Andover, the younger Lacey obeyed orders to touch Warren's arm, upon which the latter's fit immediately ceased. At this point, Lacey's testimony became rambling and contradictory (not surprising given the obvious pressure she was under). Having initially stated that she had been a witch for only a week, she then confessed to having become one more than a year earlier, at the bidding of the devil himself, who came to her while she was in bed. She acknowledged hurting Elizabeth Ballard as well as Timothy Swan (whom her grandmother had also confessed to injuring) and she went on to talk of riding a pole with others and to having prayed to the devil and served him after the devil had told her he was a god and lord to her.[10]

The devil as a god and lord to her—young Mary Lacey had offered the witch hunters the third confession in less than a week. Like her mother and grandmother, she offered further evidence against the already jailed Martha Carrier. She went further with her incriminations of Carrier than any previous witness to the latter's alleged sorcery. In her confession of July 21, Mary accused Martha Carrier of several murders (including those of Carrier's own two brothers and a brother-in-law, all of whom had died in the smallpox epidemic). She also identified a child of James Frye and the wife of Christopher Osgood as victims of Carrier. Neither of these two died in the smallpox epidemic, so Mary was accusing Carrier of additional homicides. She made it a point to mention that Osgood and Carrier had had a falling out before.[11] Lacey first said that Carrier killed her victims by directly stabbing them in the heart with pins and knitting needles, but then (prompted at least partly by the magistrates) shifted the story and declared that the murderer had pierced likenesses of her victims (in the form of poppets) with her weapons. Lacey's most damning statement, however, was her claim that Carrier had told her the devil had promised that she (Carrier) would be a "Queen in Hell."[12]

Martha Carrier as "Queen in Hell"—this was the sobriquet she would go down in history with. No less a personage than Cotton Mather designated her by that title in his writings after the trials.[13] But on that July day before the magistrates in Salem, it was the teenage Mary Lacey who labelled Carrier with that term, giving her a status among the suspected witches almost equal to that of George Burroughs, who had previously been identified as the ringleader of the growing coven. Each of the three Foster/Lacey women, in admitting her own guilt of the crime of witchcraft, added significant new wrinkles to the already volatile situation.

Two key questions arise from the confessions of the three generations of Foster/Lacey women accused. No other family had been so accommodating to the accusers and the magistrates, but this was also the first time three generations of the same family had been examined together in court. It is also necessary to assess the impact of the family's depositions on subsequent events in the persecutions. For the first question, it is possible that the judges simply tricked Ann Foster into implying her own guilt, much as John Hathorne had done with Tituba four months earlier. It is also possible that this frail old woman was simply overcome by the screams of the afflicted in the courtroom and suffered an emotional collapse under the pressure. The knowledge that their matriarch had already confessed could easily have weakened the resolve of the two younger women when they came into court with Foster three days later. It is true that plenty of other suspects had withstood the questioning and the hysteria of the afflicted, including Rebecca Nurse, who was probably nearly as feeble as Foster (at least physically). Nurse, however, had not endured the family tragedies that Foster, her daughter, and granddaughter had experienced.

Nurse was among five for whom death warrants had been issued on July 12, just three days before Foster's first confession. The five went to the gallows on July 19, the day after Foster claimed that 305 witches were in the area. It is worth noting that none of the five sentenced to death had confessed, and Foster and the two Laceys may have realized this. To assume that they confessed only to save their lives at that point in the trials is a leap of faith, however. Of more than sixty already jailed on witchcraft charges, only seven had confessed, and no previous history suggested that confessors would ultimately be spared the hangman's noose. Rebecca Nurse's own lament—"What sin hath God found out in me unrepented of that He should lay such an affliction on me in my old age?"—might actually hold the key to the most likely reason that Ann Foster confessed—and why her daughter and granddaughter followed suit.

Nurse's statement referred specifically to her arrest for witchcraft, but Foster had reasons for similar thoughts at the time of her daughter's murder three years earlier. The severe wounds suffered by her grandson would only have exacerbated her feelings. The idea that "sins unrepented of" could bring tragedy into one's life resonated with many in the seventeenth century, as did belief in witchcraft. Some people could easily have come to believe that they did, in fact, fall prey to the devil without realizing how they had done so. Someone who had experienced the emotional devastations endured by Ann Foster would be a prime candidate. Survivors of tragedies often endure horrific nightmares—and some of the experiences related by Ann Fos-

ter during her interrogations could easily have resulted from these
dreams.

On the whole, it is surprising that historians of the 1692 witchcraft
trials have not given more attention to the possible role of nightmares
in the surviving testimony. Dreams would not explain the actions of
the afflicted in the courtroom, for the teenage girls and others who
screamed that the specters of suspects were attacking them right then
and there were obviously wide awake. Depositions, however, teem
with accounts of being approached by suspects and encouraged to
sign the devil's book—on a previous occasion, not as actual testimony
was unfolding. This is a prime possibility as a dream, given the fact
that society in the seventeenth-century Massachusetts Bay colony took
such possibilities seriously and anyone who believed themselves to be
under assault by witches could dream of such an event. Other, less
commonplace events described in the testimony of witnesses seem almost certain to have been the product of dreams, primarily because
the deponents describe having been awakened during the night. Two
men who testified against Bridget Bishop—Samuel Gray and William
Stacy, both of Salem—claimed that her specter came to them in the
night. Gray claimed not to have known Bishop previously, but he described how fourteen years before the trials, he had awakened one
night after being asleep for some time and "saw the house light as if
a candle or candles were lighted in it and the dor locked,"[14] and then
saw a woman standing between the cradle and the bed. He noted that
when he rose, the woman disappeared, and when he unlocked the
door and went out, he saw her just before she disappeared once more.
He then claimed that after he returned to bed, he felt something cold
over his mouth and lips, whereupon he awakened and saw the woman
again. This was followed by a loud cry from the child in the cradle,
which was the beginning of the sickness that later claimed the child's
life. Gray claimed that only recently had he encountered Bridget
Bishop and recognized her as the woman he had seen.
  Stacy's experience was quite similar, except that he acknowledged

that he already knew Bishop, remembering having been visited by her when he had been ill with smallpox (again, fourteen years previously). He claimed Bishop professed a great love for him at the time and then noted she had hired him to work for her following his recovery. After this time, he claimed to have experienced several misfortunes, all of which he attributed to Bishop's sorcery, but the nighttime sequence he described involved a feeling of something cold pressing hard against his teeth, whereupon he sat up and saw Bishop sitting at the foot of his bed. Like Gray, Stacy blamed Bishop for the death of one of his children (a daughter Priscilla), but he did not attribute it so directly to the nighttime visit he described.

Upon reading these depositions, it seems clear that what both men described were dreams. An initial reaction might easily be that both of these men had felt physical attractions to Bishop that played out in their sleep. However Gray and Stacy (aged forty-two and thirty-six, respectively, at the time of the trials) were both significantly younger than Bishop who, having married for the first time in 1660, must have been at least in her early fifties. It may be more likely that both men somehow got the impression that Bishop had been attracted to them and were not happy about it, therefore classifying their dreams about her as nightmares—nightmares that they came to regard as actual experiences once Bishop fell under suspicion of witchcraft. Bernard Peach of Amesbury, who was forty-three in 1692, gave a similar account of Susanna Martin, who was old enough to be his mother. Again, a belief in attraction on the part of the accused witch (whether true or not) seems to have caused a bad dream in this case. Rather than lusting after older women, these men may have flattered themselves into believing the women were interested in them and feared the consequences of rejecting them—a situation that could easily turn into a nightmare.

Anyone who thought himself or herself bewitched could easily have such incidents play themselves out in dreams. By the same token, a person afraid that he or she had unknowingly become a witch could have that fear play out in nightmares. The incidents Ann Foster described in her depositions—riding on a pole with Martha Carrier to a meeting, having to hold onto Carrier's neck after the pole broke, meeting the devil in the form of a bird and then later as a man, injuring Timothy Swan by throwing a rag into a fire, and most significant, being told of the presence of 305 witches in the area—all could have happened in nightmares she experienced. Some (if not all) of the dreams may have occurred after she was arrested. If she had suspected she was guilty of witchcraft, the arrest may have confirmed it in her mind, leading her to have a series of nightmares in the days between her interrogations. It is hardly surprising that Martha Carrier, her neighbor in Andover and fellow prisoner, would play such a prominent role in her dreams.

Even if whatever nightmares Ann Foster experienced helped lead her to confess, to attribute her confession entirely to dreams would be hasty. Her frailty has already been mentioned, and the fact that she was subject to four days of intense questioning could have simply caused her to crack under the pressure. It is possible that at that stage of the persecutions, pressure to confess was intensified. Five convicted witches had been executed two days earlier, and while most of the actual trial records have not survived, there is little doubt that previous confessors had supplied evidence that helped convict them. The justices knew what suspects who acknowledged their own guilt could contribute to the prosecutions. Confessors could also help convict others in indirect ways—a piece of evidence used to convict Rebecca Nurse (hanged on July 19) was a statement she made concerning Deliverance Hobbs (who had admitted she was a witch) that she was "one of us." What Nurse had meant was that Hobbs was a fellow prisoner, but the justices and ultimately the jurors had used the statement against Nurse, interpreting it to mean that Hobbs was a fellow witch. The fact that Hobbs had confessed gave more weight to this comment by Rebecca Nurse than it would have had Hobbs not disclosed her own guilt. Ann Foster had been interrogated four times in six days. Her daughter and granddaughter would have learned this from her once they were in jail along with her. They may have confessed simply to spare themselves a similar ordeal.

✳

Breaking down the resistance of a frail, old, grief-wracked woman was one thing—wrenching affirmations of guilt from an apparently healthy forty-year-old and a vibrant teenager was quite another. Ann Foster had resisted incriminating her daughter and granddaughter, despite obvious pressure to do so from the justices. But both of the younger women did extend blame to their respective mothers in their disclosures, and the younger Mary Lacey confirmed her grand-mother's guilt as well. One fact that cannot be ignored is that confessors were being taken to the courtroom to testify against those being tried. The others in jail could not have overlooked that. Given the conditions of the jails, a few hours respite that would result from being taken to court must have been an appealing prospect. People in such dire situations who have every reason to think that death ultimately awaits them will often take desperate measures to partake in any moment of pleasure (or simple relief from pain), no matter how small. A belief in the possibility of ultimately being spared the death penalty would not have been necessary.

All the aforementioned possible reasons for the Foster and Lacey confessions could have played into later confessions as well, though other factors became more evident in the following weeks. But there may have been reasons for the Laceys' disclosures that applied specifically to them. It cannot be forgotten that Ephraim Foster, the constable that arrested them, had discovered parcels of rags, yarn, tape, and quills while searching their home. This physical evidence is not as damning as the poppets found years earlier in Bridget Bishop's cellar, but the possibility that one or both women actually practiced witchcraft with the intent of harming others cannot be ruled out. The elder Mary Lacey did specifically say that if "she doe take a rag, clout or any such thing and roll it up together and imagine it to represent such & such a person, then whatsoever she doth to that rag or clout so rouled up, the personne represented thereby will be in lyke manner afflicted."[15] If she and/or her daughter did do such things, they could have been stricken by a horror of conscience before or after their arrests that led them to fear for their destination in the afterlife—especially if they had specifically targeted Timothy Swan, who had fallen ill. These fears could have played themselves out in nightmares, and for people under such stress, the distinctions between dreams and reality can easily blur. Ministers often noted in sermons that those who confessed their sins, regardless of what those sins were, had greater reason to hope for ultimate salvation. In the case of the younger Mary Lacey, she may have also calculated that she could follow the path charted by Mary Warren three months earlier. Warren, as previously noted, had confessed to witchcraft after having temporarily betrayed the other afflicted girls in April. Upon confessing and once again accusing her master and mistress (John and Elizabeth Procter), she had been reintegrated into the ranks of the accusers. The younger Mary Lacey had not acted the part of an accuser prior to her arrest. Nonetheless, two days after her confession, she was in court falling into fits at the examination of Martha Toothaker Emerson, a newly arrested niece of Martha Carrier. Could she join the ranks of the afflicted and obtain the benefits of their status? At that stage, this would have been an open question.

Ann Foster's confession was only the third since those of Abigail and Deliverance Hobbs and Mary Warren three months earlier—the other confessors were a slave named Candy and a teenager named Margaret Jacobs. To the magistrates and others, perhaps the most significant aspect of Foster's statement was the claim that there were 305 witches in the area. No one had previously mentioned a number nearly this large. It is not certain how the judges reacted—many historians believe that they had a vested interest in keeping the trials going as long as possible—but once the word got out into the general population, it must have struck a new level of terror in their hearts. Those who still supported the activities of the witch hunters had reason to believe that the work was far from finished, for barely a fifth of the active witches had been taken into custody. Those who were starting to doubt the validity of the hunt had greater reason to believe that they, or their families and friends, would eventually fall under suspicion. For more than a month, the focus of the Court of Oyer and Terminer had been on trying those who had already been arrested.

Ann Foster's confession and those of her daughter and granddaughter sparked a new rash of arrests. The Andover witch hunt had begun.

CHAPTER SIX

The Andover Witch Hunt

S AMUEL WARDWELL, Andover's fortune teller, fearful that he would fall under suspicion, had voiced his concern to his brother-in-law, the South End's constable John Ballard. Wardwell specifically referenced the illness of Elizabeth (Phelps) Ballard, the wife of John's brother Joseph. John, in turn, told Joseph of Wardwell's trepidations, probably because he came to consider witchcraft as a likely source of Elizabeth's illness himself. The constable had, after all, been to Salem when he took accused witch Martha Carrier there at the end of May. Joseph Ballard confronted Wardwell with John's revelation, and Wardwell acknowledged having said it. The power of suggestion is high at any time in a society that believes in witchcraft, and Joseph knew all too well what was going on a few miles to the east. Seeing no relief to his wife's deteriorating condition, he undoubtedly would have seized on anything that offered the remotest possibility of a cure. The step he took was unprecedented in that fateful year—he sent for some of the afflicted girls from Salem Village, in the hope that they could determine if witchcraft was causing his wife's illness, and if so, who the witches were that were attacking her. Two of the girls came—the records do not reveal their names—and, as witch hunt critic Thomas Brattle wrote three months later, "Poor Andover does now rue the day."[1]

Ann Foster's confession, while it did offer evidence that far more witches were at large than originally thought, did not mean that a large number of them resided in Andover. If anything, her statement that she knew no one at the meeting she attended other than Martha Carrier would have suggested just the opposite. But another twist, illuminated by the testimony of the younger Mary Lacey, may have intensified the focus on Andover and the adjacent communities. Lacey designated Martha Carrier, the first Andover resident to be accused, as the future "Queen in Hell." This leadership role the younger Mary Lacey ascribed to Martha Carrier cannot be discounted as a significant factor in the explosion of accusations directed at Andover residents in general. Once the witch hunters saw Andover as the home of the future "Queen in Hell," it was no great leap for them to conclude that this leader of the coven had actively and effectively solicited her neighbors. Salem Village had been the first place attacked by the witches, but Andover led the region in producing adherents to the craft.

No such fate befell the neighbors of the minister George Burroughs, who had been identified in earlier accusations as the ringleader of the entire conspiracy. Burroughs's situation differed from Martha Carrier's in several crucial ways. For one, he lived significantly farther from Salem Village and the town of Salem than Martha Carrier did. Second, unlike Martha Carrier, he was not a native of the region (having grown up in Maryland) so he did not have a large network of relatives and longtime associates who could have been accused along with him. Third, while he was in jail, his place of residence was decimated in attacks by the Wabanaki confederacy, leaving virtually no former neighbors of his to fall under suspicion. Living in Andover, Martha Carrier was surrounded by people she had grown up with (as previously noted, her father Andrew Allen was one of the original proprietors of the town) and her extended family group. She brought far greater potential for guilt by association to the table than George Burroughs did—and the accusations flew at her associates in short order. The next three arrested after the Foster/Lacey women were Carrier's teenage sons, Andrew and Richard, and her namesake niece, Martha (Toothaker) Emerson (who resided in neighboring Haverhill). All three confessed—though Emerson's "confession" was lukewarm at best. With six arrests and confessions over an eight-day period, the first phase of the crisis in Andover was in full swing by July 23.

Despite the number of people who claimed to be afflicted by witchcraft in Salem Village, the town of Salem, and the surrounding area prior to mid-July, only one death was attributed to supernatural forces during that time. Daniel Wilkins, the seventeen-year-old grandson of Bray Wilkins (who had complained of bewitchment by his granddaughter's husband John Willard) died on May 16, 1692, after an illness that left him gasping for breath at the end. John Willard, whom several members of the Wilkins family had accused of causing the illnesses of Bray and young Daniel by occult means, was arrested the same day or shortly after. The Wilkins family was not among the leading accusers like the Putnams, however, and John Willard was the only person any of them had blamed for their sufferings. He was apprehended within a day of the teenage boy's death, and although a warrant had been issued for his arrest a week prior, it may be fortunate that he was not caught any earlier. Because Willard was not yet in custody when Daniel Wilkins died, his family had no reason to suspect that anyone other than Willard was responsible. Had he died *after* Willard's arrest, it might have caused the family to think that others besides Willard had been involved, and they may have become more active in the persecutions as a result. There were enough arrests as it was—a difference in the timing of the Willard/Wilkins case could have led to more. One shudders to think of the possible consequences if one of the afflicted girls had died while the examinations and trials were still ongoing.

By July 27, five suspects in Andover and one in neighboring Haverhill had been arrested in part due to their alleged supernatural assaults on Elizabeth (Phelps) Ballard and twenty-nine-year-old bachelor and suspected rapist Timothy Swan. But unlike the Salem Village victims of witchcraft whose symptoms were psychosomatic, Ballard and Swan were physically ill and Ballard had been for some time—even before her husband Joseph had heard the suggestion that witchcraft lay at the root of her illness. But despite the arrests, Elizabeth Ballard did not improve. On July 27, she died—the arrests and confessions of her tormentors had not saved her. More witches were still at large—and in the minds of her husband and at least some of Andover's other residents, they had to be brought to justice too before they succeeded in killing other victims.

Elizabeth Ballard's death must have terrified Swan. Whether or not he had believed himself bewitched before Joseph Ballard brought the afflicted girls to Andover, he had certainly reached that conclusion by July 27—and he must have suspected any woman who had ever given him a look of anger. Although numerous witchcraft suspects were accused of attacking him, there is no evidence that he ever made the journey to Salem to testify against any of them, most likely because he was unable to. He died in February 1693 as the witchcraft persecutions were petering out.[2] There is no known record of what sickened and ultimately killed this young man, but he and his brothers Robert and John (both of whom filed complaints on Timothy's behalf) blamed it on witchcraft.

Elizabeth Ballard's death shifted the witch hunt in Andover into high gear. Witches could kill, for they had already been blamed for several previous deaths in the testimonies of the afflicted, but now one of their victims had died even *after* some of her alleged tormentors had been confined to jail. Ann Foster's statements had already convinced many that there had been 305 witches in the area at the time of the meeting she attended. Satan certainly could have secured even more recruits since then. Not surprisingly, one of the children who later became afflicted in Andover was Sarah Phelps, the ten-year-old daughter of Samuel Phelps (brother of Elizabeth Ballard). Young Sarah might have even seen her aunt's sufferings at some point and, hearing that she had been bewitched to death, grown fearful of falling victim to a similar fate. That alone could have caused her to experience the same type of psychosomatic symptoms as the girls of Salem

Village. Her mother, Sarah, was a daughter of the Tyler family's antagonist, Thomas Chandler. Later on, Hannah (Chandler) Bixby (or
Bigsby), another of Thomas's daughters (married to Daniel Bixby),
complained of afflictions of her own and testified against suspects at
their examinations. The afflictions of young Sarah Phelps almost certainly stemmed from the terror that resulted from the death of her
aunt Elizabeth at the hands of witches (as Sarah would have believed).
Such fears again can cause horrific nightmares, especially in children.
Elizabeth Phelps Ballard was the sister of Sarah's father, but the little
girl's subsequent afflictions may, in turn, have frightened her mother's
sister, Hannah Bixby, into having similar experiences. Psychosomatic
illnesses are often just as contagious as germ-borne ones, and even
though neither Sarah Phelps nor Hannah Bixby died from their alleged bewitchments, the possibility that they suffered from physical
ailments cannot be discounted.

As already noted there were distinctions between the Salem Village
accusations and the later phase in Andover to its west. The Salem Village accusations were a continuous process, beginning in early March
and gradually gaining steam until early June, dominated by the same
group of accusers (though the number of alleged victims gradually
increased). In Andover, in contrast, the witchcraft complaints can be
divided into two distinct phases. The first phase began on July 15
with the first interrogation of Ann Foster and continued until August
19 with the examination of Rebecca (Blake) Eames of the neighboring
town of Boxford. During this time period, except in the case of
Martha Carrier, the primary accusers were some of the afflicted girls
from Salem Village, the gravely ill Timothy Swan, and, to some degree
Joseph Ballard (although his involvement seems to have been minimal
after the death of his wife on July 27). After August 19, there was a
six-day break in court actions—perhaps not coincidentally because
that was the day that five more convicted witches were hanged. When
examinations resumed in earnest on August 25, it quickly became apparent that a new group of girls claiming attacks by witches had

moved to the forefront. These girls were residents of Andover and Boxford. Although the previous accusers did not disappear from the scene, those newly afflicted took center stage during this second phase, which also saw the incrimination of a number of people much more prominent than anyone accused during the first month of allegations directed at Andover residents.

This distinction between two phases was not the only noticeable difference between Salem Village and Andover. In Salem Village, a single extended family—the Putnams—led the charge in rooting out the plague of witchcraft. In Andover, no single family group dominated the proceedings against the devil's alleged minions. The Chandler family accounted for six accusers, but its patriarchs—brothers Thomas and William—did not come close to reprising the crucial role played by Thomas and Edward Putnam in Salem Village. Another difference between the Chandler brothers and the Putnams of Salem Village is that the Chandlers later switched sides, signing petitions in support of the accused later in the year. In Andover, what emerged instead was a focus on specific families as prime candidates for suspicion, with two large family groups having the most members accused of witchcraft. Perhaps not coincidentally, both of these families had members who had played a part in the witchcraft charges against John Godfrey three decades earlier. The extended family of Martha Carrier had already seen several members accused by the time of Elizabeth Ballard's demise. The other family (the Tyler clan) began falling under suspicion immediately after the sick woman breathed her last.

Edmund Ingalls and his wife Ann were among the earliest settlers of Lynn, Massachusetts, arriving there sometime in the 1630s. They are assumed to have been from the village of Skirbeck in the English county of Lincolnshire. They had nine children, most of whom were apparently born before the family came to Massachusetts Bay. Like many of the "Great Migration" immigrants to New England, Edmund and Ann undoubtedly have hundreds of thousands of living descendants today. (Their most famous descendant with the Ingalls surname is the author Laura Ingalls Wilder, who wrote of her child-hood experiences on the American frontier in the post-Civil War era.) Edmund Ingalls himself met an untimely end, drowning in 1648 when a bridge collapsed as he rode across it on horseback. This was one of the first tragedies to strike the Ingalls family in America, but it would not be the last. The Ingalls surname is not one that is commonly associated with the witch persecutions of 1692. Before the trials were over however, fifteen descendants of Edmund and Ann Ingalls would find themselves accused of witchcraft, along with two others who had married into the family. Edmund and Ann Ingalls did not live to see the trials, but no other immigrant couple had more of their progeny charged with dealing in the black arts in 1692. Three of the Ingalls couple's children had settled in Andover, and in 1692, the families of two of them paid a terrible price for that fateful decision.

The involvement of Henry Ingalls (ca. 1627–1719), the only son of Edmund and Ann to settle in Andover, was minimal. He and three of his sons (Henry, Jr., Samuel, and John) all signed a petition in January 1693 supporting Andover residents who still faced charges of witchcraft. It was the families of two of Henry Ingalls's sisters who fell under suspicion. Faith Ingalls, born in the early 1620s, had married Andrew Allen, one of the original proprietors of Andover. Faith's younger sister Elizabeth was the first wife of Andover's longtime minister, Francis Dane (and the mother of all of his children).

Prior to 1692, the only known involvement any member of the Ingalls clan had in witchcraft accusations was the skepticism Francis Dane expressed about the charges leveled at John Godfrey in Andover and Haverhill three decades earlier. Given the circumstances of Edmund Ingalls's death, it would not have been altogether surprising if some members of the family had viewed witchcraft as a possible culprit and accused someone that Edmund had quarreled with. Other accidental deaths were blamed on witchcraft in New England at that time.[3] In the case of Ingalls, however, no one blamed anything other than a defective bridge for his untimely end, and his heirs recovered monetary damages from the town.[4] In 1692, however, the families of his two aforementioned daughters found themselves charged with all sorts of supernatural shenanigans. The family of Faith (Ingalls) Allen felt the accusers' wrath first. Faith herself apparently did not live to see the trials (her death is not recorded in Andover, but she seems to disappear from the records after the deaths of her husband and five other family members in the 1690 smallpox epidemic). But by the time of the death of Elizabeth (Phelps) Ballard on July 27, 1692, two of Faith Allen's daughters (Martha Carrier and Mary Toothaker) and four of her grandchildren (Richard Carrier, Andrew Carrier, Margaret Toothaker, and Martha Toothaker Emerson) sat confined in jail in Salem on charges of dabbling in the black arts. Mary Toothaker's husband Roger had died in the same jail six weeks earlier. Already, seven members of this family had been consumed by the hysteria that had enveloped the region and was taking firm root in Andover.[5]

Although all of the aforementioned relatives of Martha Carrier (except for her niece Martha Toothaker Emerson) had been taken into custody by the time young Mary Lacey identified Carrier as the future "Queen in Hell" (and Emerson was already under suspicion), this bit of testimony more than any other event may account for why so many members of the extended family ultimately fell under suspicion of witchcraft. After all, to the extent logic plays into the drama at all (and to those who constituted the majority that believed in witchcraft at the time, the proceedings were logical), what better way could a witch attain such an exalted status in hell as queen than to recruit as many others as possible to the devil's fold? For a disciple of Satan who wished to obtain such an honor, the obvious place to turn for these recruits would be her own relatives—not only her immediate family, but her extended kinship network as well. The town of Andover was heavily populated with descendants of Martha Carrier's long dead maternal grandparents, Edmund and Ann Ingalls. In the minds of those who thought themselves afflicted by witches, this kinship network was a fertile source of suspects.

The turn to the extended family of Martha Carrier as leading suspects did have the effect of shifting the focus away from the Foster/Lacey clan. But to ascribe that result as a calculated maneuver on the part of the distracted, youthful Mary Lacey's claims about Martha Carrier does not withstand careful consideration. The young woman may very well have been trying to transform herself from an accused witch into an afflicted person, as Mary Warren had managed to do three months earlier (some of her subsequent actions suggest this). But to credit her with enough cunning to think she could save others in her family from arrest by identifying Martha Carrier as a "Queen in Hell" is too much of a leap of faith. It is true that no others in the Foster/Lacey clan were arrested after July 21. But until the witchcraft suspicions reached Andover, no other family had experienced more than three arrests anyway. Young Mary Lacey had no reason to think she was protecting others in her family from suspicion. Her designation of royal status for Martha Carrier most likely resulted from a genuine belief. Carrier had been the first person from Andover to be accused. Lacey probably believed in Carrier's guilt long before she fell under suspicion herself, and she could easily have experienced nightmares about this woman whose reputation for malice predated the outbreak.

On July 22, the day after their original confessions, Mary Foster Lacey and her daughter were subjected to another interrogation. Martha Carrier's two sons, Richard and Andrew (arrested the day before by John Ballard), were questioned along with them. The warrant for the arrest of the Carrier brothers named Salem Village's Mary Warren as their victim—further evidence that she was one of the two unnamed afflicted girls summoned to Andover by Joseph Ballard. The transcription of the examination revealed that the teenagers were suspected of harming others besides Warren. Not surprisingly, the younger Mary Lacey continued her own profuse revelations, once again confessing to afflicting Elizabeth Ballard and Timothy Swan and accusing the elder Carrier brother (Richard, who was her age) of afflicting Swan by sticking pins in his likeness and running an iron spindle through his knee. The elder Lacey briefly denied hurting Swan, but her daughter quickly squelched that, saying, "Yes, Mother, do not deny it." The younger Lacey had transformed herself into the accusers' dream—she was confirming everything they said and dragging every other suspect down with her. When Richard Carrier denied hurting Swan and also refused to admit to injuring Elizabeth Ballard, young Mary Lacey spoke up again, insisting that Richard had choked Ballard and laid his hand on her stomach. She also detailed conversations she had with Richard Carrier when he stated his intent to kill Elizabeth Ballard and make his brother Andrew a wizard. She went on to add to the list of injuries Richard had supposedly inflicted on Timothy Swan, saying he used a pipe to burn him. Upon hearing this, the other accusers in the courtroom fell into fits.[6]

In reading this, one almost wonders if Mary Lacey had a specific grudge against Richard Carrier. They were both eighteen years old—it would be all too easy to suggest that she felt an unrequited attraction for him. It is far more likely though that the earlier reasons cited for her confession were still at work: she may have genuinely believed in her own guilt, she may *have* in a sense been guilty (if she did actually use poppets with the intent of harming others), and she certainly thought Richard's mother was not only a witch but also the designated "Queen in Hell." Whatever Lacey's motive, her accusations and young Carrier's continued denials resulted in a measure that had not, as far as the surviving records indicate, been taken before. The record of the examination specifically notes that Richard and Andrew Carrier were taken to another chamber where their hands and feet were bound a little while.[7] Upon being returned for further examination, Richard Carrier was addressed directly: "Richard, though you have been very obstinate, yet tell us how long ago it is since you were taken in this snare?" The young man's spirit had been broken by his ordeal, and he immediately acknowledged having been served the devil since May of the previous year (1691). He acknowledged hurting not only Elizabeth Ballard and Timothy Swan, but also some of the girls of Salem Village, claiming he did so by rolling up a handkerchief and imagining it to be the person he intended to victimize. He admitted to attending meetings and named more than a dozen others who were there, including his mother and his other accused relatives, along with some of those from other towns arrested in the earlier period of the witch hunt—some already hanged, some still languishing in jail. He did not name anyone new, but he gave the magistrates what they wanted, another witness. The young man also acknowledged having been baptized by the devil, just as the elder Mary Lacey had done the day before.[8]

When Andrew Carrier, three years younger than his brother, came into court, Richard told him he had acknowledged all, probably to spare the younger boy his own ordeal. Andrew unhesitatingly capitulated and confessed to signing the devil's book a month previously, agreeing to serve him five years. He did not go into the detail that his older brother had, but he did admit that his mother and brother had been with the devil when he signed the book and noted there were "pretty many names in it." He did not admit to being baptized, but Mary Warren spoke up and claimed that he had undergone the rite in the Shawsheen River (which runs through Andover, the first specific mention of baptism at that location). Andrew did tell of attending a meeting at which the already executed Rebecca Nurse had distributed bread.[9]

The arrests of the Carrier brothers had increased the number of incarcerated descendants of Edmund and Ann Ingalls to five. The next arrest, of Martha (Toothaker) Emerson, raised that number to six. Martha's father, Roger Toothaker, who had married into the family, had already died in jail, so the total number of suspects from the family stood at seven. No other family group had even approached that number of arrests. But no other family could claim the "Queen in Hell" as a member. The surviving transcript of Martha Emerson's examination on July 23 is not nearly as detailed as those of the examinations of the Foster/Lacey women and the Carrier brothers, but it does make it clear that this niece of Martha Carrier did not cave in to pressure to confess as easily as those examined the previous two days had. She stood accused of hurting Mary Warren and the younger Mary Lacey, but she denied ever having seen them. Surprisingly, no one accused her of attacking Timothy Swan. It is hard to imagine a suspect more likely to have had a vendetta against him—Martha's husband, Joseph Emerson, was a cousin of Swan's victim, Elizabeth Emerson. But in the courtroom, Richard Carrier and the elder Mary Lacey both hurled accusations at her involving others. Carrier said he had seen her hurt Warren and the younger Lacey. The elder Lacey claimed she had seen her at a witch meeting along with her mother (Mary Allen Toothaker). The two younger women fell into fits when Emerson looked at them, but the younger Lacey recovered when Emerson grabbed her wrist. Still, Emerson held steadfast.

Finally, Martha Emerson gave up when reminded that her father had said he had taught her to kill a witch by boiling the urine of an afflicted person. She admitted to having collected a woman's urine in a glass, though she did not indicate if the witch afflicting the woman had died. Upon further questioning, Emerson named her aunt, Martha Carrier, and a previously unidentified suspect (Mary Green of Haverhill) as the ones who were stopping her from confessing.[10] Though her confession was lukewarm, it was an acknowledgment of guilt nonetheless. This was the sixth confession in an eight-day period, nearly doubling the total of confessions obtained to that point in the witch hunt. It also established the family of Andrew and Faith (Ingalls) Allen as the one most heavily involved in afflicting others by witchcraft. Had Andrew and Faith been alive, it seems likely that at least one, if not both of them, would have fallen under suspicion themselves. The persecution of this clan was far from over, and eventually it was to expand into other branches of the extended family. The Foster/Lacey family, in contrast, saw no more members accused.

After the younger Mary Lacey appeared in court as a witness against Martha Emerson and helped to press her into a confession (albeit a weak one), there was a brief lull in the arrests. This did not last, and on July 28 (perhaps not coincidentally the day after the death of Elizabeth Ballard) warrants for apprehension of three other suspects were issued. One of the accused, Mary (Tyler) Bridges, resided in Andover's South End, and the other two, Hannah Bromage and Mary Green, lived in Haverhill. None of these suspects was related to anyone else already jailed, but Mary Green had been named by Martha Emerson earlier as one of those who prevented her from confessing. All stood accused of afflicting Timothy Swan, whose name had already appeared as a victim in warrants and in the recent confessions. It may be that the death of his fellow sufferer, Elizabeth Ballard, had frightened him into believing himself still tormented by others who remained at large. The actual complaints against the three arrested on July 28 do not survive, but Swan and his brothers are likely candidates to have filed them.

At that stage of the witch hunt, even a temporary turn from relatives of Martha Carrier as suspects must have been a relief for the family, but they were back in the spotlight in short order. This time, though, it was not a new victim of suspicion. Mary (Allen) Toothaker,

Martha Carrier's sister, who had been accused two months earlier and had seen her husband die in jail on June 16, endured an examination on July 30. Strangely, there is no existing record that she had been examined before, even though she had been in jail since May. Toothaker resisted confession at first, just as her daughter had a week earlier, but under unrelenting pressure from the magistrates and seeing the fits of her alleged victims, she finally caved in. Mary Beth Norton gave detailed attention to Toothaker's confession because it stressed that among the promises the supposed witch said she received from the devil was his assurance that she and her family would be kept safe from the Wabanakis.[11] The importance of this to Mary Toothaker was not surprising—her son Allen had already been badly wounded by the Indians (he would soon testify that his aunt Martha Carrier had hindered his recovery through her witchcraft). Though raised in Andover, she lived in Billerica, a town even more directly exposed to the frontier than her childhood home was.

Once Mary Toothaker's resistance broke down, she recited several familiar refrains. She had afflicted Timothy Swan by gripping a dishcloth or some other item while thinking of him. She acknowledged attending a meeting at Salem Village and claimed she was joined there by the three new suspects arrested on July 28, most of her family members who had confessed the previous week, and a few other longtime suspects such as George Burroughs, the recently executed Elizabeth Howe, and of course, her sister Martha Carrier. Toothaker admitted signing the devil's book, which she described as a pledge to set up the devil's kingdom. She denied seeing her daughter Martha Emerson sign the book but claimed that many others at the meeting signed it. She described the discourse at the meeting as focusing on "pulling down the Kingdom of Christ and setting up the Kingdom of Satan." She repeated Ann Foster's specific number of 305 witches in the region. She did not speak of undergoing baptism by the devil, but otherwise her statements mirrored other recent confessions closely.[12]

Ironically, as Norton mentions in her work, a small party of Wabanakis attacked Billerica two days after Toothaker's confession. The raiders wiped out two entire households located near her home, so had she not been "safely" in jail, she could have met her neighbors' grisly fate as well.[13] It would not be surprising if others in the area, who learned of her confession around the time of the raid, believed that she had made a pact with Satan that ultimately saved her and some of her family (including her nine-year-old daughter Margaret, who was also incarcerated on suspicion of familiarity with the black arts). At the time, the magistrates and prosecutor Anthony Checkley were selecting the next cases to try, and on the day of Toothaker's confession, the constables of Andover and Billerica were receiving summonses for witnesses against her sister. The recent evidence offered against Martha Carrier by the new confessors made her a prime candidate to go to trial immediately. As her sister, and as one who had fallen under suspicion at the same time, Mary Toothaker also appeared to be a strong candidate for a date with a jury. That, along with the fact that so many of her relatives had recently admitted guilt, may have been among the reasons she was examined then. Whether or not her confession spared her from being tried at that point, those in the area who knew of it may have believed it had. Hers was the eighth confession in less than two weeks, but it was the first one by a suspect who had already been jailed for an extended period of time. This fact is crucial: it may have been the first piece of evidence the public witnessed that one could, by confessing, at the very least postpone facing trial or perhaps avoid being tried altogether. The steady stream of confessions was not to slow down any time soon, and the perceived results of Mary Toothaker's admission of guilt could have inspired at least some of them. Regardless of the reason, over the next several days the magistrates and others focused far more attention on Mary's sister, the recalcitrant future "Queen in Hell," than any other member of the extended Ingalls clan. Martha Carrier was the only one in the family accused to that point who refused to confess. She was also the only one that would soon be facing prosecution.

On August 3, Benjamin Abbot and Allen Toothaker of Andover, both of whom blamed Martha Carrier for illnesses they suffered from, testified against her. Their symptoms, as previously noted, were probably at least partly psychosomatic in nature, resulting from their sincere belief that Carrier practiced witchcraft. Abbot's wife, Sarah

(Farnum) Abbot, vouched for her husband's statements. They were not the only ones to claim such afflictions by Martha Carrier. Twelve-year-old Phebe Chandler, daughter of William Chandler (and Benjamin Abbot's cousin), blamed Carrier for a swollen right hand and some swelling in her face. These symptoms (which her mother, Bridget Henchman Chandler, corroborated) came about after she heard Carrier's disembodied voice threaten her with poison while she was out on an errand for her mother.[14] This happened after Carrier took her by the shoulder in the meetinghouse and shook her. If this latter confrontation did happen, given Carrier's reputation, it would have terrified the child, who could then have gone on to suffer the symptoms she described as a product of her imagination.

There were others who testified against Martha Carrier. Andrew Foster, the oldest son of the jailed Ann Foster, claimed to have seen an afflicted maid (unnamed) suffer from having her neck twisted around which she blamed on Carrier. Samuel Preston, also of Andover, and John Rogers, a former neighbor in Billerica, both blamed her for the deaths of livestock that occurred after they argued with her. Others in Andover were summoned to testify against her, including Ralph Farnum, Jr. and John Farnum (brothers of Sarah Farnum Abbot) and Samuel Holt (who, like his deceased brother James, had married a sister of Martha—Sarah Allen). If any of these men ever testified, no known record of it exists. Not surprisingly, Thomas Putnam and his cousin John Putnam, both of Salem Village, accused her of hurting several of the afflicted girls of that community. Most tragically though, two more of Carrier's own children, who had been arrested themselves, blamed their mother for making them into witches. The depositions of Sarah Carrier, age seven, and Thomas Carrier, age ten, came after their mother had been convicted, so their testimony played no role in her execution, but they must have borne a heavy burden of guilt as they grew up. These two children faced examination on suspicion of witchcraft on August 10. Andover selectman and justice of the peace Dudley Bradstreet questioned them first. Both stated that they had been baptized as witches by their mother, with Sarah saying it happened in Andrew Foster's pasture and Thomas saying she did it in the Shawsheen River after removing his clothes. Both also identified some victims their mother had pressed them to afflict. The following day, poor Sarah was forced to appear before Judge Hathorne and some of the other magistrates. This time, she supplied even more details, stating that even though her mother was in jail, she had come to her in the form of a black cat and carried her along to hurt her victims.

Martha Carrier stood no chance. The jury convicted her, the court condemned her to death, and on August 19, she went to the gallows along with John Procter, George Jacobs, and John Willard (all of Salem Village) and George Burroughs, the alleged mastermind of the entire conspiracy to establish the devil's kingdom in the Massachusetts Bay colony. The supposed monarchs of hell went, in the minds of many, to their exalted places in the fiery afterlife on the same day. In his writings after the trials, Cotton Mather denounced Carrier as a rampant hag and immortalized Mary Lacey's designation of her as "Queen in Hell." Martha Carrier died without knowing the fate of her children. Of the five that were living, four (ranging in age from eighteen-year-old Richard to seven-year-old Sarah) languished in jail, charged with being among their mother's minions. Only three-year-old Hannah was spared suspicion, and even that is surprising given that four-year-old Dorothy, the daughter of the executed Sarah Good, had been charged. The toddler remained free along with her father, Thomas Carrier. His continued freedom is an even greater surprise. The accused children had to live out their lives knowing they had helped seal their mother's fate, though in the case of the two younger ones, their examinations came after she had already been condemned to death. But the extended family's tribulations had not ended—more of them were still to come under attack.

CHAPTER SEVEN

Look with an Evil Eye

ON AUGUST 10, 1692, Sarah and Thomas Carrier, ages seven and ten respectively, first answered to the charges of witchcraft in Andover. They were also the fifth and sixth of the great-grandchildren of Great Migration immigrants Edmund and Ann Ingalls to be accused of this crime. Their two older brothers and two of their cousins already awaited their fates in jail, along with their aunt, Mary Allen Toothaker. Their mother had only nine days left to live. Sarah and Thomas brought the total number of incarcerated descendants of Edmund and Ann Ingalls to eight. Mary's husband, Roger, who had first drawn the attention of the witch hunters to the family, had now been dead for nearly two months. Those seeking followers of the devil to bring to justice were not finished with the extended Ingalls family. To that point, all of those accused were daughters and grandchildren of Faith Ingalls Allen, only recently deceased. But now the persecutors were about to turn their attention to another branch of the Ingalls clan—that of Faith's long dead sister, Elizabeth Ingalls Dane. Elizabeth's widower, though not in the best of health, was very much alive and still influential in Andover. He was the town's longtime minister, Francis Dane.

Before the persecutions ended, two daughters of Elizabeth and Francis Dane, five of their grandchildren, and one daughter-in-law all found themselves accused of sorcery. Writers on the subject have generally assumed that their connection to Dane, who had voiced skepticism about witchcraft charges thirty years earlier and was eventually to do so again, caused them to fall under suspicion. There could be some validity in that assumption. There is also reason to believe that some town residents harbored some resentment of Dane because of the thirty-pound annual salary he was still receiving despite not preaching on a regular basis anymore. This hostility could have motivated some of the more vindictive parishioners to lash out at his family—or it could have also aroused genuine suspicion that the aging clergyman owed his good fortune at least partly to family members who had bargained their souls away.

Blaming the persecution of Dane's daughters and grandchildren entirely on the town's attitude toward him, however, oversimplifies the matter. The fact that Dane's progeny were all related to Martha Carrier seems more significant. His children were Carrier's first cousins, and his grandchildren were her first cousins once removed. That is not an immediate family relationship, but to the extent that witchcraft was thought to run in families, it was most often seen as passing through matrilineal lines. Martha Carrier's mother and Francis Dane's wife were sisters. There is no known record that Faith (Ingalls) Allen or Elizabeth (Ingalls) Dane ever fell under suspicion of witchcraft in her lifetime. The same is true of the family's matriarch, their mother Ann Ingalls. But once any one woman in a family fell under suspicion, others could easily follow and the fact that Martha's sister, Mary (Allen) Toothaker, had also been arrested could only have exacerbated the situation. Nonetheless, the children and grandchildren of Francis and Elizabeth Dane were not the closest female-line relatives the Martha and Mary had. There were two other Allen sisters—Sarah (married to Samuel Holt) and Hannah (widow of Samuel's brother James Holt). Sarah had no daughters, but Hannah had three. Neither of these sisters of the "Queen in Hell" was ever accused nor were any of Hannah's daughters, who ranged in age from eleven to fifteen in 1692. As the pattern of accusations in Andover was showing, people as young as seven were being accused. The youth of Hannah (Allen) Holt's daughters alone was not enough to spare them.

Nonetheless, the accusations hurled at the daughters and grand-children of Francis Dane and his late wife Elizabeth probably resulted primarily from their kinship with the by then notorious Martha Carrier. One idea espoused by some students of the Andover witchcraft outbreak can be discounted entirely. Some have suggested that it was Martha Carrier's connection to her uncle-by-marriage Francis Dane that first drew attention to her. That is patently false: her eventual arrest stemmed at least in part from the suspicion that her brother-in-law Roger Toothaker brought upon himself. The fact that she was blamed for the smallpox epidemic of 1690 did not help her cause either. While there is no evidence that she actually practiced malefic witchcraft, she did apparently have a foul temper. Martha Carrier could easily have been convicted of witchcraft if Francis Dane had never existed, but Dane's children and grandchildren suffered more from their connection to her than to him.

Whatever prompted the arrest of the first suspect from the Dane branch of the Ingalls clan, her own behavior while under examination could not have helped her nearest relatives who were charged with witchcraft later. Elizabeth Johnson was twenty-two years old in 1692. Her mother, also named Elizabeth, was Francis Dane's oldest daughter. The elder Elizabeth's husband, Stephen Johnson, had died during the smallpox epidemic nearly two years earlier, leaving his widow with at least four and maybe as many as six children at home ranging in age from ten to mid-twenties (the exact number is unclear because her twin sons, Benjamin and Joseph, born August 12, 1677, may have been dead by that time). The younger Elizabeth was unquestionably the oldest surviving daughter, but she was more of a burden to her mother than a help. A later statement by her grandfather, Francis Dane, described her as "simplish at best."[1] This Elizabeth Johnson was apparently arrested along with her second cousins, Sarah and Thomas Carrier, shortly before August 10, 1692. Like the two children, she was subjected to examination by Dudley Bradstreet on that date. It is likely that all three of them were named in the same complaint. Because the formal complaint against them does not survive, it is not possible to know who filed it. All three of these accused named ten-year-old Sarah Phelps as someone they afflicted—the first mention of her as a victim—so it is likely that an adult male close to Sarah filed the complaint. The most likely candidate is her father, Samuel Phelps, who was a brother of the deceased Elizabeth (Phelps) Ballard. It is also possible that Joseph Ballard brought the charges against the three, even though his wife had already died. If his late wife's niece was experiencing fits or suffering from some other illness, he would have had reasons to continue to involve himself in the proceedings. Elizabeth Johnson confessed to participating in the affliction of Elizabeth Ballard.

Regardless of who filed this complaint, however, the younger Elizabeth Johnson seemed a likely target for accusation. Her connection to the Carrier family cannot have helped her situation. Given that she was mentally handicapped in some way, she was probably harassed by bullies as she was growing up. The year 1692 was not a good one for anyone to be "unusual" in any way in northeastern Massachusetts. Once the witchcraft allegations spun out of control in Andover, an accusation against this developmentally challenged young woman seemed almost inevitable.

Like Sarah Carrier, Elizabeth Johnson underwent interrogations on consecutive days (if Thomas Carrier was examined a second time before the magistrates on August 11, no record of it is known to survive). Both Carrier children admitted to attacking Sarah Phelps and Ann Putnam (which indicates that the Salem Village afflicted were still involved). Thomas Carrier claimed that his mother had told him to afflict Mary Walcott, but he did not say that he had done so. Johnson, however, far exceeded her cousins in the number of people she claimed to have hurt, the number of other witches who joined her, and in the lurid details she disclosed. The confession before the magistrates on August 11 was the more thorough of the two. She corroborated the identification of Sarah Phelps, Ann Putnam, and Mary Walcott as victims, but she further admitted to having hurt Lawrence

Lacey (the husband and father of the elder and younger Mary Laceys, respectively). She named other victims—Benjamin Abbot (who had testified against Martha Carrier the previous week), an unnamed child of Ephraim Davis, two unnamed children of James Frye, and unidentified children of Abraham Foster (she did not say how many), and the deceased wife of Joseph Ballard.[2] She claimed to have been a witch for four years and that the devil and Martha Carrier had persuaded her to become one while she was at Carrier's house. She claimed they promised she would be safe and never found out. She went on to claim that they had promised her a shilling but had never delivered on that promise. She went on to describe her baptism by the devil a year later—which she said he performed by dipping her head in the water of Carrier's well, further evidence of Martha Carrier's influence. At that time, she stated, she renounced God, Christ, and her former baptism. She also told of signing the devil's book by means of scratching it with her finger and claimed that he and Carrier had threatened to tear her to pieces if she did not acquiesce. She then described a witch sacrament she attended at the village (presumably Salem Village) at which bread and wine was served and a pledge was made by all to pull down the Kingdom of Christ and set up the devil's kingdom (this part was a familiar refrain by this time).

Already Elizabeth Johnson had described events that no other confessor had previously mentioned—at least not in that exact form. She did not stop there, though—she provided more names than any other previously accused person had done. Most were already in jail—Martha Carrier, George Burroughs, Martha Toothaker, Toothaker's two children, Richard Carrier, Sarah Carrier, the elder Mary Lacey (whom she specifically accused of afflicting Mary's own husband Lawrence Lacey), and the younger Mary Lacey. She mentioned John Floyd (or Flood) who had been complained of in May, but it is not clear that he was ever arrested (no examination of him exists). But she also entered a new name into the mix—twenty-nine-year-old Daniel Eames of Boxford. She was one of two confessors to name a suspect not already in custody (at least he is not known to have been). In describing her methods of afflicting, she acknowledged using poppets, as some of the other suspects had also admitted, but she took a step

no previous confessor had taken—she actually brought out three poppets, two made of rags or strips of cloth and a third one of a birch
rind. One can only imagine the gasps in the courtroom as the sight
of these instruments of witchcraft. But the alleged sorceress did not
stop there—upon being asked, she willingly showed where her familiar (a spirit that assisted a witch) suckled her, a knuckle with a spot
that appeared to be red. She said that she had two more such places
which the examining women were immediately ordered to search her
for. They found them—or so they claimed, though they only gave
the location of one—behind the young woman's arm.[3] Perhaps the
other one was in a spot considered too personal to be mentioned.

The magistrates seated on the Court of Oyer and Terminer had
struck a gold mine. Prior to the court's establishment, Justices
Hathorne and Corwin had managed to wring confessions out of five
suspects during more than two months of examinations. Then for the
first two months of its existence, the court itself fared even worse.
Only two suspects—one a slave—admitted to the crime of witchcraft
prior to the middle of July. After July 15, the judges and others had
wrenched eleven new confessions out of those accused of witchcraft.
Of those arrested after July 15, only Mary Johnson Clark and Hannah
Bromage, both of Haverhill, had refused to admit complicity in the
black arts. Nine of the eleven new confessors resided in Andover—
the most fertile ground in the entire Bay colony for the witch hunters.
Aside from producing numerous new witches, the town's residents
had supplied the magistrates with a surfeit of evidence against suspects
already in jail, most particularly George Burroughs, the minister from
Maine, who had previously been designated as the ringleader of the
diabolical conspiracy. Andover had also "ratted out" Burroughs's female coequal—its own Martha Carrier. Witness testimony by confessors who had participated in Satanic rites, and had seen other
suspects participating, providing far stronger evidence than sightings
of the "specters" of those accused so often reported by those claiming
affliction by the witches. Physical evidence, such as the poppets previously found in the home of Bridget Bishop and the parcels of rags,
yarn, tape, and quills located in the Lacey house by Constable
Ephraim Foster, was also powerful, but rare. When young Elizabeth

Johnson willingly produced her own "weapons" of affliction at her examination, her credibility as a witch—and as a witness—was assured. More than two months earlier, at her initial examination, the recently condemned Martha Carrier had lambasted the magistrates for taking seriously the testimony of girls whom she described as being "out of their wits."[4] Those same judges now gave credence to Carrier's statement by accepting at face value the testimony of a young woman—ironically the daughter of Carrier's cousin—described as "simplish" by her own grandfather.

One must consider the evident mental shortcomings of Elizabeth Johnson when contemplating the reasons that she not only confessed, but also willingly displayed poppets that she acknowledged using as weapons. Though twenty-two years old, her intellectual capacity may have been no more than that of a child aged anywhere from about seven (the actual age of young Sarah Carrier) to early teens. Her motivation may have been simply to save or at least prolong her own life, as it undoubtedly was for others at that time, but the fact that she showed the poppets at her examination casts doubt on that idea. That is something that no previous suspect had done. As with Bridget Bishop and the two Mary Laceys, the possibility that she did actively use the poppets with the intention of harming others cannot be discounted. Then, as now, someone with a diminished mental capacity was a likely target for harassment while growing up, and the resulting emotional scars can create a desire for revenge. It is also possible that she simply tried to cultivate a reputation as a witch in order to frighten potential bullies away—a motive previously suggested for the confession of Abigail Hobbs nearly four months earlier.

Another set of possible reasons for confession is thought-provoking in the case of Elizabeth Johnson. Someone with her disabilities (whatever they were) would have been a prime candidate to be tricked by another person into testifying in a way to advance the trickster's own agenda. There is no doubt that there were those in the region who had a vested interest in continuing the proceedings as they were developing—whether they were motivated by genuine fear of witchcraft, a desire to destroy the lives of enemies, or a hope of deflecting suspicion away from themselves and their families. Such a person might have been a magistrate, an afflicted person, a malicious neighbor, or even a fellow suspect. The accusations being hurled at the extended Ingalls kinship network were drawing attention away from other families with multiple members in custody, as the Foster/Lacey women must have noticed. Someone may have even given Johnson the poppets and encouraged her to present them in the courtroom—a trick that a gullible mentally challenged young woman could easily have fallen for.

Elizabeth Johnson was the tenth member of the extended Ingalls clan to be charged with witchcraft, and the seventh to confess. The only ones who had not admitted guilt were Martha Carrier (soon to hang), Roger Toothaker (who had died after less than a month in jail), and little Margaret Toothaker who, for some reason, had never been examined—or if she had, no record of the interrogation is known to survive.[5] No other extended family group approached this clan in the number of suspected witches it had produced. The witch hunters were far from finished with the descendants of Edmund and Ann Ingalls, but the family's next victim did not bend to the will of the prosecutors as most of her relatives had done.

The same day that the justices interrogated Elizabeth Johnson, they also grilled her aunt, forty-year-old Abigail (Dane) Faulkner, the daughter of Andover's aging pastor. Unlike the mentally challenged Elizabeth, Faulkner had inherited Francis Dane's strength of will. Other factors in Abigail Faulkner's life may have toughened her up. Her husband, Francis Faulkner, came from a privileged background, but he had also suffered from an illness that caused him to experience convulsions a few years before 1692.[6] This same condition, whatever it was, had also adversely affected his memory and understanding— and apparently his financial situation. Her children were all still young at the time, so she would have borne a heavy burden, though it is likely her father helped her. By 1692, her husband had recovered, and at the time Abigail was accused of witchcraft, she was pregnant—a pregnancy that ultimately saved her life. Francis Faulkner did suffer a relapse while his wife was in jail, as she noted in her request for a pardon, but he must have once again recovered. He lived another forty years.

Abigail Faulkner stood firm in the courtroom on August 11, 1692, even as chaos reigned around her. When John Hathorne specifically told her she was there for witchcraft, she denied knowing anything of it. The court transcriber noted that with the cast of her eye, Faulkner caused Mary Walcott, Mary Warren, and others of the afflicted to fall down. Walcott, Warren, and Ann Putnam all claimed having been hurt by Faulkner for the first time on the previous night, though Warren claimed to have seen her with other witches before. The girls were, according to the transcript, "helped up out of their fits by a touch of Abigail Faulkner's hand." Sarah Phelps was there again and she also accused Faulkner of hurting her, but the minister's daughter persisted in her denials. The accusers also fell into fits if they observed the accused witch squeezing a cloth she held in her hand. Her niece, Elizabeth Johnson, urged her to confess "for the credit of her town," but she held fast—no confession or implication of others passed the lips of Abigail Faulkner that horrifying day. She did express regret for the suffering of her accusers, but the court records noted that "she did not shed a tear," which appears to have been taken as further evidence of her guilt.[7] Nonetheless, she never cracked under the pressure.

No one can deny Abigail Faulkner's courage at this stage of the witch hunt. Aside from the pandemonium in the courtroom during her examination, other reasons to acknowledge guilt and implicate others were emerging. The recent confessions had raised the total number to eighteen, and with more trials under way, one fact was becoming clear—no one who had confessed was being prosecuted. Even Tituba, who had admitted her complicity five months earlier, still languished in jail—a harsh fate, but she remained alive. It is highly unlikely that the first group of confessors in Andover—the Foster/Lacey women and the two oldest Carrier brothers—had any expectation of being spared by implicating themselves, but a later confession most likely turned the tide. Most noticeable to residents of Andover was the differing fates of the Allen sisters (Abigail Faulkner's cousins). Martha Carrier, the first resident of the town to be implicated, had been convicted well before August 11, and she died on Gallows Hill eight days later. By way of contrast, her sister Mary Toothaker (arrested at the same time), who had confessed at the end of July, remained alive—and there was no indication she was on the verge of facing trial. Confessors had no assurance that they would never be tried and executed—but it was obvious by then that they could, at the very least, buy themselves some time. They knew they brought value to the prosecutions by offering evidence against their fellow suspects, and in such a climate of hysteria, self-preservation at all costs is not a surprising strategy. Abigail Faulkner may have been aware of her pregnancy by that time—she was to give birth on March 30, 1693, less than eight months later—but her steely resolve when so many others were caving in demands admiration.

In a defense of the suspects from Andover written in January 1693, Francis Dane alluded to a rumor that spread in the town that those who confessed would ultimately be set free. But other factors undoubtedly contributed to the plethora of confessions emanating from the community. To a large degree, those targeted for suspicion during that time period were simply more vulnerable than most of the earlier suspects. As previously noted, the aged and bereaved Ann Foster stands out as possibly the most frail person accused of witchcraft in 1692—from any town. The fact that the magistrates wrung a confession from her with four days of aggressive interrogation should not surprise anyone—if anything, it would have been nothing short of a miracle if this poor widow *had* stood her ground. Of the total of twenty-one suspects examined during the period from July 15 through August 18, eleven actually resided in Andover. Six of them break from the pattern of pre-Andover accusations for a reason opposite the situation of the widow Ann Foster—their relative youth. Two of the confessors from the spring had also been two of the youngest accused to that point—fourteen-year-old Abigail Hobbs and four-year-old Dorothy Good (who never lost her status as the youngest suspect of the entire episode). Five of the eleven inhabitants of Andover examined during that five-week period beginning in mid-July had not yet reached their twentieth birthdays—Mary Lacey, who was eighteen, and Martha Carrier's four children (Richard, Andrew, Thomas, and Sarah) who were aged eighteen, fifteen, ten, and seven, respectively. Again—all five admitted guilt. The two older Carrier boys underwent physical torture. Young Mary Lacey may *have*, in a sense, been guilty as charged. For the two younger Carrier children, the mere suggestion that they could have withstood the intimidation of men like John Hathorne defies logic. To be thorough, a sixth suspect should be grouped with these young confessors—Elizabeth Johnson, Jr. Although she was twenty-two years old, her mental age was probably less than that. Her own grandfather, Francis Dane, implied that she was mentally challenged in his statement of opposition to the proceedings early in 1693.

A possible reason that younger people were targeted for accusation in Andover emerges when taking note of an order that the town's selectmen issued on March 14, 1692. The order reads as follows

> And whereas there is grievous Complaints of great prophaneness of the Sabbath both in the times of exercise and at noon time to the great dishonour of God (illegible) and all of religion & the griefe of many serious Christians, by young persons, we order and require of tything men & constables to take care to prevent such great & shameful miscarriages, which are so much observed and Complained of.[8]

This admonition to Andover's youth may very well have preceded or followed a fiery sermon by one of the town's two ministers, Francis Dane or Thomas Barnard, decrying them for their wickedness. Barnard, who appears to have assumed most of the actual preaching responsibilities by that time, is the more likely candidate to have openly chastised the community's younger population. But whether or not the town's ministers joined the chorus of voices criticizing the behavior of the local youth, the memories of the complaints about them would have lingered four months later when Andover's witch hunt began in earnest. When Ann Foster spoke of 305 active witches in the region on July 18, the general suspicion in Andover could very easily have fallen on the younger population. Some of the young residents might equally have assumed that certain peers had sold their souls to the devil or that they had unknowingly done so themselves. The Puritan idea of predestined salvation or damnation was alive and well six decades after the establishment of the Massachusetts Bay colony, and people still routinely searched for signs of their own fate in the afterlife as well as that of others. In Andover that fateful summer, residents certainly may have remembered an instance a few months earlier of a young person defiling the Sabbath. When reminded of the act himself (or herself), a guilty party could have attached greater significance to the earlier transgression than she or he previously had. Sinful behavior often portended foreordained damnation. Those who believed themselves destined for hellfire would have imagined their own vulnerability to recruitment into the growing army Satan was assembling for all-out war on the "city upon a hill." Their more pious (or perhaps more self-indulgent) neighbors could have seen them in the same light. Then, as now, children and adolescents would have more easily fallen into such a trap than self-assured middle-aged people would have. Younger adults in their twenties could have suffered from a similar lack of self-confidence. It is notable that only one Andover resident accused in this first phase is known *not* to have confessed during an examination at the time. This was forty-year-old Abigail (Dane) Faulkner, the old minister's daughter.[9] Of the eleven Andover suspects arrested during this time period, she was one of only three in middle age. This pattern continued throughout the rest of the Andover witch hunt, with only two accused—fifty-five-year-old Mary Ayer Parker and sixty-four-year-old Henry Salter known to have balked at confessing.[10]

Unfortunately, but not surprisingly, the justices gave greater weight to the testimony of the younger mentally challenged Elizabeth Johnson than to her strong-minded middle-aged aunt Abigail Faulkner. Faulkner steadfastly denied any complicity in harming anyone by occult means, but Elizabeth Johnson not only readily acknowledged her guilt, she implicated others. The new suspect Johnson had named—

Daniel Eames of Boxford (a brother-in-law of North End constable Ephraim Foster)—found himself before the magistrates two days later. The young man, perhaps inspired by Abigail Faulkner's performance, held his ground against the onslaught of the magistrates and the screams of his alleged victims all around him—including confessed witches young Mary Lacey, Richard Carrier, and Elizabeth Johnson. Johnson and Carrier, it appears, were trying at that point to wriggle their way into the ranks of the afflicted, a path the younger Mary Lacey was already following with limited success.

The interrogation of Daniel Eames was followed by a lull of sorts in the examinations. From then until August 25, only one other examination—that of Daniel's mother, Rebecca Blake Eames of Boxford—was recorded, on August 19, the same day that five recently convicted suspects, including Andover's own "Queen in Hell" Martha Carrier, died on the gallows in Salem. Rebecca confessed.

On August 25, however, actions against suspects began anew with a new set of homegrown afflicted girls supplying much of the evidence. This marked the beginning of the second phase of the Andover persecutions. Rebecca Eames's own teenage granddaughter Rose Foster was one of the newly afflicted, even though her grandmother and uncle were among the most recently examined suspects. Rose's father, Ephraim Foster, acting as the North End's constable, had already arrested several suspects. Another new accuser was Abigail Martin, a daughter of forty-one-year-old North End resident Samuel Martin, who was related to the Farnum family by virtue of the second marriage of his late father, Solomon Martin, to the widowed Alice Farnum in 1648. Alice and her first husband Ralph Farnum were the grandparents of Sarah (Farnum) Abbott, who had deposed earlier against Martha Carrier. But the afflicted girl who took center stage in Andover was sixteen-year-old Martha Sprague of Boxford, a stepdaughter of Moses Tyler, whose own family had already fallen victim to two accusations. Moses and his twenty-one-year-old son Joseph joined the ranks of the accusers as Martha Sprague's afflictions began manifesting themselves publicly.

This changing cast of accusers in Andover did not end the persecution of the extended Ingalls clan. On August 29, Moses Tyler and Samuel Martin filed a complaint against the widowed Elizabeth

(Dane) Johnson (mother of Elizabeth, sister of Abigail Faulkner, and daughter of Francis Dane) along with her eleven-year-old daughter Abigail (named undoubtedly, for her aunt, already imprisoned). The elder Elizabeth, aged fifty-one, was more than a decade older than her jailed sister and, as previously noted, had been widowed for nearly two years. The two new suspects were accused of inflicting harm upon Martha Sprague and Abigail Martin. The complaint against the two Johnson females is one of the few against Andover suspects that survive. Even though Elizabeth and Abigail lived in the North End, South End constable John Ballard apprehended them and delivered them to jail on August 30. It is possible that Ephraim Foster, the North End's constable, was preoccupied with the afflictions his daughter Rose suffered from at that point. No record of an examination of Abigail Johnson is known to exist. Her mother, on the other hand, gave the magistrates in Salem a confession that rivaled that of her namesake daughter in detail. The transcription of the elder Elizabeth Johnson's deposition does, to a large degree, include the questions posed to her and the answers she gave. As usual, the justices opened the interrogation with a question that assumed the suspect's guilt. After telling her that she was charged with "acting witchcraft," as they described it, they simply asked her, "Come tell how long you have been a witch."[11]

Johnson did not give a specific time frame, but the judges continued to press, telling her "the Devil come to you did he not?" which she acknowledged to be true. They asked if he came in the day and she said no, he had come to her in the night, awakened her, and told her he would go and afflict in her shape. This whole scenario sounds suspiciously like a nightmare—just another of many that those involved in the witchcraft scare must have experienced during the year of 1692. Pushed for details, she claimed that the devil first appeared to her as a white bird but then later took the shape of a black man. She also denied signing the devil's book at first, but then later admitted placing a spot in the book with her finger. She also broke her silence on the length of time she had been in the "snare," as she described it, saying that it had been at least three years but not yet four. Her daughter Abigail, she supposed, had been a witch for five years (meaning that the girl would have been under the influence of the devil since age six). The overwrought mother blamed the child's sorcery on the fact that she had spent time at the home of the recently executed Martha Carrier—Elizabeth's own cousin. By that point in the trials, some of Carrier's own relatives obviously believed the allegation that she was the designated "Queen in Hell." Presumably, in their minds, her reign had now begun.

The minister's daughter did not stop there. Like other confessors, she incriminated numerous others, though most of them were already in jail or at least under suspicion. She declared that her sister Abigail Faulkner—one of the few from Andover who had not confessed—had been a witch as long as she had and claimed that Faulkner threatened to tear her in pieces if she confessed. She also identified Daniel Eames, another who had held fast when pressured to incriminate himself, and four others already in custody. Finally, she named a James Howe, either the husband or father-in-law of Elizabeth (Jackson) Howe who had been executed six weeks earlier on July 19.[12] The record does not make it clear which James Howe she meant—the father or the son.[13] There is no evidence, however, that any legal action was ever pursued against either of the two men.

Elizabeth (Dane) Johnson also provided the judges with details about whom she and other witches afflicted—identifying several besides Martha Sprague and Abigail Martin, the ones she was accused of hurting in the warrant for her arrest. She claimed to have also attacked two of Martin's siblings (not named), Rose Foster, and Sarah Phelps (who had been complaining of supernatural assaults for at least three weeks by that time and perhaps longer). Strangely, the elder Johnson denied having done any harm to Timothy Swan.[14] Nonetheless she, like the other confessors, gave the witch prosecutors plenty of ammunition. Four months later, her own father described her as weak, incapacious, and fearful, while declaring that he feared "she hath falsely accused her self & others."[15] This was the same statement in which the aged minister described his granddaughter, Elizabeth Johnson, as "simplish at best." With the witchcraft terror at full strength in the late summer of 1692, however, the emotional state of anyone who was willing to confess was of no concern to the justices and the accusers.

Despite the adamant denial of guilt by the elder Elizabeth's sister Abigail three weeks earlier, the jailers brought her into court again on August 30. Perhaps the justices thought her resolve would weaken in the wake of her elder sister's confession. The clerk did not record her testimony in as much detail as had been done with Elizabeth's. Abigail Faulkner faced John Hathorne that day and initially clung to her refusal to admit to anything. Eventually though, the notorious judge (aided, perhaps, by screams of the afflicted in the courtroom) wore down her resistance somewhat. She admitted she was mad about the arrest of her niece, Elizabeth Johnson, earlier that month. She also stated the she felt even angrier when people said that her sister, the elder Elizabeth, would be next. Faulkner said that she looked "with an evil eye" on the afflicted persons and wished them ill because she blamed them for the arrests of her family members. Finally, she stated that she did "pinch her hands together" and speculated that the devil might have taken advantage of that, but she also contended that if anyone was afflicted as a result, the devil had done it and not her.[16]

Faulkner's admission of pinching her hands together echoed earlier confessions of her own relatives and others, but she gave it a different interpretation than they had. Other confessors had spoken of thinking of the person they wished to hurt while doing it and causing the harm directly. Faulkner did not acknowledge choosing any specific victims to injure—she described her action as one that the devil might simply have taken advantage of without her consent—a lesser degree of guilt or perhaps none at all. The degree of culpability did not matter to the justices, though, and Abigail Faulkner was to face trial very soon. She did not give the justices what they really wanted—incriminating evidence against others. That is the most likely reason that all of the confessors remained alive at that point. By that time, a total of eleven people had been hanged—and despite the ever-increasing number of confessors, no one who had acknowledged joining the devil's conspiracy against New England had been formally tried. Faulkner's sister, Elizabeth, certainly knew that and she may have been at least partially motivated by it—but she seems to have been more emotionally unstable than Faulkner.

Among the more shocking items in the elder Elizabeth Johnson's declaration of her own guilt was her incrimination of her own children. Her claim that her daughter Abigail, who had been arrested along with her, had been in the devil's snare since age six has already been noted. But she also expressed that she feared her son Stephen was a witch. The fourteen-year-old Stephen Johnson, named for his deceased father, is not known to have been in custody at the time his mother was examined—though it is impossible to say, as no known record of a formal complaint against him survives. At the very least, he may have already been under suspicion before his mother was examined. His examination, before Justices Bartholomew Gedney, John Hathorne, Jonathan Corwin, and John Higginson, took place two days after that of his mother in the courtroom in the town of Salem. Like his mother, Stephen described the devil as a black man and he admitted signing the devil's book by pricking a finger and marking it in blood. Unlike his mother, he acknowledged being baptized, noting that it was in the Shawsheen River near the home of Benjamin Abbot, for whom he had been working.[17] He acknowledged hurting Martha Sprague, Rose Foster, and Mary Lacey (a further indication that the younger Lacey was continuing her dual role as a suspect and a victim) by squeezing his hands. Apparently, poppets were no longer seen as necessary at this stage. Stephen Johnson also referenced a specific event that had already been mentioned in other examinations over the previous week. He mentioned having joined his company in dancing at Moses Tyler's home and making Martha Sprague sing. A few other confessors in this second phase of the Andover persecution had also acknowledged forcing Sprague to sing during a gathering at her stepfather's home in Boxford.[18] Somehow, this forced singing had caused the teenage girl to fall ill—how it could have defies explanation. More elaboration on Sprague's role in the accusations follows in subsequent chapters, but Stephen Johnson's arrest and admission of guilt brought the number of Ingalls descendants in jail to thirteen. He was also the fifth member of Francis Dane's immediate family to fall under suspicion—a circumstance that must have devastated the aging minister.

CHAPTER EIGHT

The
Touch Test

A S THE MONTH OF AUGUST DREW TO A CLOSE, those accusing others of witchcraft began lashing out at some of the more prominent residents of Andover, and at the same time, their confessions grew more elaborate. Among the first influential families to be attacked was the Barker clan, which saw William Barker, Sr. (a son of original town proprietor Richard Barker) and the former's niece, Mary Barker, interrogated on August 29. William offered one of the most detailed confessions of the entire year. Acknowledging that he had been in the snare of the devil for three years, William Barker described how Satan had first appeared to him "lyke a black man and perceived that he had a cloven foot, That the devil demanded of him to give himself up soul & body unto him, which he promesed to doe, He said he had a great family, the world went hard with him and he was willing to pay every man his own, And the Devil told him he would pay all his debts and he should live comfortably."[1]

This passage suggests that although William Barker came from a prominent family, he did not live as well as he might have expected.

His father Richard remained alive, and although William had been granted the privilege of farming some of his father's land, he would not own it outright until Richard's death in 1693.[2] William Barker, however, found himself jailed like a common criminal. His confession did not stop with his complaints about his own life situation. Like so many others, he admitted hurting those who accused him (Martha Sprague, Rose Foster, and Abigail Martin), and he confessed to signing the devil's book with blood brought to him in an inkhorn. He further described attending a meeting of witches at Salem Village, specifying that this gathering took place near the minister's house. Barker further testified that the people of Salem Village were divided and that they differed with their minister, citing that as a reason the witches intended to destroy the community.[3]

This statement demonstrates that knowledge of the conflict over Samuel Parris in Salem Village extended beyond that community's borders. By mentioning it, Barker implied that the devil exploited the dispute in the village as his starting point. Satan's design was, indeed, grandiose by Barker's account. The Dark Prince intended to "set up his own worship, abolish all the churches in the land, to fall next upon Salem and so goe through the countrey." The devil further promised "that all of his people should live bravely, that all persons should be equal; that there should be no day of resurrection or of judgment, and neither punishment nor shame for sin."[4] With this, Barker was describing a plan to dismantle everything the Puritans had worked toward since they first arrived in New England six decades earlier. He noted that additional witches had come from Connecticut to northeastern Massachusetts Bay in the spring of the year (referencing, no doubt, accusations that were occurring in Stamford, Connecticut, that year) and he also provided a specific number of witches in the region at the time—307 (increasing by two the number given by Ann Foster six weeks earlier).

But Barker was not done. He described the witches as being "much disturbed with the afflicted persones because they are discovered by them, They curse the judges because their Society is brought under, They would have the afflicted persones counted as witches."[5] Finally, Barker declared his belief in the innocence of the afflicted persons and his conviction that they performed a valuable service. He followed that up by stating that he had not known or heard of a single innocent person being imprisoned and then concluded by apologizing for his actions and begging the forgiveness of the afflicted.[6]

It is hard to imagine testimony contrasting more sharply with that of Martha Carrier three months earlier, when she castigated the justices with the comment, "It is a shameful thing that you should mind these folks that are out of their wits."[7] In defending the afflicted against charges that they practiced witchcraft themselves, William Barker also contradicted Susanna Martin of Amesbury, who had said of her own accusers, "If they be dealing in the black art, you may know as well as I."[8] Regardless of how they felt inside, the public face of most of the accused had changed drastically since the spring. That was no accident. Martha Carrier and Susanna Martin were both dead by the time of William Barker's examination, as he knew all too well. Instead of criticizing his accusers, he lauded them. Historian Mary Beth Norton offered the hypothesis that Andover residents confessed much more readily that those accused earlier because of a long-established tendency in the town to value consensus over conflict.[9] But that contention overlooks the disputes that often roiled the town in the years leading up to 1692—different from the ones in Salem Village, but nonetheless compelling evidence that Andover was no Garden of Eden of human relations. The seventeenth-century Tyler family would have scoffed at any such idealized view of Andover. Francis Dane's claim that his community's expectation that suspects who acknowledged guilt would ultimately be spared makes far more sense as a reason for the rash of confessions. That prominent citizens admitted guilt rather than using their connections to escape augments the evidence for that explanation—earlier prominent suspects often fled the region.

The witch hunt in Andover took a turn in early September 1692: the notorious "touch test" that occurred at the meetinghouse on September 7. The most complete description of the touch test comes from an undated declaration prepared and signed by six suspects just prior to the resumption of trials in January 1693. All the suspects were female and five were adults—Mary (Clements) Osgood, Deliverance (Haseltine) Dane, Sarah (Lord) Wilson, Mary (Lovett) Tyler, and Abigail (Wheeler) Barker. The sixth signer of the document was Mary Tyler's teenage daughter Hannah. The women described how, after a prayer by the minister Thomas Barnard, they (the accused) were blindfolded. The afflicted were already there and had fallen into their fits as soon as the suspects were brought into their presence. Those conducting the event had then laid the suspects' hands upon the afflicted whereupon their fits immediately ceased. The idea was that if witches laid their hands on their victims while the latter were in the throes of their torments, the torments would stop (at least temporarily). All of those who filed the declaration had been forced to participate, and the total number of suspects "tested" that day could have been as high as seventeen. This served as the evidence to arrest the suspects. It is hardly suprising that one of the signers of the declaration was Deliverance (Hazeltine) Dane, the wife of Francis Dane's son Nathaniel, who had apparently just recently fallen under suspicion at the time of the test. The persecutions of this extended family had not ended. According to the declaration, the afflicted persons were at the meeting house when they (the suspects) were brought there. To quote the petitioners directly: "After Mr. Barnard had been at prayer, we were blindfolded, and our hands were laid upon the afflicted persons, they being in their fits at our coming into their presence, as they said; and some led us and laid our hands upon them, and then they said they were well, and that we were guilty of afflicting them . . . ."[10] Those who oversaw the test, seeing the supposed victims "cured," took the results as evidence of the suspects' guilt. Not surprisingly, the afflicted persons did not exonerate anyone—all of the participating suspects "failed" the test. Andover's justice of the peace, Dudley Bradstreet, issued a warrant and all the accused were immediately seized (probably by the constables, John Ballard and Ephraim Foster, although they must have had help) and taken to the jail and Salem. The text of the declaration follows:

And, by reason of that sudden surprizal, we knowing ourselves altogether innocent of the crime, we were all exceedingly astonished and amazed, and consternated and affrighted even out of our reason; and our nearest and dearest relations, seeing us in that dreadful condition, and knowing our great danger, apprehended there was no other way to save our lives, as the case was then circumstanced, but by confessing ourselves to be such and such persons as the afflicted represented us to be, out of tenderness and pity, persuaded us to confess what we did confess.[11]

This episode is the reason why Thomas Barnard is remembered, whether justifiably or not, as one of the leading villains. Enders Robinson claims that the younger minister "masterminded" the Andover touch test, based solely on the statement in the declaration that Barnard led a prayer at the event.[12] That is no indication that he organized it. It is far more likely that the town's selectmen, under pressure from the Court of Oyer and Terminer in Salem, arranged the touch test. Bradstreet himself was one of the selectmen for that year, the others being John Chandler, John Aslebee, John Abbot, and Samuel Frye. Whether or not the selectmen unanimously approved of the test and, if not, who voted which way is not recorded. Nonetheless, by leading a prayer at such an event, Thomas Barnard was merely fulfilling an obligation expected of a town minister. Francis Dane's lack of participation is not surprising either. He had been yielding various responsibilities to the younger man for a decade by that time and may not have been expected to attend. Barnard may very well have participated willingly, but there is no way to measure his feelings on the matter at that stage.

In the same way that previous writers who have discussed the Andover witch hunt have been overly critical of Thomas Barnard and his role, they have also been too kind to Dudley Bradstreet. The reason for this is obvious. Bradstreet turned against the witch hunters after the touch test, refusing to sign any more arrest warrants, and as a result, he and his wife (Ann Wood Bradstreet) found themselves under suspicion. They fled Andover to the relative safety of the Piscataqua region of present-day New Hampshire, but returned by the end of the year to play a leading role in the resistance movement (Dudley Bradstreet's signature was the first one on a petition defending the suspects in early January 1693 and Ann also signed it). Prior to the touch test, though, there is no evidence that Dudley had any trepidations about the witch hunt.

Born in the late 1640s, Dudley Bradstreet was the third son of the town's most prominent resident, Simon Bradstreet—the oldest to remain in Andover. His given name, Dudley, was the maiden name of his mother, Anne Dudley Bradstreet (famous in her own right as the first American colonist to publish poetry). Not surprisingly, Dudley Bradstreet rose to prominence in town early in his adult life, serving almost continuously as a selectman from 1673 until the time of the witch hunt. His father, though still alive in 1692, had left Andover to assume larger roles in the colonial government (he had served the entire colony as acting governor from the time of the deposition of Edmund Andros until the arrival of Sir William Phips in May 1692). As justice of the peace in Andover, he began signing arrest warrants as soon as the accusations began in July 1692. This was his job and the fact that he carried it out does not, in and of itself, prove that he supported the witch hunt at that stage. But those accused in the early stages, as previously noted, did not belong to the town's elite, and there is no evidence that Bradstreet voiced any objections or felt any doubts about their guilt. He also conducted examinations of his own in the case of three suspects (Sarah Carrier, Thomas Carrier, and the younger Elizabeth Johnson) before they were taken to jail in Salem. As a son of an acting governor, he would have been as class-conscious as anyone else in the era, and it is likely that what raised questions in his mind was the fact that as Andover's witch hunt went on, the afflicted began targeting the town's elite. As a selectman, he would have been involved in the decision to conduct the touch test. With several leading citizens of the town among those to be tested, he and the other selectmen might have entertained the thought that these prominent citizens would be exonerated that day. If they did expect such an occurrence, it shows incredible naivete on their part—all who were tested "failed." After this event, Bradstreet did change his mind and that is to his credit. But his earlier complicity cannot be overlooked.

Deliverance Dane, one of the suspects arrested on September 7, underwent examination the next day before the judges in Salem. The surviving record of her interrogation does not reveal much, but she did state that she and Mary (Clements) Osgood (also arrested the previous day) had given Satan permission to use the old minister's shape to afflict others.[13] This fact implies that efforts to incriminate Francis Dane himself existed in the town of Andover at the time. On the same day, Mary Osgood's confession gives further evidence of this and demonstrates that there were those in the town willing to rush to Francis Dane's defense—even at the cost of incriminating themselves. After confessing to submitting to a baptism by the devil in Five Mile Pond in Boxford and to afflicting three victims, Osgood also claimed that she had attended a meeting at Moses Tyler's home for the purpose of afflicting and that she and Deliverance Dane had carried the shape of Mr. Dane, the minister, between them to make people believe he was afflicting. One of the magistrats then asked her this direct question "What hindered you from accomplishing what you intended?" Osgood's reply exonerated the minister, but gave further credence to spectral evidence: "The Lord would not suffer it to be, that the devil should afflict in an innocent person's shape."[14]

If Francis Dane knew of this testimony, it is hard to fathom how he would have reacted to it. Mary Osgood and her husband John (1630–1693) were two of Andover's leading citizens, John having served numerous terms as a selectman. The minister obviously valued their support, but it must have hurt him to see Mary not only incriminate herself, but also to give validity to the spectral evidence that he and numerous other Essex County ministers had so vociferously rejected. He may have known at that point, though, that an admission of guilt was Mary's best hope to, at the very least, prolong her life. He must have also realized that her defense of him probably reduced the chances that he would have to make the choice between belying himself and facing an immediate risk of dying on the gallows. It may very well be that she did spare him that predicament. The accusers were not yet done with his family and he knew that he stood a better chance of ultimately saving them if he remained free of suspicion himself. The last two members of the extended Ingalls clan to face the

Court of Oyer and Terminer were both children—daughters of the already jailed Abigail (Dane) Faulkner and, therefore, granddaughters of the longtime clergyman. Dorothy Faulkner and young Abigail Faulkner, aged twelve and nine respectively, came into the notorious Salem courtroom on September 16, not only to answer allegations against themselves, but also to address the question of their mother's guilt or innocence.

These two frightened girls may have been in jail as long as nine days by the time of their examinations. It is equally possible they had been arrested as recently as the day before. Some scholars believe that as many as seventeen Andover residents were taken into custody on the occasion of the touch test at the meetinghouse. Others think that only the six women who filed the declaration the following January were first jailed on that terrible day. Ultimately no documents exist to prove the exact number of arrests that occurred on September 7. Two things can be ascertained. First, the six women who signed the document describing the events of the touch test were imprisoned at that time. Second, seventeen residents of Andover were arrested sometime after September 1. All of those arrests could have occurred on the occasion of the touch test—but unless some as-yet-unknown documentation surfaces in the future, the specific facts will forever remain a mystery. But regardless of how long these two young Faulkner sisters had been in jail, coming before these magistrates who had already sent eleven people to their deaths could only have been a nightmare—and indeed, it is conceivable that real nightmares had convinced these girls of their own guilt and that of their mother. In their briefly summarized examination, both girls declared that their mother had appeared to them and made them witches. Three other accused girls—Martha and Joanna Tyler (twins, aged eleven) and young Sarah Wilson (aged fourteen) also blamed their venture into sorcery on the elder Abigail Faulkner. A twenty-one-year-old male suspect named Joseph Draper followed suit.[15] As pitiful as this scene appears—two terror-stricken young girls quavering in front of hardened judges and joining a chorus damning their own mother for enticing them into the service of Satan—a greater horror awaited the very next day when their mother went on trial for witchcraft.

Though few records of witchcraft prosecutions before the Court of Oyer and Terminer survive, the trial of Abigail (Dane) Faulkner stands out as one of the best-documented ones of the entire disastrous year of 1692. Two indictments of Faulkner (for afflicting Sarah Phelps and Martha Sprague) were presented in court September 17. Six depositions against her survive—three by Sarah Phelps, Martha Sprague, and Rose Foster, all key figures in the cluster of afflicted girls from Andover, all of whom presumably participated in the touch test ten days earlier. Three longtime stalwarts of Salem Village—the younger Ann Putnam, Mary Walcott, and Mary Warren—testified against Faulkner, too. In addition to themselves and the others who deposed, Foster and Sprague accused this middle-aged mother of afflicting Phelps's aunt, Hannah (Chandler) Bixby. The statement made by the five girls and Joseph Draper the day before was sworn to in the courtroom. Once in deliberations, the jury did not need long to come to a guilty verdict. Chief Justice Stoughton wasted no time in pronouncing a sentence of death.

Of course Faulkner was not going to the gallows—and everyone in the courtroom knew she would not, at least not immediately. Her pregnancy would have been evident by that time, and executing her would have also terminated the life of her innocent unborn baby. Elizabeth Procter, whose husband John had met his end a month before, remained alive for that very same reason. She, too, would survive the trials. Others who were sentenced that day faced death in short order and they knew it.

September 17 stands out as one of the most significant dates in the entire witchcraft episode of 1692. For the first time of the entire ordeal, beginning on September 10, confessors were being tried—and convicted. On the seventeenth, the Court of Oyer and Terminer condemned nine people to death by hanging—included six who had acknowledged their guilt, although one of them (Samuel Wardwell, of fortune-telling fame) had retracted his confession. Not surprisingly, five of the people sentenced that day were residents of Andover—in addition to Faulkner and Wardwell, Ann Foster, the elder Mary Lacey, and Mary (Ayer) Parker were condemned. Rebecca Eames, a resident of neighboring Boxford who was ensnared as part of the Andover phase of the persecutions, also heard the sentence of execution pronounced against her that day. Of that group, only Mary Parker had not confessed. All of those condemned from Andover were adults, but the judges also sentenced Abigail Hobbs, the teenaged confessor from Topsfield, on September 17—the first indication that, ultimately, underage suspects could also expect to die on the gallows.

As it turned out, the confessors were not executed. The next hanging took place on September 22, and of the Andover group, only Wardwell and Parker died that day. Had Wardwell not renounced his confession, he undoubtedly would have lived. In all, eight people hanged on the twenty-second, including four of the ones sentenced five days earlier. The living confessors, though, still had reason to expect that death awaited them. As far as they knew, they were only being spared temporarily to give them time to redeem their souls. One of those condemned earlier in September, Dorcas Hoar of Beverly, had not previously admitted guilt. She only confessed *after* being sentenced—and her date with the executioner was postponed. None of the jailed suspects were safe—and they knew it.

Of the extended Ingalls clan, two had died and fifteen more were still incarcerated. Sixteen of the sixty-three accused of witchcraft during the Andover phase of the witch hunt descended by bloodline or marriage from the Great Migration immigrants Edmund and Ann Ingalls of Lynn—slightly more than a quarter of the number from that area. When considering the entire episode of 1692, 11 percent of all the suspects came from this clan.[16] No other kin group had suffered more, and at that stage no one knew how many more arrests lay ahead or whether those still free—even personages as significant in the community as Francis Dane—could do anything to halt the chain of events.

As things turned out, the proceedings were interrupted after the executions of September 22 when several leaders in the Massachusetts Bay colony began to raise questions about the actions of the Court of Oyer and Terminer. These issues prompted Governor William Phips to disband the court in late October, thereby putting any further prosecutions on hold until a new court could be established—which it was in December. No more members of the extended Ingalls clan were arrested and, as it turned out, none of those already in custody was to die. But the delay in the proceedings, while buying time, did not free anyone already arrested from the fear of prosecution, nor did it spare their family members from the prospect of losing them— whether to a hangman's noose or the deprivations of life in jail.

But this family group did not suffer alone. Another large extended clan with ties to Andover also saw itself ripped apart by the horrors of 1692.

Two woodcuts from the *History of Witches and Wizards: Giving a True Account of All Their Tryals in England, Scotland, Swedeland, France, and New England: With Their Confession and Condemnation*, by "W. P.," and published in 1720 by T. Norris, London. The top shows witches riding on broomsticks, and the bottom illustrates a feast with devils. Ann Foster confessed that she and Martha Carrier "rode sticks" to a meeting of witches in Salem Village. (*Welcome Institute*)

"Witchcraft at Salem Village." This 1876 illustration shows one of the "afflicted" girls of Salem—possibly Mary Walcott. Thomas Carrier confessed that his mother, Martha Carrier, had told him to afflict Mary Walcott, but he had not done so. (*William A. Crafts,* Pioneers in the Settlement of America)

Spofford Pond in Boxford, known as Five Mile Pond in 1692. Some of those who confessed to witchcraft in 1692 claimed to have undergone baptism by the Devil in this pond. It is located near Witch Hollow Farm, the home of Moses Tyler and his family. (*Cassandra Michael*)

Thomas Barnard House in North Andover, constructed about 1715 to replace the earlier parsonage that was destroyed by fire about 1707. Thomas Barnard (1657-1718), the younger of the two ministers in Andover at the time of the 1692 witchcraft trials, led a prayer on the occasion of the touch test on September 7, and listened to confessions, but he also played a leading role in the opposition to the witch hunt. The house is now the property of the North Andover Historical Society. (*Cassandra Michael*)

The Shawsheen River in Andover, near the home of Benjamin and Sarah Farnum Abbot. Several confessors claimed to have been baptized by the Devil in this river and one of them specifically stated that this baptism occurred when he was going home after having worked for Abbot. (*Cassandra Michael*)

Home of Benjamin Abbot (1662–1703) and his wife, Sarah Farnum Abbot (1661–before 1720) in Andover. Benjamin testified against Martha Carrier in 1692, claiming to have been afflicted by her. Sarah gave testimony supporting her husband's allegations. (*Cassandra Michael*)

Home of Sherebiah Ballard (born 1688) and his wife Lydia Osgood Ballard (born 1695) in Andover. Sherebiah was a son of South End constable John Ballard and Lydia was a daughter of suspect defender Christopher Osgood. (*Cassandra Michael*)

Foster's Pond, in Andover and Wilmington. This pond is on land owned by Andrew Foster and his wife Ann, original proprietors of Andover. Andrew died in 1685, allegedly aged 100 years. Ann, accused of witchcraft in 1692, died in jail in December of that year aged about seventy-five. Her son Abraham retrieved her body and according to family tradition, she was buried somewhere on her land. (*Cassandra Michael*)

The monument in Salem erected in 2017 to those hanged for witchcraft. The hill in the background is the site of the executions. (*Richard Hite*)

The Old Burying Ground in modern-day North Andover, established about 1660 for the First Church of Andover. Buried here are accused witches, accusers, and defenders of suspects from 1692. This cemetery may contain more marked graves of people involved in the 1692 witch hunt than any other cemetery. (*Cassandra Michael*)

Gravestone of Moses Tyler (ca. 1641–1727) in the old burying ground in North Andover. Moses filed formal complaints against some suspected witches in 1692, even though his sister and several other close relatives were among the accused. Moses was also the stepfather of the Andover witch hunt's leading afflicted girl, Martha Sprague. (*Cassandra Michael*)

Gravestone of Timothy Swan (1663–1693) in the old burying ground in North Andover. Timothy Swan was one of the leading accusers of suspects in Andover. Apparently sick at the time of the witch hunt (an affliction he attributed to witchcraft), he died on February 2, 1693, shortly after the reprieve of the remaining convicted witches by Governor William Phips. The death date carved into his tombstone (February 2, 1692) is based on the Julian calendar, which designated March 25 as the first day of a new year. By modern calculations, his year of death was 1693. (*Cassandra Michael*)

Gravestone of Abigail Martin Safford (1676–1768) in Ames Cemetery, Lisbon, Connecticut. Abigail was one of Andover's afflicted girls in 1692. She later married John Safford of Ipswich and they moved to Connecticut. Abigail may have been the last survivor of all the afflicted children of the 1692 witch hunt. (*Cassandra Michael*)

Gravestone of Thomas Barnard (1657–1718) in the old burying ground in North Andover. Thomas was the younger of two ministers in Andover at the time of the witchcraft trials. He has often been unjustifiably stereotyped as a zealous witch hunter. In reality he signed petitions defending witchcraft suspects in Andover late in 1692 and in early 1693, along with the older minister, Francis Dane (1615–1697). (*Cassandra Michael*)

Gravestone of Ephraim Foster (1657–1746) in Mount Vernon Cemetery in Boxford, Massachusetts. Ephraim was the constable for Andover's North End at the time of the 1692 witch hunt and arrested several of those accused. He also filed complaints against some suspects accused of afflicting his daughter, Rose Foster, and testified against Samuel Wardwell at his trial. (*Cassandra Michael*)

Gravestone of Rebecca Blake Eames (ca. 1640–1721, spelled Rebekah Eams on the stone) in Mount Vernon Cemetery in Boxford, Massachusetts. Rebecca was charged with witchcraft in August 1692 and confessed. She was tried in September, convicted, and sentenced to death, but was reprieved by Governor Phips in October. In December, she retracted her confession. She was, nonetheless, among those slated for execution in early February 1693 before Governor Phips intervened again. Her gravestone may be the only contemporary one in existence for a person convicted of witchcraft in 1692. Those executed were buried in unmarked graves near the site of the execution. Among those convicted and sentenced to death but not hanged, Rebecca is the only one known to have a surviving tombstone that was placed on her grave soon after her death. She was also the mother-in-law of Constable Ephraim Foster of Andover's North End and the sister of Moses Tyler's first wife, Prudence Blake Tyler (1647-1689). (*Cassandra Michael*)

Gravestone of Christopher Osgood (1643–1723) in the old burying ground in North Andover. Christopher signed petitions defending witchcraft suspects late in 1693. His oldest daughter, Mary Osgood Marston, was among the accused. Christopher was a militia captain and a frequent selectman in Andover. (*Cassandra Michael*)

Gravestone of Andrew Carrier (1677–1749), Colchester Burying Ground, Colchester, Connecticut. Andrew, a son of Martha Carrier was tortured into confessing to witchcraft in 1692. He and his siblings, along with their widowed father Thomas, all moved to Connecticut a few years after the trials.(*Cassandra Michael*)

CHAPTER NINE

The Tribulations of Job (and Moses)

THE CONFLICTS JOB TYLER and his family experienced in Andover from the time of their first arrival there are well chronicled (see Chapter 4). Job had taken permanent leave of the town by 1692 and settled permanently in Mendon. He had first tried to put down roots there in the 1660s before being driven back by the ravages of King Philip's War. By the late 1680s, though, that area was safer from Indian attacks than Andover was. Despite the family's less than stellar history in Andover, three of Job's children resided there in 1692. Mary, the oldest of those three, had married her second husband (John Bridges) there in 1678, three years after her first husband, Richard Post, was killed at the outset of King Philip's War in Mendon. Mary and John resided in the North End with their large blended family consisting of some of Mary's children and stepchildren with Post, John's children by his first wife Sarah Howe, and the children they produced together. Hopestill Tyler, whose apprenticeship to Thomas Chandler had stirred so much controversy three decades earlier, resided in the South End, plying the trade of blacksmith that he had learned from his father's nemesis. John Tyler, who had married into the same Parker family involved in the controversy, made his home in the North End with his wife Hannah and their children. His now widowed mother-in-law, Mary (Ayer) Parker, lived nearby. With Job away in Mendon, the patriarch of the family in the area was the oldest Tyler brother, Moses, who resided in neighboring Boxford (formerly Rowley Village) but attended the church in Andover. This was the same Moses Tyler who had, in company with John Godfrey, seized his brother Hopestill's indenture from the home of Nathan Parker, the now deceased father-in-law of his brother John. Moses and his sister Mary had also testified against Godfrey when their father accused him of witchcraft in 1659. Now, more than thirty years later, witchcraft came into their lives again. By the time the trials ended, the whole family may have wished they had followed their parents back to Mendon.

Mary Tyler (Post) Bridges, the oldest daughter of Job, became the first of the family to be apprehended on sorcery charges. A warrant for her arrest was issued on July 28, accusing her of committing "sundry acts of witchcraft" on the body of Timothy Swan and others.[1] Although she lived in the North End, it was John Ballard rather than Ephraim Foster who took her into custody in Salem. The division of labor between the two constables must not have been strictly regimented. It is hardly surprising that Timothy Swan was named as Bridges's "victim" on the warrant. At that stage, he remained the most visible of the afflicted in Andover, although the Salem Village girls still played a significant role and the younger Mary Lacey continued her efforts at transforming herself from a suspect into an accuser. For Bridges, no record of an examination is known to survive, but she must have quickly confessed because two days later she gave evidence against Hannah Bromage of Haverhill, who had been arrested the same day that she had. Bridges testified that Bromage had been with her and others at the house of Joseph Ballard and that she had hurt Ballard's wife (Elizabeth, who had died three days earlier) by sitting on her breast. The young Ann Putnam was, as always, in the courtroom, and when she fell into a fit, Bridges and the younger Lacey claimed they saw Bromage upon her. Bridges urged Bromage to confess, telling her the devil would not leave her until she did.[2]

Despite the pressure Bromage faced, she resisted, saying only that the devil appeared to her but denying that she accepted him. Mary Bridges, however, had established herself as another confessor who was willing to testify against other suspects. Not surprisingly, suspicion quickly extended to a member of Bridges's immediate family. Her eldest daughter, twenty-eight-year-old Mary Post, resided in the town of Rowley rather than in Andover with her family, even though she was unmarried. On August 2, Timothy Swan, Ann Putnam, and Mary Walcott complained to Andover's justice of the peace, Dudley Bradstreet, that Post had "sorely afflicted them." Swan gave a bond of twenty pounds, whereupon Bradstreet issued a warrant for Post's arrest. Rowley's constable, Joseph Jewett, apprehended her and delivered her to Salem the next day.[3] Post's case echoes that of her mother in two ways. First, no record of an examination of her is known to exist. Second, it is obvious that she confessed because almost immediately, she testified against another suspect. The very day after her own arrest, she appeared in court and claimed that she had seen Mary Johnson Davis Clark of Haverhill afflict her own accuser, Timothy Swan, though she gave no specific details of this attack. She also identified Clark as one of those she saw at the village witch meeting (presumably Salem Village) and said that Clark ate and drank with the others. Several of the Salem Village girls also testified against Clark, but like Bromage a few days earlier, Clark resisted self-implication. Post had not demonstrated the strength of will that these two Haverhill women displayed and neither had her mother. Instead, these first two members of the Tyler clan to fall under suspicion added themselves to the growing litany of confessors.

Determining why the accusers turned their attention to the Tyler family does not seem difficult. Due to the earlier conflicts with Thomas Chandler, who was still alive and well, the family's reputation in Andover was less than sterling. It is true that no member of the Chandler family took any direct action against either of these women at that early stage, even though Sarah Phelps (a granddaughter of Thomas Chandler) and Hannah Chandler Bixby (Thomas's daughter) later joined the ranks of the afflicted.[4] The Tyler family's own reputation is the most likely reason they came under attack. Even without such family connections, Mary Post stood out as a prime candidate for suspicion in her own right. Writing a few years after the trials, Boston merchant Robert Calef (a leading critic of the proceedings) described Mary Post and the younger Elizabeth Johnson—whose own grandfather Francis Dane had called "simplish at best"—as two of "the most senseless and ignorant creatures that could be found."[5] Given that Calef described Johnson accurately, there is little reason to doubt the veracity of his comments on Mary Post. This poor young woman, nearing the age of thirty and still unmarried (yet no longer living with her own nuclear family), presented a viable target for accusation. Her family connection could only have made matters worse. She may have been bullied as a child and, if she ever voiced any threats or mere wishes of harm to those who harassed her, those utterances would have sounded like curses to any who remembered hearing them in 1692.

Mary Post and her mother, Mary Tyler (Post) Bridges, both went to jail after their own confessions and sat there with the others awaiting trial. From that time until the beginning of the second phase of the Andover persecutions, no other direct Tyler family member was arrested. Two collateral relatives came into the Salem courtroom for examination, though. Daniel Eames of Boxford, examined on August 13, was a first cousin of Moses Tyler's children. Tyler's late first wife, Prudence Blake Tyler, had been a sister of Rebecca Blake Eames (then aged fifty-one), Daniel Eames's mother. Six days later, Rebecca herself faced the justices and readily confessed to afflicting Timothy Swan and some of the Salem Village girls, among others. She even acknowledged giving her son to the devil when he was two years old—even though he was there urging her not to admit guilt.[6] She also admitted to hurting Swan, some of the Salem Village girls, and the younger Mary Lacey.[7] But Moses Tyler and his immediate family had not yet entered the fray, and the connection between the Eameses and Moses Tyler's sister and niece were too distant to be considered significant. The confession of Rebecca would assume greater importance in the second phase of the Andover accusations though. She mentioned Five

Mile Pond in Boxford as the place of her baptism by the devil. Previous confessors from Andover had primarily been citing the Shawsheen River. Five Mile Pond was near the property of her brother-in-law, Moses Tyler, whose role was to grow soon after.

The examination of Rebecca Eames marked the end of the first phase of the Andover persecutions. To that point, the involvement of the Tyler family had been limited. In the second phase, they took center stage, both as accusers and accused. No other family in any community involved in the 1692 witch hunt played such prominent roles on both sides of the issue.

The extended Tyler clan actually touched off the second phase, acting as accusers and accused on August 25. On that day, two more daughters of Mary Tyler (Post) Bridges underwent examination in the Salem courtroom, along with two stepdaughters—one from each husband. Hers was a complex blended family. The eldest of these newly accused, Susannah Post, had been born to Richard Post and his first wife, Susannah Sutton, sometime prior to 1662. Though over thirty, she remained single. Hannah Post, a daughter of Richard Post by Mary Tyler (and therefore a full sister of the already jailed Mary Post), was almost twenty-six, having been born in Woburn in 1666. The other two were much younger. Sarah Bridges, a daughter of John Bridges by his first wife, Sarah Howe, was probably about seventeen in 1692.[8] The youngest, Mary Bridges, was only thirteen, having been born to John Bridges and Mary Tyler (Post) Bridges in 1679. All of them except Hannah Post (whose examination record did not specifically name any of her alleged victims) stood accused of hurting (among others) Martha Sprague, the stepdaughter of Moses Tyler. Moses, as previously noted, was the oldest brother of the previously accused Mary Tyler (Post) Bridges and therefore the uncle (or step-uncle in two cases) of all of the women and girls examined on August 25.

On the same day that his nieces were examined, Moses Tyler (along with Samuel Martin of Andover) filed a complaint against William Barker, Sr., Mary (Osgood) Marston, and the adolescent Mary Barker (niece of William), charging that all three had "woefully afflicted and abused Abigail Martin (Samuel's daughter) and Rose Foster of Andover and Martha Sprague of Boxford by witchcraft."[9] Ephraim Foster, the North End's constable and father of Rose Foster, arrested the three the same day. In Enders Robinson's *Salem Witchcraft and Hawthorne's House of the Seven Gables*, which places Moses Tyler at the head of a conspiracy that fueled the witchcraft accusations in Andover, the author assumes that Martha Sprague merely acted as her stepfather's tool, accusing those he wanted to see jailed, including his own close relatives.[10] In Robinson's work, Moses Tyler emerges as the central villain of the entire drama in Andover. Robinson writes:

> His motivations could have sprung from some twisted form of sibling rivalry, from a paranoid delusional personality, or from a hundred other possibilities. Clearly his character was disordered; here was a man who lacked a conscience, who lacked any sense of guilt. And it is the absence of these very traits which explains how he and his cronies became such cunning and successful witch hunters.[11]

This damning description of Moses Tyler rivals the vilification of Cotton Mather by some nineteenth- and early twentieth-century writers, who viewed him as the leading instigator of the entire drama of 1692. Author Diane Foulds, possibly taking her cue from Robinson, describes Martha Sprague as doing her stepfather's bidding, whether it was willingly or by coercion. She further states that Martha "unflinchingly backed him [Moses]" just as Moses had supported his father (Job Tyler) thirty years earlier in his feuds with John Godfrey and Thomas Chandler.[12]

Moses Tyler is by no means without guilt in the Andover witchcraft drama. He did file a complaint against three suspects on August 25, the same day his nieces were examined. He and Samuel Martin were also the ones who swore out the warrant against the elder Elizabeth Johnson and her daughter Abigail five days later. Given that so few documents of the formal complaints filed against Andover suspects survive, it is possible that Tyler was responsible for more of them. But it cannot be taken for granted that his stepdaughter acted merely as his willing tool. The complaint against Mary Tyler (Post) Bridges's daughters and stepdaughters, probably filed a day or two before their examinations, does not survive. It is true that Martha Sprague was specifically named as a victim of three of them. That does not, however, prove that her stepfather filed the complaints. It is equally plausible that someone else filed them on her behalf and she may have accused these women and girls partly due to malice she bore against her stepfather.

Martha Sprague's entire world had turned upside down in the nineteen-month period before she first complained of affliction by witches. She had been born about 1676 in Malden, where she lived with her parents, Phineas and Sarah (Hasey) Sprague, and six siblings (four brothers and two sisters) until her father's untimely death on January 23, 1691. As the oldest daughter, Martha (aged about fourteen when her father died) would have borne a heavy burden of responsibility regardless of the family's circumstances. Sarah Sprague, who gave birth to another daughter (Abigail) five weeks after Phineas's death, remarried almost immediately, probably out of financial necessity. The daughter closest to Martha's age was nine-year-old Katherine and the other sister (aside from the newborn baby) was still a toddler, so Martha might have been hoping for some new stepsisters to ease her workload. Instead Sarah's new husband, Moses Tyler, brought her into what had been, since the death of his first wife Prudence (Blake) Tyler nearly two years earlier, an all-male household. It is somewhat surprising that he waited that long to remarry, though he may have taken in nieces and neighborhood teenage girls to help out prior to his second marriage. The Sprague children not only lost their father, but were also uprooted from the only home they had ever known in Malden. They now found themselves in the far less-established community of Boxford. Moses Tyler had eight sons, ranging in age from twenty-four-year-old Moses, Jr. to three-year-old Joshua, by the time he married the widow Sprague in 1691. Instead of additional help, Martha found herself saddled with the responsibility of providing for the needs of a new stepfather and eight new stepbrothers. If all four of her own brothers followed them to Boxford, there may have been as many as thirteen males in this newly blended family's home. With Sarah nursing a new baby, young Martha's workload would not have lessened in any way by the time of the outbreak of witchcraft accusations in neighboring Andover. Though the family lived in Boxford (on land known today as Witch Hollow Farm), they attended church in Andover and would have had ample firsthand exposure to the events plaguing that town in the summer of 1692. Martha, undoubtedly still grieving from the loss of her father and perhaps understandably nursing a grudge against a new stepfather, was primed to see herself as a victim of malefic magic.

The differences between the situations of teenage girls living with biological parents and those residing in the households of others as domestic servants manifested themselves in Salem Village earlier in the year of the witch hunt. As noted previously, the younger Ann Putnam and Mary Walcott both lived with their respective biological fathers, Thomas Putnam and Jonathan Walcott, who took their claims of bewitchment seriously and swore out warrants against their daughters' alleged tormentors. Mary Warren and Sarah Churchill, on the other hand, lived as domestic servants to John Procter and George Jacobs, respectively, who ridiculed the young women's claims of victimization by witches. A stepdaughter/stepfather relationship fell somewhere between those two situations. Moses Tyler, if he genuinely loved his new wife, might have extended that affection to her children to some degree. It is also possible he simply saw the teenage girl as a new maid for himself and his numerous sons. Regardless of what bond (or lack thereof) existed between Martha Sprague and Moses Tyler, there can be no doubt that the upheavals in her life over the previous year played a significant role in the afflictions she suffered. She began testifying against suspects on August 25 and continued until May 1693 when the trials ended. Evidence from her testimony during some of the September trials suggests that her stepfather did not immediately embrace her suffering.

On September 17, Sprague was deposed in the trial of Abigail Dane Faulkner, who had first been examined on August 11, two weeks before Sprague's first appearance in court. The testimony against Faulkner is particularly revealing in that Sprague claims that this minister's daughter had been afflicting her since the beginning of

August 1692.[13] Sprague had not been mentioned as a victim in either of Faulkner's previous examinations, and no record of her claiming affliction is dated prior to August 25. This discrepancy may shed light on her relationship with her stepfather, Moses Tyler. If her afflictions did start in early August, Moses might have initially reacted to them in the way that John Procter and George Jacobs did when their respective servants (Mary Warren and Sarah Churchill) first showed signs of bewitchment in Salem Village: assuming their servants were playacting to avoid their responsibilities. Moses Tyler might easily have thought the same of Martha Sprague. If he did, he had obviously changed his attitude by August 25 when he and Samuel Martin first filed witchcraft complaints naming Martha as a victim. But it is quite possible that his motive for action was simple self-preservation. Tyler knew all too well the fate of Procter and Jacobs. Both had died on the gallows on August 19, six days before Tyler filed his first complaint. Their fate could await him if he dismissed his stepdaughter's afflictions as an effort to dodge her household chores. It is also noteworthy that Moses was not the only member of the Tyler family who filed formal complaints against new suspects for supposedly bewitching Martha Sprague.

On the same day that Moses Tyler and Samuel Martin filed their complaint against the Barkers and Mary Marston, Joseph Tyler (Moses's third son, who was less than a month shy of his twenty-first birthday) and Ephraim Foster filed a complaint against three men from Rowley for bewitching Martha Sprague and Rose Foster (Ephraim's daughter). Ephraim's wife, Hannah (Eames) Foster, was Joseph Tyler's first cousin.[14] The men they accused were John Jackson, Sr., his son John Jackson, Jr., and John Howard. The elder Jackson was the brother of the previously executed Elizabeth (Jackson) Howe, which made him and his son likely candidates for suspicion. But the significance of this complaint regarding the Tyler/Sprague blended family is the fact Joseph acted independently of his father in filing it. Joseph also concerned himself with the alleged afflictions of his stepsister. The fact that the supposed victims named in this accusation were Martha Sprague and Rose Foster (and *not* Abigail Martin) hints at who accused Mary Tyler (Post) Bridges's daughters and stepdaughters. In the warrants sworn out on August 25, Moses Tyler and Samuel Martin acted in tandem for one, while Joseph Tyler and Ephraim Foster joined forces for the other one. As previously noted, the elder Tyler and Martin again teamed up five days later to file a complaint against Elizabeth Dane Johnson and her daughter Abigail. August 25 was also the day that the four young women and girls from the Bridges/Post/Tyler clan came before the magistrates in Salem for examination. In the cases of Mary Bridges and Susannah Post, the justices began the interrogations by declaring that they stood accused of afflicting Martha Sprague and Rose Foster. For Sarah Bridges, they stated that she was charged only with inflicting Martha Sprague. They did not name Hannah Post's alleged victims. But one name is conspicuously absent in these accusations—Abigail Martin. That is a clue—though not proof—that Samuel Martin was not among the accusers of these young suspects. Since Martin acted in tandem with Moses Tyler in the two surviving complaints they filed, it is not unreasonable to think they did not file the complaint against Moses's family members. Instead, the more likely formal accusers of the four suspected witches who were questioned on August 25 are Joseph Tyler and Ephraim Foster.

If that is the case, then why would Joseph Tyler have been any more likely than his father to have taken such action against his own cousins? As is evident by this point, it is very possible that Martha Sprague's symptoms were real to her—whether they were genuinely physical or simply psychosomatic. Whatever was wrong, in those circumstances both Tyler men could have eventually concluded that she suffered from witchcraft. If she did, in fact, resent her new stepfather, she could have blamed his nieces as an indirect attack on him. So why would Joseph have taken her at her word if she accused his own family? He was almost twenty-one and she was about sixteen. Perhaps he had fallen in love with her. For a young man in the grip of passion to echo every whim of the object of his affection, even a direct assault on his own kin, is a story as old as time. But no one will never know.

A little over a month after the last executions of 1692 (which occurred on September 22), Governor William Phips abolished the Court of Oyer and Terminer. In December, the colony established a

new court—the Superior Court of Judicature and Court of Assize—
to try the remaining witchcraft cases. This court began hearings in
January 1693. The records of this new court consistently referenced
Martha Sprague as "Martha Sprague alias Tyler." Researchers have
most commonly assumed that she had simply taken the name of her
stepfather Moses—perhaps because a bond formed between them as
a result of his persecution of her presumed tormentors. When she
married Richard Friend in 1701, she appeared in the marriage record
as Martha Tyler—even though the marriage records of all of her sisters
gave their maiden name as Sprague. It was, however, highly unusual
for a child of a widowed mother who remarried to assume the surname of his or her stepfather in that time period in New England.
On the other hand, it was not unusual for married women—particularly recently married women—to be referred to in legal documents
by their maiden names, alias their married names. As an example, the
division of the real estate of Robert Swan of Haverhill (father of Timothy) after Robert's death in 1698 refers to his daughters as Ann Swan
alias Ayer, Sarah Swan alias Hartshorn, Dorothy Swan alias Dalton,
Ruth Swan alias Hartshorn, and Elizabeth Swan alias Herriman. The
aliases are the daughters' married names. There is no reason to think
that the references to Martha Sprague, alias Tyler, in the 1693 court
cases were any different. In addition to the fact that her mother had
married Moses Tyler, she had probably also married a Tyler. Sixteen
was an unusually early marriage age for women in colonial New England but the man whose approval Martha Sprague would have needed
to marry that young was none other than Moses Tyler. If his son
Joseph had fallen in love with her, he might very well have granted
that permission.

The best evidence that Martha Sprague did marry Joseph Tyler by
the end of 1692 comes from the record of the trial of Hannah Post
before the reconstituted court on January 12, 1693. The document
includes the following accusation against Post:

> For that shee the said Hannah Post, of Boxford, single woman, in
> and upon the 23d day of August last in the Year of our Lord 1692
> and diverse other dayes, and times, as well before, as after, certain
> detestable arts, called witchcrafts, and sorceries, wickedly, mali-

tiously, and ffeloniously hath used, practiced, and exercised, at, and in the town of Boxford, in the county of Essex aforesaid, upon and against, one Martha Sprague, of Boxford, aforesaid, now wife of [space left blank] by which said wicked arts, the said Martha Sprague alias Martha Tyler, was, and is tortured, afflicted, consumed, wasted, pined, and tormented against the peace of our Soveraigne Lord and Lady the King and Queen, their Crowne and dignity, and the Lawes, in that case made, and Provided.[15]

Post was acquitted, as were all but three of the suspects who faced this reconstituted court in 1693, but the most significant aspects of this document are what they reveal about Martha Sprague. It is one of several 1693 documents that refer to her as "Martha Sprague alias Martha Tyler" but the only one that identifies her as "now wife of" someone. There is space after that phrase to fill in a name, but it is left blank. It is, of course, possible, that the clerk mistakenly thought she was married because she was using a different name than she had before. However, it is equally possible that he simply did not know the given name of her husband and simply left space to fill it in later, but never followed through. It is also noteworthy that this record did *not* refer to Martha Sprague, alias Tyler, as a single woman, nor did any other document from the court records of 1693. Others, accused and afflicted, some of them Martha's age and younger, were often (though not necessarily always) referred to as "single woman."

Joseph Tyler died in 1699, aged only twenty-seven or twenty-eight. His only immediate survivor was a widow named Martha—no children. There is no known record of the marriage of Joseph and Martha—whatever her maiden name was. The probate record demonstrates that Joseph had business ties to the West Indies, and it may be that he died there. Among those he collaborated with was his stepbrother, Phineas Sprague, Jr. The fact that the two men were stepbrothers was reason enough for this interaction—but if they were also brothers-in-law, the reasons were amplified. Two years after the death of Joseph Tyler, Martha Sprague (listed as Martha Tyler in the record) married Richard Friend in Andover. By that time, she was about twenty-five—a bit late for a first marriage for a New England woman of that era, though not unheard of. The assumption that she had simply adopted her stepfather's surname may be an oversimplification. She might very well have been Joseph Tyler's widow. If she did marry Joseph at the end of 1692, they would have been married for six to seven years by the time of his death. Joseph, however, died childless. Martha also had no children by Richard Friend. The possibility that she was infertile cannot be discounted. Perhaps she, like Timothy Swan, was genuinely sick at the time of the witchcraft trials of 1692. Unlike him, she survived the trials, but if she was unwell, perhaps the malady she suffered from left her barren—even though she was certainly not too incapacitated to appear in court on a regular basis. Regardless of Martha Sprague's physical condition in late August 1692, there is no question about her mental state—she believed herself to be under supernatural assault. Six of her stepfather's close relatives had been arrested on witchcraft charges, four of them at least partly because of her.

Enders Robinson writes that Moses Tyler incriminated his own close relatives due to a long-standing intra-family quarrel, but there is more circumstantial evidence that if anyone in the Tyler family swore out warrants against the Post and Bridges women, it was Joseph Tyler. So, this raises the question of why Moses Tyler involved himself at all. Like others in the community, he must have genuinely believed in witchcraft. He had, after all, willingly accused John Godfrey more than thirty years earlier. As previously noted, his actions may have served, at least in part, as self-preservation. If his afflicted stepdaughter resented him, it is likely he sensed it. His sister Mary's daughters and stepdaughters were in court that very day being examined for afflicting Martha Sprague and Rose Foster. They had probably been arrested the day before, most likely on the basis of a complaint filed by Joseph Tyler and Ephraim Foster. This accusation of some of his nearest kin, probably instigated by his own son and the constable of Andover's North End, would have given Moses Tyler reasons to fear that he and his own household could be next. If Joseph Tyler was in fact besotted with his afflicted stepsister, there was no certainty that he would not lash out at his own father on her behalf—particularly if Moses had not treated Martha as kindly as he should have and had accused her of playacting in the early stages of her fits. If Moses did ignore

Martha's earliest symptoms, she might have turned to Joseph instead, perhaps having already sensed that he was interested in her.

If the protection of his own family was Moses Tyler's motive for steering accusations toward others, he was only partially successful. No one accused him, his new wife, or any of his children. But the afflicted, including Martha Sprague, had not finished with the extended Tyler clan. Mary (Lovett) Tyler, the forty-year-old wife of Moses's brother the blacksmith Hopestill Tyler, fell victim to suspicion early in September along with three of her daughters—Hannah (aged fourteen) and twins Joanna and Martha (aged eleven). Mary and Hannah definitely stood among those subjected to the touch test on September 7—they signed the document describing their experience the following January.[16] The two younger girls were probably also there. The mother and all the daughters can be documented as having confessed to the crimes they were accused of. There is no doubt that Martha Sprague was among the afflicted at the Andover meeting house on that fateful day. What role, if any, she played in the initial accusations against Mary (Lovett) Tyler and her daughters is not reflected in any of the surviving documentary evidence. But given her prominent role among the town's victims and the fact that she had already accused others of her stepfather's near relations, there is no reason to believe she would have hesitated to attack his brother Hopestill's family. She could have done so without his cooperation, just as Mary Warren and Sarah Churchill claimed spectral assault by members of the families they served. Others in town might have taken Martha Sprague at her word when she claimed supernatural abuse by her newly acquired relatives. When one of those who believed her was the North End's constable, Ephraim Foster, the accusations carried weight.

Ultimately, ten members of the family of Moses Tyler's aged parents (Job and Mary Tyler) fell under suspicion of witchcraft in 1692— one daughter, one daughter-in-law, six granddaughters, and two step-granddaughters. No other family except the extended Ingalls clan saw so many of its progeny charged with witchcraft that year. This round of accusations seems to relate more to the family's earlier troubles in Andover than to an alleged vendetta against siblings by a vengeful older brother. Years earlier, the family had tarnished its reputation in the town by feuding with one of its leading citizens, Thomas Chandler. If anything, Moses Tyler may have been attempting to live up to his biblical name by leading his own people away from suspicion. He failed—and his method of turning the accusations against others does not inspire admiration. In reality, the distracted eighteen-year-old Mary Lacey succeeded to a far greater degree in staving off accusations against her own family than the middle-aged Tyler did—even though no real evidence suggests that as her intention. After the youthful Mary designated Martha Carrier as the future "Queen in Hell," no one else in her family was accused. The accusations against the Tyler clan continued despite Moses's efforts.

Moses Tyler also did not cast doubt on the fits of his stepdaughter Martha Sprague, and he may never have intended to. Even though the idea that he deliberately targeted the families of his own siblings does not withstand a careful examination of the evidence, there is little doubt he did nothing to quell the tide of persecution in general. Indeed, one of the suspects Martha Sprague identified as an attacker had direct ties to the Tyler family's dispute with Thomas Chandler thirty years earlier. Mary (Ayer) Parker of Andover, examined on September 2, was the widow of Nathan Parker, who had drawn up the indenture confirming Hopestill Tyler's apprenticeship to Thomas Chandler. Moses Tyler, in company with the notorious John Godfrey, had taken the document from the Parker home in 1662 in an effort to extricate his brother from the contract. There may very well have been lingering tensions between Moses Tyler and Mary Parker over that incident. Young Martha Sprague, though not necessarily her stepfather's puppet, was still in the throes of belief that witches were tormenting her. As with the Salem Village girls, the power of suggestion would have been high. If her stepfather did influence her to name Mary Parker, it might have happened indirectly. Joseph Tyler, who may have been in love with Martha, might have been the one who actually suggested Parker as a possible tormentor. Born in 1671, Joseph might have been hearing grumblings about Nathan and Mary Parker throughout his life and, when he saw his stepsister bewitched, Mary Parker could have immediately come to his mind as a likely suspect. The complaint against Mary Parker does not survive, but there is little doubt that one of the Tylers (Moses or Joseph) was among those who filed it. Mary Parker herself balked at confessing, bucking the trend of suspects from Andover at the time. Instead, she tried to shift the blame, making it a point to note that another Mary Parker lived in Andover.[17] But Martha Sprague confirmed that this Mary Parker was the one who had afflicted her.[18] Eventually, Parker paid with her life, going to the gallows three weeks later.

The Tyler clan's wrath next came crashing down on Samuel Wardwell and his family. The complaint filed against Wardwell, his wife Sarah, his daughter Mercy (age nineteen), and his stepdaughter, Sarah Hawkes (age twenty-two), has not survived. Because all of them admitted to diabolical acts and the first "victim" named in all of their confessions was Martha Sprague, it is most likely that Moses or Joseph Tyler (possibly both) was among the plaintiffs. Ironically, the man who would have borne the responsibility for arresting the Wardwells was none other than John Ballard—the husband of Sarah Hooper Wardwell's sister Rebecca. The Wardwells resided just south of the divide between the North and South Ends so it is possible that Ephraim Foster took them into custody. All four of them appeared in court on September 1 and they all confessed. The stories the various members of this family told varied drastically, however. Sarah Hawkes described a gathering at Moses Tyler's home. The afflicted (not named at the beginning of the examination) accused Hawkes and others there of forcing them to dance and sing for several hours. In acknowledging her guilt, Hawkes specifically noted that Martha Sprague "sung at Mr. Tyler's almost all day till she was almost killed." She acknowledged dancing at the event herself and forcing Ephraim Foster's wife (Hannah Eames Foster) to dance at home.[19] On the same day Stephen Johnson, the recently arrested son of Elizabeth Dane Johnson, also acknowledged dancing at the Tyler home and making Sprague sing.[20]

Samuel Wardwell resisted confessing at first before acknowledging that he knew himself to be in the devil's snare. Describing his history of fortune telling, he admitted that his predictions sometimes came true and he also noted that if any creature (presumably an animal) came into his field that he bid the devil take it and he expressed his concern that perhaps the devil had taken advantage of his habit of making such declarations. He went on to admit that twenty years or so previously (apparently just before his marriage to Sarah) he had encountered a man who called himself "a prince of the air" who had made several promises to him if Samuel would honor him. Samuel agreed to do so until he reached the age of sixty (he was about twenty-nine when he supposedly made that promise and forty-nine when arrested though he gave his age as about forty-six in the deposition). He noted having been discontented at the time because of being in love with a maid named Barker who slighted his love (presumably Sarah Barker, 1647–1729, daughter of founders Richard and Joanna Barker, who married John Abbot in 1673). He described having seen a cat behind Captain Bradstreet's home (presumably Dudley Bradstreet), and a week after that declared that a black man appeared, calling himself prince and lord, telling him (Samuel) he must worship and believe him which Samuel had agreed to do. Samuel further stated that this "black man" had promised him he should never want for anything but had not delivered on his promise even though he had signed the man's book.[21]

Samuel Wardwell still had more to say. He implicated two other newly arrested suspects, Jane Lilly and Mary Taylor from his wife's birthplace of Reading, saying that they were of his company.[22] He also claimed to have begun afflicting four days previously (August 28) and that Martha Sprague was the first person he afflicted, accomplishing the task by pinching his own coat and buttons and by giving the devil a "commission" to afflict her. He also acknowledged being baptized in the Shawsheen River by the black man and renouncing his former baptism.[23]

Sarah Hooper Wardwell appeared before the magistrates the same day as her husband. The documents are separate, so it is not possible to know who underwent examination first. Sarah's confession mirrored that of her husband in important ways, in that she claimed that a man appeared to her requiring her to worship him and that he enticed her by offering things she wanted such as clothing. She also acknowledged signing a piece of paper by putting a black mark to it and undergoing baptism in the Shawsheen River. She differed from Samuel in that she spoke of attending a meeting in Salem Village where she had seen the long-imprisoned Ann Foster, the late Martha Carrier, and a certain "Goody Lawrence" (probably Mary Foster Lacey, whose husband's first name was Lawrence). She then emulated her husband again by confessing to afflicting Martha Sprague, but unlike Samuel, she offered a motive. She described Sprague as "a means of taking up her husband and because he was gone from home and she much vexed at it."[24] Sarah apparently suspected her husband of being infatuated with the youthful Martha Sprague and may also have suspected Sprague of encouraging the attraction. There is, of course, no direct evidence that anything inappropriate occurred between Samuel Wardwell and Martha Sprague. Nothing even hints at a flirtation between the two, mutual or otherwise. But for Sarah Wardwell to suspect such a thing would not be surprising. Her description of her method of hurting Sprague is profoundly disturbing. She stated that she "suddenly catched up her child in her arms and wished Sprague might be afflicted and little after said she squeezed the child with an intention that the persons should be afflicted."[25] In effect, Sarah Wardwell confessed that she used her own child as a weapon to harm Martha Sprague and some of the others, just as earlier confessors claimed to have used poppets. Such an act, if actually carried out, could not have failed to cause pain to the child.

Sarah Wardwell's youngest child at the time of this statement was her daughter Rebecca, who was born September 10, 1691, and was thus nine days away from her first birthday. Sarah had been permitted to take Rebecca to jail with her in order to keep nursing her. Since her second youngest was a five-year-old son named Eliakim, the child she referenced could only have been baby Rebecca. Why would Sarah admit to such a shocking action? At that point in the witch hunt, confessions were growing more and more elaborate on a daily basis, perhaps because each confessor hoped to prove his or her usefulness to the magistrates. But there is no reason that an admission of using one's own baby as an instrument of affliction would give that impression. Had the whole situation driven Sarah to the point of madness? That is certainly possible. The claim does point very strongly toward one conclusion—Sarah Wardwell bore an intense animosity toward Martha Sprague. The fact that Sprague had played a role in her arrest and that of her family members could, in and of itself, account for this. But one wonders—did she hate the teenager enough to experience a nightmare about using her own baby as an instrument of torture? If she suspected her husband of lusting after the girl, perhaps so—particularly if she thought the attraction was mutual.

After that particularly unnerving statement, Sarah's confession reverted to more typical admissions. She acknowledged that she knew her husband to be a witch but indicated that she had not known him to be one until she became one herself. She also said that she thought her daughters had been witches for no more than a month. Finally, she expressed regret at what she had done and promised to renounce the devil and serve God. No fewer than seven of the afflicted (including Sprague, of course, and confessors young Mary Lacey, Hannah Post, and Sarah Bridges) spoke against Sarah Wardwell and/or gave indications of being afflicted by her in the courtroom. If she did hate Martha Sprague, the feeling appears to have been shared.

The Wardwells' daughter, Mercy, examined on the same day, also confessed but her statement evokes more despair than anger. She acknowledged having been in the snare of the devil for a quarter of a year and said that he had come to her while she was discontented because she had been told by others that no young man would ever love her. Finally, as previously stated, Sarah Hawkes (Sarah Hooper Wardwell's daughter by her first marriage) was one of the suspects who admitted to making the afflicted dance at Moses Tyler's farm and to forcing Martha Sprague to sing.

Others in the extended Tyler family also claimed affliction. Hannah Post, Susannah Post, and Sarah Bridges all attempted, with varying degrees of success, to follow the path charted by the younger Mary Lacey in Andover and transform themselves into afflicted persons. Hannah Post, the only one of the group who was a Tyler by blood (the biological daughter of Mary Tyler Post Bridges), claimed bewitchment by no fewer than six other suspects, including one she named during her own examination—Martha (Toothaker) Emerson. A mere two days later, she stood alongside some of the very people who had accused her and claimed she was attacked by John Jackson, Sr., of Rowley, one of the suspects complained of by Joseph Tyler and

Ephraim Foster. She later complained of spectral attack at four other examinations—Sarah (Hooper) Wardwell (September 2), Mary Taylor of Reading (September 5), Henry Salter (September 8), and Mary (Clement) Osgood (September 8). Among those accused of witchcraft in the Andover phase of the witch hunt, only the aforementioned Mary Lacey exceeded Hannah Post in her efforts to change from a suspect into an accuser. Sarah Bridges and Susannah Post both complained of affliction by John Jackson, Jr., when he was examined on August 27, and Susannah claimed victimization by one other suspect—Mary Taylor. Another person who was a Tyler by marriage joined the chorus, however briefly. John Bridges, the husband of the accused Mary Tyler (Post) Bridges, deposed against Samuel Wardwell on September 14. His testimony was brief and he did not speak of enduring an attack on himself. He only mentioned that Wardwell had correctly told the fortune of Bridges's son James by revealing the young man's love for a fourteen-year-old girl. Nonetheless, the fact that the elder Bridges testified against anyone comes as something of a surprise, considering the fact that his wife, daughters, and step-daughters had all been accused.

In the final analysis, no family became more thoroughly involved on both sides of the witchcraft persecution of 1692 than the extended Tyler clan—in Salem, Andover, or anywhere else. Altogether fourteen descendants, step-descendants, and in-laws of Job and Mary Tyler were caught up in the collective disaster that engulfed Essex County that year. Job and Mary themselves had moved a safe distance away from the community that they and their children had so often quarreled with three decades earlier. Their children who remained probably regretted that choice many times during and after the witch hunt.

A monument to Job Tyler still stands in the community's oldest cemetery, now within the limits of North Andover.

IN MEMORIAM
JOB TYLER IMMIGRANT
FIRST ANDOVER SETTLER
ABOUT MDCXL
BORN MDCXIX DIED ABOUT MDCC
DEDICATED BY HIS WHOLE CLAN
SEPTEMBER 4, 1901[26]

The actual grave of his much-maligned son Moses lies alongside it. Nothing on either marker reveals the family's tumultuous history in the town of Andover in the seventeenth century.

CHAPTER TEN

The
Resistance Grows

O N OCTOBER 8, 1692, Thomas Brattle (a Harvard graduate and Boston-based mathematician and astronomer) penned a lengthy letter to an unidentified clergyman that sharply criticized the conduct of the Court of Oyer and Terminer—particularly regarding the acceptance of spectral evidence. Brattle, who may have been a classmate of the young minister Thomas Barnard (they were the same age) was well aware of events in Andover, noting the fact that Joseph Ballard had summoned some of the afflicted girls of Salem Village to determine whether or not witchcraft was responsible for the sickness of his wife that summer. Brattle also referenced the fact that Dudley Bradstreet had recently fled the town. In referencing the court's proceedings, Brattle specifically stated "Excepting Mr. Hale, Mr. Noyes, and Mr. Parris, the Rev'd Elders [the region's ministers], almost throughout the whole country, are very much dissatisfied."[1] Notably, Brattle does not name Thomas Barnard here as one who agreed with the use of spectral evidence.[2] Brattle was unquestionably well-acquainted with events in Andover and had Barnard been the dedicated witch hunter he is sometimes stereotyped as having been, his fellow Harvard graduate certainly would have taken him to task for it. As it was, Brattle did not mention Barnard or Francis Dane by name—indicating that he did not regard either of them as among the villains in the drama he criticized.

The first direct indication of any stance Barnard took came on October 18, when he (and Dane) signed a petition defending some of the town's accused. This in and of itself belies any effort to pigeonhole Barnard as having played the same role in leading the charge against suspects as his counterpart (Samuel Parris) did in Salem Village. Another noteworthy omission of Barnard and Dane can be found when reading the detailed confession of William Barker, Sr., recorded on August 29. Barker, like so many others, described attending a meeting of witches at Salem Village, specifically upon "a green peece of ground neare the minster's house" (obviously the home of Samuel Parris). Barker went on to say "they mett there to destroy that place by reason of the peoples being divided & theire differing with their minister."[3] Although Barker went on to describe how Satan's design was to "set up his own Worship, abolish all the churches in the land, to fall next upon Salem and soe goe through the country," he never mentioned any conflict over the two ministers in Andover. Once again, this omission speaks volumes. Considering the thoroughness of William Barker's admissions, it is hard to fathom that he would have neglected such a dispute had it been a significant factor by that time. There can be no doubt there were some hard feelings in Andover on the occasion of Barnard's hiring a decade earlier, but by 1692, the town's residents might have put most of that dispute behind them. Dane may have remained on the scene longer than Barnard had bargained for, but there is no credible evidence that the younger man seized on the witch trials as a chance to destroy his mentor's family.

In his letter, Brattle described Andover as "an object of great pity and commiseration." The witch hunt critic hit the mark with his comment. For the previous month, no town in the Massachusetts Bay colony had wrestled with more regret. Three residents had been hanged and three others lived under suspended sentences of death.

An additional thirty-nine languished in jail with those condemned—more than a quarter of the remaining suspects. Eighteen other accused witches from surrounding communities had ties to Andover, even if their own connection involved nothing more than having been accused by someone from the community. Altogether the cases of sixty people complained of during the two phases of the Andover witch hunt hung in abeyance. All of them—and their families—knew that a hangman's noose loomed as a legitimate threat. Brattle offered the opinion that some family members of the accused initially believed in the guilt of their loved ones. In particular, he cited Captain Osgood (John Osgood, husband of Mary Clements Osgood) and Deacon Frye (John Frye, Jr., husband of Eunice Potter Frye) as "having taken up that corrupt and highly pernicious opinion, that whoever were accused by the afflicted, were guilty, did break charity with their dear wives, upon their being accused, and urge them to confess their guilt; which so far prevailed with them as to make them say, they were afraid of their being in the snare of the Devill."[4] In this passage, Brattle stresses that these two Andover men (and others) thought their wives were guilty as charged and talked the accused women into believing it themselves. Brattle apparently visited some of the suspects in jail, and this may be what he was told in some cases. There probably is some truth in it—in such an environment, people can easily fall into a trap of thinking themselves culpable, however unwittingly.

For those on the outside, the risk of arrest had not passed. On October 3, Sarah Aslebee Cole of Lynn was arrested and examined. No one from Andover played a role in accusing her but she was a sister of Andover's own Rebecca Aslebee Johnson, jailed for nearly a month by that time. Some of those still free felt compelled to resist the madness that had ruled their community since mid-July, but they had to tread lightly. Spouses of those jailed had to take particular care, especially if they still had children at home. Throughout the trials, those married to people already under suspicion were among the most vulnerable to accusation themselves—and no one wanted to leave his or her children alone while joining a spouse in jail.

Such a fate was exactly what had befallen the household of Samuel and Sarah Hooper Wardwell. The jailing of the Wardwells and subsequent execution of Samuel had left four children, ranging in age from fifteen-year-old Samuel, Jr. to five-year-old Eliakim, uncared for (the infant Rebecca remained in jail with her mother). In late September, selectmen John Abbot, John Aslebee, and Samuel Frye received permission from the General Court in Ipswich to place the children. Ironically Samuel Wardwell, Jr. was placed in the home of his uncle and aunt, John and Rebecca (Hooper) Ballard. (John Ballard had probably been the one who had arrested Samuel's parents and sisters a month earlier.) Frye (along with his wife Mary, another Aslebee sister) took twelve-year-old William Wardwell into his home and committed to teaching the boy the trade of weaver. The selectmen placed Elizabeth Wardwell (age uncertain) in the home of young John Stevens and his wife Ruth Poor Stevens, and the five-year-old Eliakim was assigned to the household of Ruth's brother Daniel Poor and his wife Mehitabel Osgood Poor (a daughter of the imprisoned Mary Clements Osgood).[5] This action by the selectmen did not hint at sympathy for arrested witchcraft suspects—it was simply a show of charity to the impoverished children of an executed felon.

But these children were not the only ones that certain citizens of Andover took action to assist. As noted previously, the Andover witch hunt distinguished itself from the earlier phase centered in Salem by the added tendency to accuse children. Several still suffered in the confines of Essex County jails, awaiting trial. On October 6, eight townsmen presented four separate recognizances to the court taking various accused minors into their custody with the promise of delivering them for trial upon being ordered to do so. John Osgood, Sr. and Nathaniel Dane, for example, posted a bond of five hundred pounds for the release of Dorothy Faulkner and young Abigail Faulkner, whose mother awaited execution upon the birth of her unborn child.[6] Both of these men were the husbands of accused witches who remained in jail, and Dane was the girls' uncle. John Osgood's wife Mary was the suspect who had exonerated Francis Dane while confessing her own guilt, so interaction between the Osgood and Dane families continued. Another such action freed the younger Johnson children (Stephen and Abigail) and Sarah Carrier (the youngest of the executed Martha's children to have been arrested), who went into the care of the Johnsons' oldest brother, Francis, and Sarah's father, Thomas Carrier, respectively. Walter Wright, who had preceded John Ballard as the South End's constable the previous year, joined this effort—perhaps his financial status was needed to guarantee the bond, as neither Carrier nor Francis Johnson was in the best of economic circumstances. Wright also bailed out his own thirteen-year-old stepson, John Sadie, who was probably among those arrested on the day of the touch test. Francis Faulkner, the husband of the condemned Abigail, supported Wright in this latter action. Finally, in a surprisingly magnanimous move, Faulkner joined John Barker in posting bond for young Mary Lacey, whose loose tongue during her own examination had contributed so much to fanning the flames of the witch hunt in Andover. This recognizance document, like the others, included a promise to keep the suspect "secure."[7] Perhaps one of these men (most likely Barker, who was a militia lieutenant) actually did keep Lacey under guard until she came to trial before the newly constituted court three months later.

Nothing in any of these bond postings suggests an effort to free the suspects from eventually facing their day in court. The actions these men took had no design other than to free juvenile suspects from the conditions in jail. John Bridges, joined by John Osgood, took a similar step on October 15 to free his twelve-year-old daughter Mary, one of the suspects from the extended Tyler clan. Others in the community may also have posted similar bonds to free youthful suspects—some of the documents may not survive. John Osgood, the most prominent resident of Andover after Dudley Bradstreet (who had fled to avoid arrest the previous month), was emerging as a leader in the growing effort to obtain the freedom of the town's accused. His name topped a petition submitted on October 12 by nine of the town's residents, all of whom had immediate family members in jail on suspicion of witchcraft. This petition marked the first recorded effort to secure the release of adult suspects, though it also included some more children. The petition specifically stated: "We do not petition to take them out of the hands of Justice but to Remain as prisoners under bond in their own familys where they may be more tenderly cared for: and may be redy to appear to Answer farther when the honored Court shall Call for them."[8] Joining John Osgood in this were John Frye (on behalf of his wife Eunice), John Marston (husband of Mary Osgood Marston), Christopher Osgood (father of Mary Osgood Marston), Joseph Wilson (husband of Sarah Lord Wilson, father of Sarah), John Bridges (husband of Mary Tyler Bridges and father or stepfather to four others), Hopestill Tyler (husband of Mary and father of three accused daughters), Ebenezer Barker (husband of Abigail Wheeler Barker), and Nathaniel Dane (husband of Deliverance). Several of these men were among the most prominent in Andover. Though none of them was yet disputing the charges of witchcraft (at least not publicly), their efforts to obtain the release of suspects on bond exceeded any resistance effort being attempted in any other affected town at that point—including Salem Village and the town of Salem, where no one had gone any further than creating petitions on behalf of certain individual accused witches. The Andover petition did not achieve the desired results, at least not immediately, as no adult suspects were released from jail that month. Other events at higher levels of the clergy and government of the colony would soon embolden the growing resistance movement in Andover to further action.

In early October 1692, Increase Mather made his recently completed work on the witchcraft trials available to numerous prominent ministers in the Massachusetts Bay colony as well as the justices on the Court of Oyer and Terminer. This work, titled *Cases of Conscience Concerning Evil Spirits Personating Men, Witchcrafts, infallible Proofs of Guilt in such as are accused with that Crime*, is widely considered (and deservedly so) the single most significant piece of writing that led to the eventual end of the witch hunt. Mather did not dispute the existence of witches in the book. He did, however, cast serious doubts on the validity of spectral evidence, contending that it was impossible to know that the Devil could not take the shape of an innocent person. In making this case, Mather refuted the testimony of confessors from Abigail Hobbs on April 19 (who said the Devil afflicted in her shape after she granted him permission to do so) to Mary Osgood on September 8. Osgood said she had tried to afflict in the shape of Francis Dane, but had been unable to do so because the Devil could not appear in the shape of an innocent person.

Mather did not denounce the actions of the Court of Oyer and Terminer, and he mentioned having attended the trial of George Burroughs, of whom he said: "Had I been one of his judges, I could not have acquitted him."[9] But most famously, Mather included the statement: "It were better that Ten Suspected Witches should escape, than that one Innocent Person should be Condemned."[10] The most immediate result of Mather's work was that Governor Phips, having returned from leading the fight against the Native Americans on the Maine frontier, suspended the actions of the court he had established in May. In a letter to the Privy Council in England, he stated that "on enquiry into the matter I found that the devil had tak(en) upon him the name and shape of severall persons who were doubtlesse innocent and {to} my certain knowledge of good reputation, for which cause I have now forbidden the Comitting of any more that shall be accused with(out) unavoydable necessity; and those that have b(ee)n Comitted I would shelter from any proceedings against them wherein there may be the least suspicion of any wrong to be done unto the innocent I would alsoe waite for any particular directions or Comands if their Majesties please to give mee any for the fuller ordering this perplexed affaire."[11]

This action by Phips, dated the same day as the aforementioned petition of nine Andover residents, at least temporarily reprieved those confessors who remained jailed under sentence of death—Abigail Hobbs, Dorcas Hoar, Ann Foster, the elder Mary Lacey, and Rebecca Eames. Until the governor suspended legal proceedings, these five convicted witches expected to be informed of their date with the executioner at any time. Their family members, whether in jail or out, also knew more time had been bought. But Phips had not pardoned them, nor had he taken any action to drop charges against any others who had not yet faced trial. He also did not rule out further arrests. Nonetheless, the governor's suspension of legal proceedings gave hope to those who wished to bring the process to a halt without any more executions or the jailing of any further suspects. Defending the accused remained a risky proposition, but a determined corps of residents of the beleaguered town of Andover took the fight to new levels.

On October 18, 1692, twenty-six Andover residents submitted a petition to the governor, the Council, and the colony representatives, challenging the validity of the charges against the accused inhabitants of Andover, a stance no other previous petition had put forward.[12] The first statement after the perfunctory introduction declared: "It is well known that many persons of this Town, have been accused of witchcraft, by some distempered persons in these parts, and upon complaint made have been apprehended and committed to prison."[13] This statement echoes Martha Carrier's declaration in her examination on May 31: "It is a shameful thing that you should mind these folks that are out of their wits."[14] The signers of the petition—Francis Dane's name appeared first followed immediately by that of Thomas Barnard—were taking a risk, as Martha Carrier had been dead for two months by that time, but perhaps they sensed safety in numbers and believed that the tide was turning. The petition did state that the signers did not wish to advocate for anyone "found guilty of so horrid a crime" and expressed their hope that the area be "purged from that great wickedness." They wished to speak on behalf of those falsely accused. The petition further stated: "We can truly give this Testimony of the most of them belonging to this Town, that have been accused, that they never gave the least occasion (as we hear of) to their neerest relations or most intimate acquaintances, to suspect them of witchcraft." The document described some of the suspects (not named) as members of the church in full communion and described them as "walking as becometh women professing godliness." While acknowledging that most of the suspects from Andover had confessed, they expressed the concern that the confessors had been frightened into belying themselves and also noted that some of them had subsequently denied the truth of their statements. The document also described the financial difficulties incurred by the families of the jailed suspects and expressed the concern that some would be impoverished as a result. The petitioners denounced the methods previously used for detecting guilt, declaring in another attack on the accusers: "We know not who can think himself safe, if the Accusations of children and others {who are} under a Diabolicall influence shall be received against persons of good fame."[15]

This second statement attacking the credibility of the afflicted reiterates another comment made by one already executed for witchcraft. Susanna Martin, by then dead three months, said of the accusers in her examination: "If they be dealing in the black art, you may know as well as I."[16] Again, these petitioners risked drawing suspicion on themselves. But their statement did not end there. They noted that in addition, "persons of good credit among ourselves, but some Honorable and worthy men of other places, do suffer in their names by the accusations of the afflicted people in this Town."[17] For the first time since the accusations began in Salem Village the previous winter, a significant group of citizens of one community devastated by the witch hunt had denounced the actions of the accusers within their own ranks. In Salem Village and other towns, many individuals had signed petitions on behalf of particular suspects. Those documents only vouched for the good character of people accused of witchcraft—they did not denounce the accusers. These Andover residents broke new ground.

The men who signed this petition knew the risk they were taking. Those who had loved ones awaiting trial probably did not give their own peril a second thought. Francis Dane's name appeared first on the document and the fact that eight members of his own family had been accused has been noted. His son Nathaniel Dane, whose wife Deliverance was among those under suspicion, also signed the petition, the fifth name on the list. Thomas Barnard, despite the fact that his own family had not suffered, penned his name immediately below that of the senior pastor.

John Osgood, the husband of the incarcerated Mary, signed the petition along with his sons Timothy and Samuel and his nephew Hooker Osgood. The afflicted in Andover had aimed too high by accusing Mary Osgood. The revelation that her confession would not necessarily save her life jolted her husband and others into action. These Osgoods, every bit as powerful in Andover as the Porter family was in Salem Village, took a much stronger public stand against the witchcraft accusations in their town than the Porters ever did in the home community. If John Osgood had encouraged Mary to acknowledge her culpability, his own guilt over that action would have given him added impetus to denounce the alleged victims of the witches, even at his own peril. These Osgoods, primarily associated with the North End (though Hooker had moved to the South End), were joined in signing the petition by their distant cousin, Christopher Osgood, who had risen to a leadership position in the South End and had also previously served as a selectman. As already noted, Christopher's daughter Mary Osgood Marston languished in jail on suspicion of witchcraft. Others with close family members in jail signed the petition but, as will be seen, some of the signers appear to have acted entirely because of personal convictions. Some of them (or their family members) had played a role in the accusations and may have regretted it by October. The most surprising signer was none other than Samuel Martin, who had filed at least two complaints and whose teenage daughter Abigail was among the afflicted. By affixing his signature to the petition, Samuel was denouncing his own daughter as "distempered."

The day after the Andover men signed this petition, Increase Mather reported a series of recantations by women from Andover who had previously confessed. Mather had visited the women in jail, most likely accompanied by Thomas Brattle. Not surprisingly, Mather quoted Mary Osgood first. The powerful minister would have been conscious of rank, and Osgood was the most prominent suspect from Andover in the jail at that time, if not the most influential of all of the prisoners. Mather gave her renunciation of her previous confession the most detailed attention of any. According to his account, she declared her statement of guilt to be "wholly false, and that she was brought to said confession by the violent urging and unreasonable pressings that were used toward her; she asserted that she never signed to the devil's book, was never baptized by the devill, never afflicted any of the accusers, or gave her consent for their being afflicted."[18] In her confession, Osgood had specified that she had been baptized by the devil about twelve years before. When asked why she had specified that time frame, she replied that she had been pressed to give a specific time, and twelve years had been as likely as any because that was when she had given birth to her last child, after which she had suffered from sickness and melancholy (probably what is known in the twenty-first century as postpartum depression). Mather or Brattle also asked her about her statement that the devil had appeared to her in the shape of a cat, and she responded that this was again something that occurred to her under pressure. She had seen a cat when walking out of her house recently and had not at the time "any whitt suspected the said cat to be the devil" but had named the first creature that occurred to her at the time.[19]

Mather wrote fewer details on the confessions of most of the other women. He did stress how Abigail Barker "bewailed and lamented her accusing of others, whom she never knew any evil by in her lifetime; and said that she was told by her examiners that she did know of their being witches and must confesse it."[20] She acknowledged that she had finally given in and was by then in "great horrour and anguish of soul." Mary Lovett Tyler noted that she "had no fears upon her" when first apprehended, but said that her brother Bridges (John Bridges, husband to Mary Tyler Post Bridges, who was a sister of this Mary's husband Hopestill Tyler) rode with her from Andover to Salem and kept telling her that she must be a witch because her touch had stopped the fits of the afflicted. Once in Salem, he had continued to press her along with the minister John Emerson, saying, "God would not suffer so many good men to be in errour about it and that she would be hang'd, if she did not confesse,"[21] This statement is further evidence of the idea that had taken root in Andover prior to the September trials that the lives of confessors would be spared. Tyler, like the others, suffered from the guilt of lying. The same sentiment was expressed by Eunice Frye, Deliverance Dane, Sarah Wilson, the elder Mary Bridges, and Mary Osgood Marston. All these women except Bridges and Marston (both jailed prior to the end of August) had probably been arrested at the time of the touch test. Not all their actual confessions survive, but this document proves that all of them had previously acknowledged their guilt. Sarah Churchill, Hannah Post, and Mary Post, mentioned briefly at the end, did not recant, and it appears that Mather and Brattle spoke only briefly to them. For those that did retract their confessions, having the sympathetic ear of men as prominent as Mather and Brattle may have emboldened them. They also knew that Governor Phips had suspended any further legal proceedings for the time being even though they remained incarcerated.

Perhaps encouraged by the actions of Andover residents, petitioners from other towns began to press for the release on bail of their own family members in jail, though no other surviving document so strongly condemned the afflicted. In other cases, prisoners took action on their own behalf. Ten suspects housed in the jail in Ipswich petitioned for release on bail in later October, citing the facts that winter loomed and they did not expect to be tried until the following spring. They expressed a willingness to answer the charges when the time came.[22] Among the petitioners were Mary Green and Hannah Bromage of Haverhill, both of whom had been accused of attacking Timothy Swan (among others, mainly Salem Village girls) during the first phase of the Andover witch hunt. Initially, the document must not have achieved the desired result because Green's husband, Peter Green, and James Sanders bailed her out on December 16. Others in this group might also have gained their freedom eventually—not all of the documents survive.

The denunciation of the afflicted by those who signed the petition of October 18 and the visit of Increase Mather gave renewed hope even to those who had been convicted and awaited execution. On December 3, a still-pregnant Abigail (Dane) Faulkner petitioned Governor Phips directly for a pardon. She stated that she had been "condemned to die having had no other Evidences against me but the Spectre Evidences and the Confessors which Confessors have lately since I was condemned owned to my selfe and others and doe still own that they wronged me and what they had sa(i)d against me was false." She declared herself "innocent and Ignorant of the crime of witchcraft which is layd to my charge" and noted that she knew that she would have already been executed if she had not been pregnant. Faulkner also described the sufferings of her family, noting that her husband Francis was suffering a relapse of the fits he had endured five years earlier, fits that "did very much impaire his memory and understanding, but with the blessing of the Lord upon my Endeavours did recover of them againe, but now through greife and Sorrow they are returned to him again as bad as Ever they were:"[23] She went on to express her concern that she would die in jail and her six children would also die for lack of care. She obviously did not think her husband could handle the situation at their home because of his mental state. Phips did not grant the requested pardon despite his own skepticism of spectral evidence. The danger to those convicted but not yet executed had by no means passed. The other suspects still had every reason to expect to face trial eventually.

Faulkner had not confessed to the crime of witchcraft, although she had admitted to some lesser actions that might have been interpreted by some as sorcery. Another convicted witch, Rebecca (Blake) Eames of neighboring Boxford, had admitted guilt and was among those confessors sentenced to death on September 17, a fact that had jolted other confessors into the understanding that they were not safe. Eames petitioned Phips for a pardon on December 5, making one of the same claims that Faulkner advanced (the unreliability of spectral evidence). Eames also described her confession as

> altogether false and untrue I being hurried out of my Senses by the A{ff}licted persons Abigail Hobbs and Mary Lacye who both of them cryed out against me charging me with witchcraft the space of four days mocking of me and spitting in my face saying they knew me to be an old witch and IF I would not confess it I should very Spe{e}dily be hanged for there was some such as myself gone before and it would not be long before I should follow them which did so amaze and affright me that I knew not what I said or did which was the occasion with my owne wicked heart of my saying what I did say.[24]

Eames went on to say that when Increase Mather and Thomas Brattle came to the jail, Hobbs and Lacey (presumably the younger Mary Lacey, a much more active accuser than her mother) disowned their accusations against her, calling them "the Devil's delusions."[25] Unlike Faulkner, Eames did not cite her family circumstances as a reason for asking for a pardon. She simply maintained her innocence, denying that she deserved to die (at least not by the hands of man) for witchcraft or any other sin. Eames, of course, knew that she faced possible execution at any time the governor might decide to permit legal action to resume. Faulkner knew she still had time (until her child was born) regardless of what happened.

Aside from the fact that Faulkner did not confess and Eames did, the two women differed in other significant ways. Faulkner lived in Andover, Eames in Boxford. Faulkner, as already noted, was from the extended Ingalls clan, which owned the dubious distinction of having seen seventeen members accused of witchcraft—the largest number of any family group in 1692. Eames's only near relative to face accusation was her son Daniel, who was accused before she was. Eames did have the odd circumstance of a close connection to several of the accusers. Her daughter Hannah Eames Foster and her granddaughter Rose Foster were among the afflicted, Rose being second only to Martha Sprague among Andover's "victims" in the number of suspects she complained of. Hannah's husband Ephraim, the North End's constable, filed complaints, arrested suspects, and testified against Samuel Wardwell. Furthermore, Rebecca's late sister Prudence had been the first wife of Moses Tyler, making Joseph Tyler the accused witch's nephew. Rebecca must have become acquainted with Martha Sprague, who had joined Moses Tyler's household the year before. In terms of their involvements with the witchcraft persecution, the family situations of Abigail Faulkner and Rebecca Eames could not have been more different. Faulkner's near relatives were among the leaders of the growing resistance. None of Eames's family stepped up in that effort according to surviving documents. Regardless of their sharply contrasting circumstances though, both of these women faced the possibility of execution and were making concentrated efforts to save themselves, with or without assistance from their families.

No assistance came for the frail and aged Ann Foster. Like the two petitioners, this woman had heard the sentence of death pronounced against her three months earlier. In the end, no rope was needed. On December 3, the bereaved widow breathed her last in the squalid conditions of Salem's jail. Given Foster's general physical condition and emotional turmoil, it is surprising that she survived nearly five months in those crowded cells. Having lost one daughter to an act of violence three years earlier, she had long known that she faced a real possibility of seeing another daughter hang alongside her. For all practical purposes, this elderly woman, who had told tales of 305 witches to horrorstruck examiners the previous summer, may have willed her own death. Whether intentional or not, she had resisted the hangman the only way she knew. Her younger son Abraham found himself forced to pay two pounds and ten shillings to recover her body for burial. Despite his efforts, her resting place is unknown. If her grave is in the town's oldest cemetery in modern-day North Andover, it is unmarked. Having died a convicted felon, though, she was probably not granted the dignity of burial in sacred ground. Far more likely is the possibility that her bones lie somewhere on property the family owned in 1692. For those not yet tried, with the cold of winter rapidly approaching, the prospect of dying like Ann Foster had appeared a more immediate threat than death on the gallows. Family members in Andover and other towns knew that as well as anyone.

With that consideration in mind, eight of the nine men who had petitioned the General Court for the release on bail of their wives and daughters on October 12 sent a similar document on December 6, this time to Governor Phips and the council then sitting in Boston. Some of the younger suspects had been freed on bail after the first petition, but the adult females all remained incarcerated. The previous petition had only asked for their release. This one went beyond that, asking for the opportunity to prove that the prisoners were innocent of the charges against them. This document included all of the women who had recanted on October 19, a week after the submission of the first petition this group of men filed. Each of those women was the wife or daughter of one of the signers. For unknown reasons, John Marston (the husband of Mary Osgood Marston) did not sign this second document. Perhaps the group decided that only one family member of each suspect should sign, and Mary's father, Christopher Osgood, did so for her. The document addresses accused neighbors as well, though it does not mention the names of any suspects in the text.[26] This petition did not move the governor and council to immediate action, although they may have set an amount for bail of each of the suspects concerned. On December 20, John Osgood and John

Frye joined forces and bonded themselves in the sum of four hundred pounds (two hundred for each of their wives) and secured the release of both women on the condition that they return for trial when summoned. There is no similar documentation regarding other adult suspects from Andover—Osgood and Frye may have been the only petitioners who could afford the bond—but some of the suspects from the surrounding towns who were accused during the Andover witch hunt left jail under similar circumstances. Peter Green and James Sanders of Haverhill posted bond for Mary Green, Peter's wife. Frances Hutchins, also of Haverhill, went free after her son Samuel and neighbor Joseph Kingsbury bailed her out. Other suspects from different communities tasted freedom for the first time in many months that December. One of the suspects bailed out was William Hobbs of Topsfield, the father of the confessor Abigail Hobbs, who now lived under a sentence of death. Ironically, one of the men who posted recognizance for him was John Nichols, the father of the two Nichols girls who had deposed against Abigail. Another, Joseph Towne, was the youngest brother of the already executed suspects Rebecca Nurse and Mary Esty.

This release of prisoners on bond did not, however, mean that any of them or the ones remaining in jail were safe. No one could have known at that time that no more were to be executed. On December 14, the legislature passed a new law that it termed "A Bill against Conjuration, Witchcraft, and dealing with evil and wicked Spirits." The stated purpose of the law was "for more particular direction in the Execution of the Law against Witchcraft." The first paragraph contained this provision:

> That if any person or persons shall use, practice, or Exercise any Invocation or Conjuration of any evil and wicked Spirit, Or shall consult, covenant with Entertain, Employ, ffeed, or reward any evil and wicked Spirit to or for any intent or purpose; Or take up any dead man woman or Child, out of his, her, or their grave or any other place where the dead body resteth, or the Skin, bone, or any other part of any dead person to be Employed or used in any matter of Witchcraft, Sorcery, Charm {or} Inchantment, Or shall use, practice or Exercise any Witchcraft, Inchantment charm or

Sorcery, whereby any person shall be killed, destroyed, wasted, consumed, pined, or lamed in his or her body or any part thereof, That then every such Offender or Offenders, their Aiders, Abetters, and Counsellors being of any of the Said Offences duly and lawfully convicted and attainted, shall suffer pains of death as a Felon or Felons.[27]

The law also mandated milder punishments of a year's imprisonment, time in the stocks, and wearing a sign around one's neck confessing the sin for less egregious acts performed by witchcraft such as destroying cattle and goods, locating stolen items, or inciting people into what was termed "unlawful love." This punishment was to suffice for a first offense, bur a second conviction commanded a death sentence. The council approved the law and Governor Phips signed it.

The passage of this law removed all doubt that at the very least, the colony authorities intended to prosecute those already charged with witchcraft—not that there had ever been reason to believe otherwise. Two days later, another legislative action permitted the Superior Court to hold what was termed a Court of Assize and General Goale Delivery beginning on January 3, 1693, because so many persons accused of capital offenses were in custody in Essex County. Resumption of the trials loomed in less than three weeks. Those already convicted faced the possibility of their sentences being carried out soon after the beginning of the new year. Governor Phips's next action sent a clear message that the future trials, while not allowing spectral evidence, were likely to be conducted as harshly as the previous ones. He appointed William Stoughton, who had so ruthlessly presided over the Court of Oyer and Terminer, to serve once again as chief justice. The other three justices appointed that day were Samuel Sewall, Waitstill Winthrop, and John Richards, all of whom had served on the previous court. Sometime before the actual resumption of the trials, Phips added Thomas Danforth, the only judge of the new court not to have participated in the earlier trials.

Jonathan Elatson, who had performed clerical duties in the earlier examinations and trials, took on the role of clerk of the new court. He promptly sent orders to the constables of the various towns to assemble town meetings to select jurors for the grand jury and the trial juries. Ephraim Foster complied for Andover and the town selected Joseph Marble and Henry Holt for the grand jury and Christopher Osgood and Samuel Frye as trial jurors. The choice of Osgood would be unthinkable in modern-day America because his daughter was among those accused. But every town in Essex County named men to serve in this capacity—it was, in effect, a jury pool, not a group that was to serve in its entirety for the duration of the remaining trials.

The pieces were all in place by the beginning of the year, and no town had more reason to dread the resumption of the trials than Andover. Four of its residents had already died. Two others had been sentenced to death. Thirty-nine others still faced this possibility. Knowing this, even more residents of Andover joined the resistance on behalf of their jailed friends and neighbors.

On or around January 2, 1693, with the trials about to resume, Andover's aged senior minister penned his statement defending those from his congregation who had been accused. This statement is worth quoting in its entirety.

> Wheras there have been divers reports raysed, how, and, by what hands I know not, of the Towne of Andover and the Inhabitants, I thought it my bounden duty to give an account to others, so farr as I had the understanding of anything amongst us. Therfore doe declare that I beleeve the reports have been Scandalous, and unjust, neither will bear. the light, As for that, of the Sive, and Cisers I never heard of it, thill this past Summer, and the Sabboth after I spake publiqly concerning it Since which I beleeve it hath not been tryed. As for such things of Charmes, and way's to find their cattle, I never heard, nor doe I know any Neighbour that ever did So, neither have I any grounds to beleeve it. I have lived above Fortie fower years in the Towne and have been frequent among the Inhabitants, and in my healthfull years oft at their habitations, and Should certainly heard if so it had been. That there was a Suspicion of Goodwife Carrier among Some of us before she was apprehended I know. As for any other persons, I had no suspicion of them, and had Charity been put on, the Divel would not have had Such an advantage against us, and I beleeve many innocent persons have been accused, & imprisoned, the Conceit of Spectre Evidence

as an infallible mark did too far prevaile with us Hence we So easily parted with our neighbours, of honest, & good report, & members in full Comunion, hence we So easily parted with our Children, when we knew nothing in their lives, nor {any of} our neighbours {to Suspect them} and thus things were hurried on; hence Such strange breaches in families, Severall that came before me, that Spake with much Sobrietie, professing their innocency, though through the Devil's Subtlity they were too much urged to Confesse, and we thought we did doe well in so doeing, yet they stood their ground professing they knew nothing, never Saw the devil, never made a covenant with him, & the like; & Some Children, that we have cause to feare that dread has overcome them to accuse themselves in that they knew not. Stephen Johnson Mary Barker the daughter of Lieftenant Barker, and some others by what we had heard from them, with Suitable affections we have cause to beleeve they were in the truth, and {So} held to it, if after many indeavors they had not been overcome to Say what they never knew.

This hath been a trouble to me, considering how oft it hath been Sayd, you are a witch, you are guilty, & who afflicts this maid or the like, & more than this hath been Said, charging persons with witchcraft, and what flatteries have passed from; & threats and telling them they must goe to prison, et. this I feare have caused many to fall. our Sinne of Ignorance wherin we thought we did well, will not excuse us when we know we did amisse but whatever might be a Stambling block to others must be removed, else we shall procure divine displeasure, & Evills will unavoidably breake in upon us.

Andover Jan 2, 92²⁸ Yours Sir who am {though unworthie} a friend to them that are friends to Sion

Francis Dane, Senior

* * *

Concerning my Daughter Elizabeth Johnson, I never had ground to suspect her, neither have I heard any other to accuse her, till by Spectre evidence she was brought forth, but this I must say, She was weake, and incapacious, fearfull, and in that respect I feare she hath falsely accused herself {& others}. Not long before {that} she was sent for {she} Spake as to her own particular, that she was sure she was no witch, and for her Daughter Elizabeth, she is but Simplish at the best, and I feare the comon speech that was frequently spread among us, of their liberty, if they would confesse, and the like expression, used by some, have brought many into a snare, the Lord direct & guide those that are in place, and give us all Submissive wills, & let the Lord doe with me, & mine, what Seems good in his owne eys.

Francis Dane[29]

One of Francis Dane's daughters had already been condemned to death and another faced trial. A daughter-in-law and five grandchildren were among the accused. All of them except the already convicted daughter had confessed to the crime of witchcraft, and he feared that the confessions would serve as the best evidence against them. Dane would have known that prior to 1692, every person who had confessed to witchcraft in New England had ultimately been hanged for the crime. On January 3, 1693, fifty-five inhabitants of the town submitted a petition to the newly seated court in Salem on behalf of their fellow residents. The petition specifically named five suspects, but included a defense of the others in the town who had been accused without naming them. The names mentioned must have been very carefully chosen to show that accusations had been leveled against people considered to be of the highest quality. To that end, the names of four of the signers of the aforementioned declaration that described the touch test appear on the petition—Mary Osgood, Deliverance Dane, the elder Sarah Wilson, and Abigail Barker. The fact that Mary Tyler and her daughter Hannah were not included probably reflects the Tylers' dubious reputation in Andover. The fifth suspect named on the petition was none other than Eunice Frye. Whoever chose the names to list (possibly Dudley Bradstreet, who had returned from hiding, or perhaps one or both ministers) probably did so with the intent of maximizing the number of residents who would be willing to sign on their behalf. The Osgood, Frye, and

Barker families had been prominent in the town since its founding. Deliverance Dane's status as a daughter-in-law of Francis Dane made the case for her. Sarah Wilson's husband Joseph was not affluent, but there was no known taint on the family's reputation.

The petition began by briefly mentioning how the five suspects had suffered while in jail, but then went on to describe their character, focusing on how highly regarded all of them were in the community and in the town's church. The author (or authors) then noted how shocked the signers were to learn that these women were accused of the crime of witchcraft, not realizing at the time "that the most innocent were liable to be so misrepresented and abused." The women, according to the document, continued to deny guilt for a time despite being so strongly urged to confess. Finally, they gave in and admitted to the charges against them but despite that, the petitioners still thought them innocent. This statement is quite telling: "And, it is probable, the fear of what the event might be, and the encouragement that it is said was suggested to them, that confessing was really the only way to obtain favour, might be too powerful a temptation for timorous women to withstand, in the hurry and distraction that we have heard that they were then in."[30]

This statement serves as another indication that the residents of Andover had come to believe that there was never any intention of executing those who confessed. Unlike the petition of October 18, this one did not impugn the character of the afflicted accusers. Instead, it focused entirely on the perceived integrity of the suspects, stressing that the signers would not have defended them if they believed the confessions of witchcraft. They did acknowledge that false confessions were sinful, but they also stressed that since admitting their guilt, the suspects had retracted their statements while in a calmer mood, away from the pressure they had previously been under. The suspects were also enduring intense guilt for having belied themselves. Finally, after defending only the five named suspects throughout the document, the petitioners concluded with this statement: "As for the rest of our neighbours, who are under the like circumstances with those who have been named, we can truly say of them that while they lived among us, we have had no cause to judge them such persons as, of late, they have been represented and reported to be, nor do we know that any of their neighbours had any just grounds to suspect them of the evil that they are now charged with."[31]

This last statement in the petition makes it clear that the author(s) intended for it to serve as a defense of all of the town's suspects—not just the five named. In that regard, this newest overture repeated the motive for the petition of October 18. As previously noted, though, this document said nothing about the virtue (or lack thereof) of the accusers, while the earlier appeal had described them as "distempered." This document differed from the previous one in other noteworthy ways. One obvious distinction is that not all of the signers of the new petition were men—women also signed it. Another noticeable difference was that immediate family members of the accused specifically named in the petition did not sign. Perhaps that was because they had signed earlier petitions and that the leaders of the resistance felt, by that point, that attestations by others would be more effective. Even without immediate family members, fifty-five townspeople signed the document—the largest number to affirm any statement defending the Andover suspects. Those signers included twelve of the twenty-six who had given their support to the petition of October 18. The remaining forty-three had not previously affixed their signatures to any petitions, although a few had posted recognizances for the release of certain suspects. Dudley Bradstreet, the town's justice of the peace, who had previously signed numerous arrest warrants, was the first to inscribe his name to the new petition. The experience of seeing some of the town's leading residents arrested and falling under suspicion himself had changed his attitude about the trials, and he and his wife Ann both signed the petition defending their neighbors. Not surprisingly, the second and third signatures on this petition were those of the ministers, Francis Dane and Thomas Barnard. Dane, having seen so many of his family jailed on suspicion, had now reasserted himself as Andover's father figure, and his protégé gave the venerable old parson his unqualified support.

With witchcraft trials on the verge of resumption, it would be a mistake to say that everyone in Andover now opposed the process. No other community affected by the trials, however, had seen such strong public opposition to the proceedings. That is not surprising considering the large number of suspects from the town who awaited trial. The pattern of extensive family connections, far stronger among the accused in Andover than in Salem Village or any other community ensnared in the tragedy of 1692, manifested itself just as clearly among those who rose to the defense of the suspects. (See Appendices for detailed discussion of families of resisters, supporters, and bystanders in the proceedings.)

With the trials for witchcraft about to resume, seventy-two residents of Andover had, in one fashion or another, taken a stand on behalf of their accused neighbors. As the newly constituted court convened for the first time in January 1693, none of these defenders knew if their signatures carried enough weight to prevent the conviction of the suspects—or if they had placed their own lives in jeopardy.

CHAPTER ELEVEN

The
Trials Resume

T RIALS OF WITCHCRAFT SUSPECTS resumed under the newly constituted court on January 4, 1693. The stern face of William
Stoughton once again greeted the accused as they were marched into
the Salem courtroom to face their accusers. Spectral evidence was no
longer admitted into the record. Nonetheless, this court did not act
just as a formality to clear the docket. The possibility of conviction
and hanging remained very real as far as the suspects and their families
knew. For those who had confessed, their confessions were to be admitted as evidence against them. With the claims of spectral attacks
by the shapes of suspects having been disallowed, those confessions
could serve as the strongest indications of guilt available, as in earlier
New England witchcraft prosecutions.

The surviving records of the grand jury appearances and trials before this newly constituted court are sparse. They generally include
only indictments against the alleged witches, the names of supposed
victims (usually only one per case), whether or not indictments were

returned ignoramus (meaning there was not sufficient evidence to warrant a trial), and the verdicts when trials did occur. Four trials and two grand jury appearances were noted the first day. The only one involving an Andover resident was the grand jury appearance of the teenage Sarah Bridges, but no further action was taken against her for a week. The next day, two more Andover residents faced indictment. One of those was Henry Salter, the only remaining Andover suspect known not to have confessed who had not yet been convicted.[1] The other suspect from Andover indicted that day was Hannah Tyler, one of the imprisoned daughters of blacksmith Hopestill Tyler. The specific victim named for both of them was Rose Foster, the daughter of the still-resolute accuser Ephraim Foster. The initial actions in both cases offered a hint of how things had changed.

The case of Henry Salter, who had not confessed, was returned ignoramus, meaning the charges against him were dropped. Hannah Tyler, however, was ordered to face trial later that same day. The apparent difference in the treatment of confessors and nonconfessors by this new court struck a new fear in the hearts of those who had admitted guilt. Most of them had undoubtedly done so in the expectation of mercy. Now they had reason to believe that they might have sealed their doom. Increase Mather had, after all, written "that a free and voluntary confession of the crime made by the Person Suspected and accused after Examination, is a sufficient ground of Conviction."[2]

Some of that newly established concern may have been mitigated by the immediate trial and acquittal of Hannah Tyler. In her case, her confession did not serve as evidence strong enough to convict her. Over the next two days the court continued trying suspects, including four from Andover—Mary Osgood Marston, Abigail Wheeler Barker, Elizabeth Dane Johnson, and Mary Lovett Tyler (the mother of Hannah). All were acquitted. The court also dismissed an indictment against Rebecca Aslebee Johnson for lack of sufficient evidence. This dismissal was significant because Johnson had acknowledged guilt—although her confession was one of the least convincing. She had only admitting to turning the sieve and scissors to determine whether her brother-in-law, Moses Haggett, was alive or dead (he apparently had been missing for some time).[3] Nonetheless, the dismissal of the charges against Rebecca Johnson without bringing her to trial gave further hope that the confessions of the previous year might not be taken too seriously by the court. John Jackson, Sr. and John Jackson, Jr. of Rowley—both accused by people from Andover in the second phase of the witch hunt there—also saw charges against them dismissed. The elder Jackson had never admitted guilt so in his case, like that of Henry Salter, no confession existed to serve as evidence against him. The son did confess, but despite that, he never faced trial either, another beacon of hope for those who acknowledged the validity of charges against them.

That all changed three days later. January 10 saw the dismissal of charges against Martha Toothaker Emerson, another confessor whose admissions could be described as lukewarm at best. But that date also saw the trials of Sarah Hooper Wardwell and her daughters, Sarah Hawkes and Mercy Wardwell. The court acquitted both daughters, but the jury brought in a guilty verdict against their mother—the first conviction since the new court convened. The next two days brought two more convictions—young Elizabeth Johnson on the eleventh and Mary Post on the twelfth. Post, still single at the age of twenty-eight, lived in Rowley, but she was a daughter of Mary Tyler (Post) Bridges of Andover and had first appeared in court on August 2—the second member of the extended Tyler clan to fall under suspicion. Several acquittals also occurred on the twelfth—including those of Mary Post's mother and three other Andover residents (Post's sister Hannah, her stepsister Sarah Bridges, and the prominent Mary Clements Osgood).

Acquittal could no longer be taken for granted, though. January 13 was a busy day for indictments and not surprisingly, Andover suspects were most heavily represented. Children appeared at the forefront. The court indicted Mary Barker, William Barker, Jr., Richard Carrier, and Stephen Johnson that day—all minors. Indictments also came down against William Barker, Sr. and Edward Farrington—both of whom had fled, apparently after having escaped from jail or being bailed out. A long-awaited trial also took place on January 13, that of suspect-turned-accuser young Mary Lacey. The indictment against the teenage Stephen Johnson even listed Lacey among his victims that day. During the first phase of the Andover accusations, no afflicted person from the town played a more prominent role in terms of actual appearances in court (Timothy Swan, the most frequently cited victim by confessors, never testified). Young Mary Lacey, despite being a suspect, led the way in the courtroom in late July and early August. It was she who first called Martha Allen Carrier the future "Queen in Hell." But if her efforts at transforming herself into a victim of the witches were designed to protect herself, she only partially succeeded. The still gravely ill Timothy Swan was named as her victim in her trial record. Yet the jurors did bring in a "not guilty" verdict in her case. Her fate was happier than that of her mother, Mary Foster Lacey (who still awaited execution) and her grandmother, Ann Foster, who had died in captivity the previous month. Having been acquitted, she was free to walk away once her expenses were paid. Others indicted that day, but not yet tried, still awaited their ultimate fates.

Aside from the Andover residents, Hannah Bromage of Haverhill (accused in the first Andover phase of attacking Timothy Swan and some of the Salem Village girls) also faced indictment on January 13. The court dropped the charges against her. More famously (though probably not more noteworthy in the larger scheme of things), the court declined to indict Sarah Towne Cloyce on January 13. Cloyce was a sister of Rebecca Towne Nurse, included among the group of five hanged in July, and Mary Towne Esty, hanged along with seven others on September 22.

Several recognizances for accused children also occurred on January 13. John Barker posted bond for his daughter Mary and his nephew, William Barker, Jr., both under indictment. John Osgood, Sr., who could now rest easily after the acquittal of his wife, joined Barker in this action. Francis Faulkner took a similar action to free his daughters Dorothy and Abigail. Joseph Marble, the husband of Faulkner's sister Mary, joined him in this. Hopestill Tyler acted to free his daughters Martha and Joanna, with help from his brother-in-law, John Bridges. Joseph Wilson posted bond for his wife and daughter (both named Sarah), also with the assistance of John Osgood, Sr. Osgood, who had played a leading role in the Andover resistance from its very beginning, was continuing his work on behalf of his accused neighbors even though the danger to his own wife had passed. He had similarly aided John Frye, Jr. a day earlier on behalf of Frye's wife, Eunice Potter Frye.

The two-week period after January 13 saw a break in court actions. Dozens of suspects still filled the jails awaiting trial. The surviving records do not note when it occurred, but the newly convicted suspects would have been sentenced to death by that time. The countdown to their executions, along with those of the confessors sentenced in September, had begun. Again, no record of a date set for the next hangings is known to exist, but circumstantial evidence strongly suggests February 1.

The convictions of Johnson and Post can probably be explained by their mental impairments. The guilty verdict in the case of Sarah Hooper Wardwell requires another explanation. Robert Calef offered the supposition that she may not have denied her previous confession so stringently as the others because of the fact that her husband had gone to the gallows after retracting his.[4] Calef gave no indication that he witnessed her trial though and his interpretation is clearly speculative. As was the case with young Elizabeth Johnson, Sarah's confession contained an element not found in any other admission of guilt. Instead of admitting to afflicting her supposed victims by squeezing cloth or her own hands, she claimed to have hurt Martha Sprague by squeezing her own infant daughter and imagining the baby as Sprague. It is hard to fathom today that Sarah actually did this, but anyone who heard the account in the courtroom in early September must have believed there was some truth in it. The jurors for her trial of January 10 must have heard it or read it as well, and it would have repulsed them just as strongly. No other suspect admitted using her own child as a weapon of affliction. This admission seems the most likely reason for her conviction. By the end of January, her execution seemed imminent. She and her deceased husband Samuel seemed on the verge of joining Giles and Martha Corey, the only husband-and-wife tandem executed prior to that time. Only Elizabeth Bassett Proctor's pregnancy had spared her and her husband John that fate.

Contradictions exist in contemporary accounts about the number of suspects slated for execution at the end of January. Calef wrote that seven were reprieved by Governor Phips on January 31.[5] Cotton

Mather wrote that graves were dug for the three newly convicted witches and about five others who had previously been convicted at Salem (for a total of eight).[6] Obviously, the three convicted in January were among those about to be hanged. The others almost certainly included Mary Foster Lacey of Andover, Rebecca Blake Eames of Boxford, Dorcas Hoar of Beverly, and Abigail Hobbs of Topsfield. Abigail Dane Faulkner had still not given birth. Elizabeth Bassett Proctor's situation at that time is not entirely clear, as no primary source gives the birthdate of her son (named John for his late father, even though he already had a much older half-brother named John). Some secondary sources date the birth of this baby as having occurred on January 27, 1693. If that date is correct, a grave may have been dug for Elizabeth as well—the most likely scenario.

Regardless of how many convicted witches were slated for immediate execution, Phips reprieved all eight on January 31. He explained his action in a letter to the Earl of Nottingham on February 21.[7] He noted that the King's Attorney General (Anthony Checkley) told him that the three newly convicted suspects were under the same circumstances as those who were cleared (whether by acquittal or having the charges dropped without trial). He had therefore reprieved the convicted suspects until their Majesties' (William and Mary) pleasure be known.[8] Phips also noted that Lieutenant Governor Stoughton had been so incensed by this reprieve that he had refused to involve himself with any further court actions. Phips further castigated Stoughton for having rushed things while presiding over the previous court (the Court of Oyer and Terminer) as well as the new court and for having caused property of suspects to be seized illegally.[9]

Phips was obviously trying to cast himself in the best possible light and may have, to some degree, been using Stoughton as his scapegoat in this letter. But one cannot deny Stoughton's role as one of the leading perpetrators of the tragedy of 1692. Had the newly constituted court of 1693 been free to consider spectral evidence, there is a very good chance that far more trials (perhaps all) would have resulted in convictions. Without the intervention of Governor Phips, at least eight more suspects would have died at the end of a rope on February 1. Five trials occurred on that day (including that of Mary Allen

Toothaker, jailed since the previous May), all resulting in acquittal. Trials resumed in May 1693 (three months after Phips's reprieve), but no more suspects were convicted. The absence of Stoughton from the bench probably contributed to that outcome. Jurors in May acquitted Susannah Post, Eunice Potter Frye, young Mary Bridges, Mary Barker, and William Barker, Jr., all residents of Andover. Daniel Eames of Boxford, accused by residents of Andover, had the charges against him dropped. Though some suspects remained in custody because they did not have the funds to cover their legal expenses, the prosecutions of suspects had effectively ended.

In what was possibly just a coincidence, Andover's most prominent sorcery victim from the first phase of the town's witch hunt, Timothy Swan, died February 2, 1693. Though he was not quite thirty years old, his death would not have surprised anyone—he had been sick with some undisclosed illness at least since the middle of the previous July. One cannot help but wonder, though—was his death on that date entirely happenstance? Or did Phips's reprieve of some of those he considered his tormentors finish him off? For someone so extremely ill for such a long period, it may be possible that a fear of renewed attacks hastened him to his grave.

CHAPTER TWELVE

Aftermath

A T ANDOVER'S ANNUAL TOWN MEETING on March 6, 1693, Christopher Osgood served as moderator. The town elected him, John Osgood, Sr., Dudley Bradstreet, Andrew Peters, and John Chandler as selectmen. Peters, though hardly a young man at the age of about fifty-eight, took on this responsibility for the first time. Two new constables, Benjamin Stevens and William Abbot, were chosen for the North and South Ends, respectively. These men all had one thing in common—each of them had signed at least one of the petitions defending the witchcraft suspects. Even though the signers of those documents did not constitute a majority of the town's adult population, it is clear that by this time those opposing the trials held sway in Andover. Supporters of the accused also filled nearly all the other offices in Andover that year—Ephraim Stevens became clerk of the market, John Barker assumed the role of commissioner of the assessments, and George Abbot was designated sealer of leather. Some lesser officeholders were men who declined to take any public stand— Henry Holt was a surveyor for the South End and Nathan Stevens served as a tithing man. Samuel Martin, also named as tithing man, was the only known accuser to be named to office in 1693, and he

had shifted his position before the end of the episode. The only Andover officeholder in 1693 to have a tie to the accusations and who
did not later voice opposition to the proceedings was Samuel Phelps,
the father of afflicted Sarah Phelps and brother of the deceased Elizabeth Phelps Ballard. His position in 1693 was a "fence viewer,"
which did not equal selectman or constable in terms of responsibility.
There is no certainty that Phelps ever filed any complaints on his
daughter's behalf; in fact, the only strike against him evidenced by
any surviving documentation is his failure to join his Chandler in-
laws in signing petitions defending the suspects.

This pattern—naming men to office who defended the suspects
or opted not to take a stand—continued for the next several years,
particularly in regard to choosing the selectmen and constables. In
1694, the aging Samuel Blanchard secured a seat as a selectman for
the first time. A year earlier, he had signed the last of the petitions
from Andover that condemned the prosecutions, even though no one
in his family had been accused. John Osgood, Sr., who had risen to a
leadership role in the resistance after the confession of his wife Mary,
died August 21, 1693, but his son John succeeded him as a selectman
the next year. Andrew Peters served again, a role he was to fill frequently for the next decade, and he also assumed the responsibility
of town treasurer on an almost uninterrupted basis until his death in
1713. The other two selectmen named in 1694—John Abbot and
James Frye—also defended the suspected witches. With two exceptions (out of a total of thirty-four positions chosen) other offices went
to men who had joined the resistance or who, at the very least, played
no role in accusations. The two exceptions were Benjamin Abbot
(who accused Martha Carrier) and John Ballard, who had served as
the South End's constable during the terrible summer and fall of
1692. Both men served in the relatively minor capacity of "field
driver" (one responsible for catching and confining roaming animals)
in 1694.

Indeed, if John Ballard had any hopes that he would be able to follow in the footsteps of his older brother Joseph by parlaying his service
as a constable into an eventual election as a selectman, he never
achieved that ambition. He did occasionally serve in lower level of-

fices, such as tithing man and surveyor, but others (usually witch hunt resisters) obtained those offices far more frequently. Joseph never served as a selectman again, either, even though he and John lived out their lives in Andover. Neither brother signed a petition defending the accused, and John's inaction is particularly glaring considering that Sarah Hooper Wardwell was a sister of his wife Rebecca. The rest of the town probably never forgot the role these two brothers played in bringing the witch hunt to Andover in the first place. The Ballards continued operating the system of mills they had constructed in the section of town that bears their name today, but they never achieved the prominence in the town they may have hoped for.

Benjamin Abbot had greater success in advancing himself in the power structure than the Ballards did, even though he also played a role in the witchcraft accusations. His role was limited to accusing Martha Carrier (who had numerous accusers and whose guilt was not entirely discounted even by Francis Dane), but he had declined to join his siblings and his Chandler cousins in endorsing the resistance to the witch hunt when it formed. Nonetheless, he managed to obtain the position of South End constable in 1698 and then rose to the role of a selectman in 1702 and 1703. The prominence of his family must have helped him achieve that status—his older brothers John and George had both served previous terms as selectmen and both did resist the witch hunt. They may have supported their younger brother. But Benjamin's career ended abruptly soon after his election to a second term as selectman—he died March 30, 1703, aged forty-one.

Not until nearly two decades after the trials did anyone who had played a major role in them rise to the position of selectman in Andover. In 1711 Ephraim Foster, the North End's notorious constable of 1692, achieved that honor. A few years earlier, in 1705, Foster did serve the town as a surveyor, a responsibility he once again assumed in 1708. Throughout the decade of the 1710s, this former accuser of witchcraft suspects acted in this role of decision maker for the town he had settled in as a young adult. No major accuser enjoyed greater prominence after the witch hunt in Andover than Ephraim Foster— but only after nearly two decades. By the end of the decade, he was in his early sixties, by no means too old for the role, but the position was gradually being passed on to younger men. In 1731, he saw his eldest son, Ephraim Foster, Jr., elevated to the post of town selectman. The younger Foster, only four years old at the time of the witch hunt, had been born only after his mother Hannah had given birth to at least four daughters during the first decade of her marriage to his father—one less than the number of girls Samuel Wardwell had supposedly predicted the Fosters would have before producing a son.

Coincidentally, another selectman elected in 1731 was Hezekiah Ballard (aged ten at the time of the trials), the third son of Joseph Ballard, whose invitation to the Salem Village girls touched off the witch hunt in Andover. This marked the first time since before the trials that anyone with the Ballard surname had served as a selectman in Andover. The last Ballard to serve in that capacity had been Joseph himself who filled the position in 1688.

In the years after the trials, those who joined the resistance effort clearly controlled town politics. Yet one should be careful not to read too much into that dominance. With few exceptions, the most prominent citizens in Andover did join the resistance effort by January 1693. Some of them (or their fathers) had served numerous terms as selectmen in the past. But from 1693 until 1702, with five selectmen chosen each year, only one slot was ever filled by a man who did not sign the petitions. Samuel Frye, the lone selectman in 1692 not to sign any opposition documents, secured a seat in 1698. After that, he did not serve in that capacity again until 1706. In that same time frame his brother James, who did sign petitions, served six terms. Samuel did not even participate in the accusations—he simply declined to oppose them. As previously noted, the first accuser to serve as a selectman after the trials, Benjamin Abbot, did not obtain the position until 1702. In contrast, Andrew Peters served his first term as a selectman in 1693 after having signed the resistance documents and remained prominent in the town's politics for the remaining two decades of his life. His participation in the resistance to the witch hunt must have helped to fuel his rise.

One would expect the effects of the witch hunt to have extended into the personal sphere in Andover as well as the political. Personal interactions are harder to measure, but one area to examine is the town's marriage patterns in the years after the trials. One might expect to find accusers and their families intermarrying with other accuser families and the resisters and accused and their families intermarrying with other resister and accused families. The probable yet unrecorded wedding of Martha Sprague and Joseph Tyler before the end of 1692 has already been discussed. The first marriage in town after Governor Phips's reprieve of the convicted witches occurred on the same day that the execution of those suspects was probably scheduled. This marriage certainly echoed the circumstances of the witch hunt. Sarah Hawkes (an acquitted suspect), the daughter of reprieved witch Sarah Wardwell, married Francis Johnson on February 1, 1693, in Andover. Johnson's grandfather, Francis Dane, performed the ceremony. This marriage represented the union of two severely persecuted families. Francis Johnson had seen his mother and three younger siblings arrested along with an aunt and numerous cousins. In October, he joined Thomas Carrier and Walter Wright in posting bond for his brother Stephen, his sister Abigail, and his cousin Sarah Carrier. His new bride, Sarah Hawkes, had lost her stepfather Samuel Wardwell on the gallows and had suffered in jail herself along with her mother and half-sister Mercy Wardwell. Mercy herself married four years later, on October 31, 1697, to John Wright, a cousin of Francis Johnson and a son of the same Walter Wright who joined Francis in the recognizance posting and played a major role in the resistance. Mercy defied those who had told her that she would never have a man to love her. John himself, not yet eighteen in early 1693, must have shared his family's sympathies. Thomas Barnard performed the wedding, Francis Dane having died earlier that year. From the time ministers began performing marriage ceremonies in Andover in 1686 (prior to that they had always been performed by government officials) until Dane's death, the elder minister performed the majority of the wedding ceremonies in town (thirty-three to only ten for Barnard, with no appreciable difference before and after 1692). This may represent an agreed-upon division of labor between the two men, but it may also reflect the possibility that most lifelong residents of Andover preferred to be joined in marriage by the man they had known as their spiritual guide since early childhood.

A later marriage in Andover demonstrated bonds formed during the witch hunt even more strongly. On April 20, 1704, cousins William Barker, Jr. and Mary Barker, jailed together twelve years earlier, exchanged marriage vows. At the time of their incarceration, William had been only fourteen and Mary thirteen. Marriages between first cousins did not occur that frequently in the Massachusetts Bay colony, but they did happen. In this case, their shared experience in jail created a bond far stronger than the usual one between cousins. The witch hunt brought these two together just as it had with Martha Sprague and her stepbrother Joseph Tyler, even though the latter couple stood on the side of the witch hunters.

Marriages connected to the witch hunt also crossed town lines. Among the many accused from the extended Ingalls clan was Dorothy Faulkner, jailed at the age of twelve in 1692 along with her mother Abigail Dane Faulkner and her younger sister, also named Abigail. On November 25, 1708, Dorothy married Samuel Nurse of Salem Village, a grandson of the executed Rebecca Towne Nurse, one of the most famous victims. Members of the Preston family, intermarried with the Nurse clan, resided in both towns, and this connection may have helped to facilitate this marital alliance. John Preston, whose brother Thomas was married to a daughter of the martyred Rebecca, signed petitions defending the suspects in Andover. Six months after this wedding Dorothy's father Francis Faulkner joined his new son-in-law and several other members of the Nurse clan in signing a petition to restore the reputations and estates of convicted witches.

Two of John Preston's own nephews also entered marriage alliances with accused witches. Samuel Preston, Jr. married Sarah Bridges on April 2, 1694. Samuel's younger brother Jacob married young Sarah Wilson eight years later. The Preston family had not presented a united front during the witch hunt, however. These two young bridegrooms were sons of John's brother Samuel Preston, who had deposed against Martha Carrier. The elder Samuel Preston does not appear to have been among the more zealous of the witch hunters though. He was one of several who testified only against Martha Carrier, although it is noteworthy that he did not join his brother John in signing petitions. Other marriages in the 1690s and early 1700s simply strengthened unions among families who joined the resistance to the witch hunt—Peters and Frye, Osgood and Blanchard, Chandler and Abbot, Ingalls and Russell, and Osgood and Dane, just to name a few.

Some weddings did join people on opposite sides of the witch hunt. On August 17, 1698, the younger Rebecca Johnson (accused of witchcraft along with her widowed mother Rebecca Aslebee Johnson six years earlier) married none other than Joseph Ballard, Jr., the eldest son of the same Joseph Ballard who invited the afflicted girls of Salem Village to Andover. The extended Johnson clan had suffered grievously during the witch hunt, and the fact that one of them married a son of Joseph Ballard only six years after the trials seems shocking. Time must have healed at least some of the bitterness the family may have felt. On May 3, 1705, Rebecca Johnson Ballard's brother Timothy Johnson, Jr. married Katherine Sprague, a younger sister of the notorious Martha Sprague. At least one other Johnson family member found a spouse among the suspects: Timothy and Rebecca's cousin Susannah Johnson was married on June 19, 1705, to Thomas Carrier, Jr., one of the accused sons of the Queen in Hell herself. Ironically, Susannah's father William Johnson had not joined his relatives in signing petitions supporting the suspects. William Johnson's wife, Mary Lovejoy Johnson, may have been a Ballard cousin.

For his own part, the younger Joseph Ballard had seen his mother die, allegedly at the hands of witches, six years before, although he may have moved beyond believing in that by the time of his marriage. The Ballards may very well have let go of the idea that Elizabeth Phelps Ballard's death resulted from witchcraft by 1698. More than a generation later, in 1721, Jeremiah Ballard (a much younger half-brother of Joseph, Jr., born to Joseph, Sr. and his second wife Rebecca Rea Ballard in 1697) married Mary Dane, a daughter of Francis Dane, Jr. and Hannah Poor Dane. More such marriages crossed those lines as time went on. On May 25, 1708, James Frye, Jr. (born 1682), a grandson of the accused Mary Clements Osgood and a son of witch defender James Frye, married another of Martha Sprague's sisters, Joanna Sprague. The next month, Samuel Phelps, Jr., a brother of afflicted girl Sarah Phelps and nephew of Elizabeth Phelps Ballard, joined in matrimony with Hannah Dane, a granddaughter of the old minister by his son Francis, Jr.

The Johnsons were not the only persecuted family who formed marriage alliances with people who took actions on both sides of the matter. Two of Christopher Osgood's children had married into branches of the extended Hooper clan that had been directly affected by the witch hunt and resisted it. Mary Osgood Marston, the oldest daughter of Christopher Osgood, had been arrested in 1692. Christopher himself made his presence felt in the resistance movement. On December 18, 1707, another of Christopher's daughters, Priscilla, married James Russell. James, age twenty-five in 1692, had joined his parents Robert and Mary Marshall Russell in signing petitions supporting the suspects. (Mary Marshall's father, Thomas Marshall, was named as "brother" in the will of Hooper patriarch William Hooper, indicating that they must have been brothers-in-law, half-brothers, or stepbrothers.) Now James was finally marrying at age forty. Just over three years later, on February 20, 1711, Christopher Osgood's son Ezekiel married Rebecca Wardwell, the daughter of the executed Samuel Wardwell and the convicted (but reprieved) Sarah Hooper Wardwell. Rebecca, only a baby at the time of the trials, went to jail with her mother despite the fact that Sarah confessed to squeezing the child in an effort to hurt her accuser Martha Sprague. Twelve years Rebecca's senior, Ezekiel Osgood remembered the jailing of his sister very well, though at thirteen he had been too young to participate in the opposition.

Six years later though, another member of this Osgood family continued the growing connection with Hooper descendants, but she bucked the trend of marrying relatives of witch trial opponents. Lydia Osgood, born three years after the trials (thirty years younger than her accused half-sister Mary), married Sherebiah Ballard, a son of the South End's constable John Ballard, on January 2, 1717. Sherebiah's mother, Rebecca Hooper, had been a sister of Sarah Hooper Wardwell. This marriage came slightly more than a year after John Ballard, his wife, and their three youngest daughters (Ruth, Sarah, and Elizabeth, all born after the trials) died in a mysterious epidemic that confined itself to their household in November and December 1715. John, who died December 18, saw the others all go before him and hastily wrote a will before his own end. Perhaps with John dead,

Christopher Osgood lost any possible reluctance to see his daughter wed the son of one of the men responsible for bringing the witch hunt to Andover in the first place. A quarter of a century had passed by that time, and resentments over the trials must have diminished. Despite the opposite-side witch trial connections of some of these these marriages, the ultimate Romeo and Juliet match in Andover occurred in 1708.

In 1692, twelve-year-old Phebe Chandler testified against Martha Carrier. Her mother Bridget, the second wife of Phebe's father William Chandler, supported her in this. Soon after, the Chandler family turned against the proceedings with several of them (including William and Bridget) signing petitions in support of the accused. Another Chandler who switched sides was Phebe's uncle, Thomas Chandler, who deposed against Samuel Wardwell in September but then later joined the resistance movement. (It was Thomas Chandler who had feuded with the Tyler clan in the 1660s.) On June 14, 1708, however, the former witch "victim" Phebe Chandler married Jonathan Tyler, a son of Moses Tyler. The extended Tyler clan saw members acting on both sides in the terror of 1692, but for one of their own to marry a Chandler would have seemed unthinkable in prior decades. Phebe's father William died ten years before the marriage, and the Tyler family's nemesis, Thomas Chandler, did not live to see his niece's marriage either. Again, the passage of the earlier generation of Chandlers might have lessened Moses Tyler's trepidations at seeing one of his sons marry into the family that he blamed for the tribulations of his own father Job.

Because so many young people were included among the suspects in Andover, the question of whether being accused of witchcraft adversely affected their marriage prospects is worth examining. At first glance, the evidence suggests probably not. The marriages of Sarah Hawkes, Mercy Wardwell, Sarah Bridges, Dorothy Faulkner, Rebecca Johnson, Sarah Wilson, and Thomas Carrier, Jr. have all been mentioned previously. All except Dorothy Faulkner were under the age of twenty-five at the time of their marriages. Another accused Carrier brother, Richard, married only two years after the trials (at age twenty) to Elizabeth Sessions, also of Andover, whose family had not involved itself in the proceedings in any way. It should be noted that Elizabeth's reputation was less than stellar since she had conceived a child out of wedlock in 1690. At the time, she had been working in the home of Daniel and Hannah Chandler Bixby and had identified Hannah's brother, Joseph Chandler, as the father. The Bixbys, however, had provided evidence that young John Russ, a neighbor not nearly as affluent as the Chandlers, had been their servant's seducer.[1] The possibility that they were just trying to protect the good name of Hannah's brother cannot be ruled out, of course. Neither can the thought that Elizabeth Sessions regarded Joseph Chandler as a more desirable match (or at the very least, a man better equipped to support her and her child). In any event, Richard Carrier's new bride was not one many Andover families would have regarded as a good catch for a young adult son. The other Carrier children married after moving to Colchester, Connecticut, about 1705. Sarah Carrier, arrested at the age of seven, married a man named John Chapman. She did not die until 1772 (aged eighty-eight), almost certainly the last survivor of those accused of witchcraft in 1692.

Abigail Faulkner, a sister of the aforementioned Dorothy, married Thomas Lamson of Ipswich at age twenty-five in 1708. Young Elizabeth Johnson did not marry, but she was said to be mentally challenged. Her accused younger siblings, Stephen and Abigail, both married eventually, but their marriages are not recorded in Andover. One of the accused who may have hurt her prospects by her actions was young Mary Lacey. Aged eighteen when accused in 1692, she gave evidence against more suspects than any other confessor. She did not marry until age thirty, in 1704, and then her bridegroom was her cousin Zerubbabel Kemp (son of her mother's sister, Sarah Foster, and Samuel Kemp). The Kemp couple lived in the town of Groton and were still there in 1748 when Zerubbabel wrote his will. Perhaps they were not overly welcome in Andover in the wake of Mary's string of accusations.

It is also worthwhile to examine the marriages of the accusers. The fact that Martha Sprague probably married her stepbrother Joseph Tyler has already been discussed. Joseph's younger brother Jonathan married another accuser (though a far less active one) in Phebe Chandler. Jonathan himself had never joined the ranks of the accusers, although Joseph did. Rose Foster, second only to Martha Sprague in the number of accusations in Andover, died at age thirteen in February 1693. Abigail Martin, sixteen at the time of the trials, was married in 1702 to John Safford of Ipswich. The fact that she married a non-resident of Andover may be significant. Abigail and John moved to Lisbon, Connecticut, where Abigail died at the age of ninety-one in 1768, probably the last surviving accuser of 1692. Sarah Phelps remained in Andover but did not marry until 1720 at age thirty-seven. Her actions in 1692 may have limited her desirability as a bride. In general, acting as an accuser in 1692 appears to have hurt a young person's marriage prospects more than being accused did, but the sampling is too small to draw definitive conclusions.

Although marriage stands out as one of the best indicators of social interactions in colonial New England towns discussions over building a new meetinghouse in Andover in 1705 also illuminated personal relations. The issue revolved around the fact that the town could not agree on a location. Prominent North Enders wished to rebuild at the site of the existing structure, even though the population center had shifted southward over time. The dispute continued for four years before the decision to divide the town into two parishes, each with its own meetinghouse and minister, resolved the situation.[2] One might expect that this dispute, arising only a little more than a decade after the witch hunt, would pit accusers against suspects and their defenders. The evidence does not bear this out. The two distinct Osgood families, for example (the John Osgood family in the North End and the Christopher Osgood clan in the South End), both defended witchcraft suspects in 1692, with the former playing a particularly significant role. In the meetinghouse debate, though, Samuel Osgood (one of the sons of the accused Mary who signed the petitions) acted as a leader in the North End while Christopher Osgood played a prominent role in the South End. A committee formed in 1707 to facilitate funding the construction of the new meetinghouse included

John Chandler and George Abbot (signers of resistance petitions) and Moses Tyler, a leading accuser. The matter went to court in 1707, and the following year, the ruling came down that Andover had grown large enough to justify two separate precincts. The first meeting of the new South End precinct in 1709 was called by a committee of seven leading citizens—George Abbot, John Abbot, Francis Dane, Jr. (all witch hunt opponents), Joseph Ballard (who invited the afflicted girls to Andover), Henry Holt, William Lovejoy, and John Russ (none of whom involved themselves in the witch hunt). Thomas Barnard remained in the North Parish while the new parish hired Samuel Phillips as its minister. The initial membership of the South Parish (admitted October 17, 1711) included several witch trial opponents (the aforementioned Abbot brothers with their wives, Dorcas Graves Abbot and Sarah Barker Abbot, Thomas Chandler, Jr. with his wife Mary Peters Chandler, Christopher Osgood, and Mary Marshall Russell). Just reading these names is enough to convince someone to see this parish as a haven for former witch hunt resisters. Accused witch Sarah Bridges Preston joined early the following year on March 23, 1712.

Accusers also swelled the ranks of the early membership of the new church. Joseph Ballard, though not among the very first to enroll, joined the new meeting on April 6, 1712, along with his wife Rebecca, whom he had married after the death of his first wife in 1692. His brother John, the South End's constable in 1692, soon followed along with *his* wife Rebecca. Hannah Chandler Bixby, another accuser, enrolled along with her husband Daniel. Sarah Farnum Abbot, the widow of Benjamin Abbot whom she had supported in his accusations of Martha Carrier, involved herself in the South precinct. Her brother, Ralph Farnum, who was also summoned to testify against Carrier, became an early member with his wife Sarah Sterling Farnum. The new meetinghouse did not exclude anyone on either side of the witch hunt. Perhaps most symbolic of this was the fact that Rebecca Johnson Ballard, the accused witch who had married Joseph Ballard, Jr., joined on January 4, 1713. Simply put, there is no clear indication that the push for a separate meetinghouse in the South End grew out of anything other than the inconvenience of the North End location for the residents of the southern section of the town. If anything, the witch hunt and other tumultuous events of the 1690s (particularly the Indian War) may have delayed the process—the town's population had been drifting southward for more than three decades by the time of the construction of the new meetinghouse. An earlier effort to relocate the existing facility in 1680 had gone nowhere. Francis Dane's leading role in the resistance to the trials regained for him any prestige as the town's father figure that he might have lost in the process of the hiring of Thomas Barnard a decade earlier. The fact that Barnard joined forces with the senior minister in defending the suspects in the fall of 1692 may have helped to mitigate the type of factionalism in Andover that endured in Salem Village in the years after the trials. Dane lived on until February 1697 and the idea of dividing the parish did not resurface until several years after his death.

Ultimately, the best evidence that undermines the idea of Thomas Barnard as a wild-eyed fanatic, steering the accusations toward his opponents in Andover, is the documentation of his life after the crisis had subsided. Quarrels over Samuel Parris in Salem Village continued after the trials ended and ultimately, he found himself forced out of the town's pulpit five years later. Barnard, on the other hand, spent the rest of his life in Andover as a minister. Several events in the years after the witchcraft trials demonstrate that even some of those most affected by the crisis held the younger pastor in high regard. In his own account book (not a sermon book), he noted that in 1702 Betty Faulkner (Elizabeth Faulkner, the oldest daughter of convicted witch Abigail Dane Faulkner) came to live with him.[3] The Faulkner family had, of course, suffered much during the witch hunt, with Abigail and two of her daughters being jailed. Abigail herself had been convicted and had survived only due to her pregnancy. At that time, the family's travails had not yet ended. Abigail, though never executed, still labored under attainder as a convicted felon, a situation not reversed until 1703. It seems highly unlikely that the Faulkners would have accepted the idea of one of their daughters taking up residence with Barnard if they held him responsible for the trauma of 1692.

Further, on July 8, 1703, Barnard headed a list of twelve area clergymen who presented a petition to the governor, council, and representatives of the colony to clear the names of those convicted of witch-craft, noting that some of their "neighbours of a good conversation, were apprehended upon Suspicion of Witchcraft, upon the complaint of some young persons under Diabolicall molestations; and upon their Tryall at the Court at Salem were condemned; great weight being layd upon the Evidence of the Afflicted persons, their Accusers. Sentence of Death was executed on severall of them, but others were re-prieved."[4] Thomas Barnard signed the petition first. The name of Joseph Green, who had replaced Samuel Parris in Salem Village in 1697, appeared second. The petition declared that there had been errors in the trials, that the evidence had not been sufficient for conviction, and asked that action be considered to restore the reputations of those convicted. While the trials had been widely discredited by this time, not all the ministers responsible for parishioners accused in 1692 signed this document. Nicholas Noyes, who continued active in Salem Town, opted not to sign. Barnard not only endorsed the document; his name appeared first.

More evidence for Thomas Barnard's good standing in Andover surfaced in 1709 when the South End got its wish for its own parish. The congregations of both churches were willing to have him as their pastor. Eventually, the South End wearied of waiting for him to choose (or perhaps they had some advance inkling he would opt for the North Parish) and hired a new minister, Samuel Phillips. At the time of the division, some residents of the newly established South Parish who lived near the border petitioned the governor, the House of Representatives, and the General Court to be allowed to remain with the North Parish. Altogether, thirteen people signed this document and ultimately remained as members of the North Parish. The greater convenience of the location of the meetinghouse in the North End was of paramount importance to the signers and it is also clear that they wished to avoid contributing to the construction of the new one in the South End. Nonetheless, they also stressed the "hardship" of having to leave their minister (Thomas Barnard), to whom they obviously felt an attachment.[5] Ebenezer Barker, whose wife Abigail had been arrested at the touch test seventeen years earlier, was the first to sign the petition. Two sons of the executed Samuel Wardwell and the convicted but reprieved Sarah Hooper Wardwell (Samuel, Jr. and William) joined Barker in this, along with their brother-in-law John Wright (husband of their accused sister Mercy). The list of signers also included at least three men (Hooker Osgood, Ephraim Stevens, and Stephen Barnard, the latter not related to the minister) who had defended the accused witches in 1692. A fourth signer, Joseph Marble, may or may not have been the man of that name who resisted the witch hunt that year (by 1709, the elder Joseph Marble's son, also named Joseph, was an adult and it is not clear which one signed that year's petition). The wife of the elder Joseph was Mary Faulkner, sister of Francis Faulkner who was married to the convicted Abigail Dane. The younger Joseph's wife, Hannah Barnard, was a daughter of the aforementioned Stephen Barnard. It is implausible that any of these residents, particularly the immediate family members of witchcraft suspects, would have held Thomas Barnard in such high regard had they believed that he played a leading role in the arrests in 1692. None of the signers of this petition had played any role in the persecution.

When Barnard died suddenly in 1718, aged sixty, the North Parish much lamented his death and they hired his son, John Barnard, as his replacement. At the time of his death, Thomas Barnard had served the town for thirty-seven years. His stone remains in the old cemetery in modern-day North Andover, Massachusetts.

The fight that the accused and their families did undertake in the years after the trials was outside Andover: some of them pressured the colony's courts for restitution for losses incurred because of their arrests. Those who were convicted, but reprieved, sought removal of the attainders against them and families of some of those who had been executed sought reversals of the convictions. Not surprisingly, the first to seek an overturning of her conviction was Abigail Dane Faulkner, the spirited daughter of the stalwart pastor Francis Dane. On June 13, 1700, she petitioned the General Court of the colony to reverse her conviction which remained on record despite the fact that Governor Phips had first reprieved and then pardoned her. She noted that she lived as what she termed a "malefactor convict" which, aside from ruining her own reputation remained as "a perpetuall brand of Infams [infamy] upon my family."[6] The court did not act immediately so three years later, Abigail and her husband Francis (who had apparently recovered his mental health by that time) led efforts to secure pardons not only for Abigail but also for eight others convicted of the crime of witchcraft. Six of the total of nine named in the petition had died on the gallows in 1692. Abigail, Elizabeth Bassett Proctor, and Sarah Hooper Wardwell remained alive. In addition to Faulkner and Wardwell, two others from Andover appear on the list—Mary Ayer Parker and Samuel Wardwell, both of whom had paid the ultimate price. This petition bore twenty-one signatures—nine from Andover. The names of Abigail Faulkner, her husband Francis, and her sister Phebe Dane Robinson led the list. Abigail's brothers Nathaniel and Francis also signed. Sarah Wardwell signed along with her eldest son, Samuel Wardwell, Jr. John and Joseph Parker signed on behalf of their mother. Not surprisingly, another of the executed suspects whose name appeared on the list was that of Rebecca Towne Nurse. Her sons, Samuel and John Nurse, her daughter, Rebecca Nurse Preston, and her son-in-law John Tarbell, all signed for her and for their aunt, Mary Towne Esty. The bonds forged between the Faulkner and Nurse families at that time may have led to the marriage of Dorothy Faulkner and Samuel Nurse, Jr. five years later. The petition was read in the House of Representatives on March 18 and the immediate result was the proposal in the House of Representatives for an act reversing the attainders of the three living convicts on May 26 of that year.[7]

Most of the ministers of the hometowns of the convicted witches rallied behind their parishioners, living and dead. As noted previously, on July 8, 1703, twelve clergymen presented a petition to the governor, council, and representatives of the colony, asking for restoration of the reputations of those convicted, whether executed or not.[8] The names of Thomas Barnard and Joseph Green (pastor of Salem Village) headed the signatures. In the end, the representatives reversed the attainder on the three living suspects—Abigail Faulkner, Sarah Wardwell, and Elizabeth Proctor—but took no action on behalf of those who were executed. The act passed on July 27—the first legal action taken to invalidate convictions for witchcraft during the trials of 1692. Seven years went by before colony officials took any more action on behalf of the accused. Two petitions by family members (and a few of the suspects) in May 1709 asked the governor, council, and the General Assembly for restoration of the suspects' reputations and some restitution for monetary losses sustained.

The families of the Towne sisters (Rebecca Nurse and Mary Esty) led the way, but four Andover men joined the effort—Francis Faulkner, John Parker, Joseph Parker, and John Johnson (son of the elder Rebecca Johnson). These petitions, because they sought financial compensation in addition to reversals of attainders, applied to all of those jailed on suspicion, not just the convicted. More than a year passed before colony officials took any action, but in September 1710, the General Court formed a committee to hear appeals for restitution. Family members represented those executed and those who died in jail. (For some of the accused, however, no family members came forward.) Next of kin also spoke on behalf of many of those who survived, some of whom went before the committee themselves. Not surprisingly, a number of Andover suspects participated. Ebenezer Barker petitioned on behalf of his wife Abigail Wheeler Barker. John Barker acted on behalf of his daughter Mary, his son-in-law (and nephew) William Barker, Jr., and his brother William, Sr. (even though the latter remained alive and presumably well). Sarah Bridges Preston, though married, spoke for herself. The aging Thomas Carrier petitioned for restitution for the execution of his wife Martha and the money he had spent to maintain his jailed children. Nathaniel Dane acted for his wife Deliverance. Abigail Faulkner, Sr., whose conviction had been overturned seven years earlier, applied for restitution for herself and her two accused daughters. Abraham Foster asked for compensation for the funds he paid to retrieve the body of his mother Ann after she died in jail. Francis Johnson petitioned on behalf of his wife Sarah Hawkes Johnson and his mother and sister, both named Elizabeth. Francis's cousin John Johnson also acted for his mother and sister, both named Rebecca. Christopher Osgood had been the most persistent defender of his daughter, Mary Osgood Marston, in 1692, but in 1710 it was her husband John Marston who acted to restore her good name and obtain compensation (Mary herself had died in 1700). The equally persistent Parker brothers asked for compensation for the loss of their mother Mary. Samuel Osgood petitioned for compensation for his accused mother Mary (his father having died the year after the trials). Mary Clements Osgood herself may have been too ill to appear—she was to die on October 27 of that year. Mercy Wardwell Wright was another married woman who took matters into her own hands. Her brother Samuel Wardwell, Jr. spoke for their convicted parents, their mother having also died sometime before September 1710.

Even the two Lacey women, whom no family member defended in 1692, had a champion in 1710. The elder Mary's husband Lawrence, silent eighteen years earlier, asked for compensation for the sufferings of his wife (who had died in 1707) and for the benefit of his daughter. No one in this family publicly joined the resistance movement that formed in the fall of 1692 despite the death of their matriarch, Ann Foster, in December of that year. Their elaborate confessions, especially those of the grandmother and granddaughter, had fanned the flames sparked by Joseph Ballard's invitation to the afflicted girls that summer. Others in the family may have felt the need to lay low at that point. By 1710, those concerns were gone and the younger Mary Lacey (married to Zerubbabel Kemp and living in Groton at that time) needed help to obtain the compensation she was entitled to. Her father's actions on her behalf were also for his own benefit since he, as the widower of a convicted suspect, stood to gain.

One of the least likely candidates to speak for herself ultimately did so. Rebecca Blake Eames of Boxford, one of the convicted confessors who escaped the noose when Governor Phips reprieved her, was seventy years old in 1710. Her husband Robert, like John Osgood, had died the year after the trials. Rebecca's son Daniel, accused along with her (but not convicted) brought shame to the family two years later when he abandoned his wife, Lydia Wheeler Eames, and their children.[9] In January 1695, Daniel appeared before the court in Hartford, Connecticut, charged by an unmarried woman named Mary Case with fathering her as yet-unborn child. The court sentenced Daniel to be whipped and ordered him to return to his wife in Boxford. Apparently, he never followed that order. Rebecca's son-in-law, Ephraim Foster, was destined to be chosen as a selectman in Andover the next year and would have been a likely person to act on her behalf. Nonetheless, this aging widow spoke for herself and asked for compensation. A note on the back of her petition described her as "Rebeccah Eames not Executed an Extraordinary Confessor."[10]

There was another suspect who seemed even less likely to act on her own behalf. Writing in 1697, witch trial critic Robert Calef described Mary Post and Elizabeth Johnson, Jr. as "two of the most senseless and ignorant creatures that could be found."[11] But in 1710, Mary Post, age forty-six and still single, asked for compensation for her own expenses that she apparently had managed to pay herself at the time. She did ask John Barker, who was already acting on behalf of his immediate family, to deliver her petition, but she must have developed more self-sufficiency by 1710 than could have been imagined in 1692. Like the others, her request for restitution was brought back to officials by the committee. When she was granted some compensation, she authorized Joseph Parker, a son of the executed Mary Ayer Parker, to claim her funds for her.[12] The next three years saw a series of compensatory payments to those who suffered in 1692.

Colony officials finally took additional steps toward reversing attainders in 1711. On October 17 of that year, the General Assembly passed an act invalidating the convictions of fourteen of those who were put to death (including Giles Corey, who was crushed rather than hanged) and eight others convicted but not executed. Six of those executed were not included,[13] probably only because no one spoke up on their behalf. Nearly all of those convicted but not executed in 1692 (and not pardoned in 1703) were included in the reversal of attainder in 1711.[14] The document made a point of stating that "Some of the principal Accusers and Witnesses in those dark and severe prosecutions have discovered themselves to be persons of profligate and vicious Conversation."[15] Opinion against the witch hunt had hardened by that time.

For most of those omitted by the reversals of attainder in 1703 and 1711, the book finally closed centuries later. In 1957, the Commonwealth of Massachusetts acknowledged legal errors in the case of Ann

Pudeator. A similar action was taken in 2001 for the other executed suspects who had not been included in the overturning of convictions in the early eighteenth century. Acting governor Jane Swift declared all the pardons official on October 31 of that year. But one name, missed in the actions taken by the colony and later the commonwealth, remains on the books as a convicted witch to this day (2018). Young Elizabeth Johnson, the granddaughter Francis Dane described as "simplish at the best," did not see her attainder reversed in 1711, even though her brother Francis acted on her behalf. In the twentieth- and twenty-first-century proceedings, she somehow escaped the attention of the General Assembly and the acting governor—perhaps mainly because she was not executed. The fact that she never married and has no direct descendants cannot be discounted, either. It is perhaps only fitting that the one convicted witch who remained unpardoned by the Commonwealth lived in Andover.

In 1692, the town of Andover saw more residents accused of witchcraft than any other community did. By July, Andover residents had known for months what was happening in Salem. So did the residents of every other community in Essex County, and what happened in Andover could have happened in any other town if an appropriate combination of events had come together. Throughout the late summer of 1692, confessions fed the growing flames of accusation in Andover, culminating in the touch test of September 7.

The first trials of confessors in mid-September jolted Andover into reality. Prior to that, the general belief that suspects could save themselves by confessing held sway in the town. The convictions of a few confessors shook the town to its core. The resistance movement sprang up almost immediately and continued until the newly constituted court began trying suspects again in January 1693. The town's two ministers, Francis Dane and Thomas Barnard, led the movement that eventually included seventy-two people who signed at least one of the petitions defending suspects. Close relatives of the accused, many of whom had undoubtedly encouraged them to confess earlier, rushed to endorse the petitions once they realized that admitting guilt had endangered the suspects' lives rather than ensuring their safety. No other town saw such a concentrated rejection of the accusations of witchcraft that so thoroughly defined the year of 1692 in northeastern Massachusetts Bay.

Early in the fall of 1692, a young resident of the town of Gloucester—Ebenezer Babson—took a step like the one taken by Joseph Ballard that summer. Believing himself bewitched, he invited some of the afflicted girls from Salem Village to Gloucester to determine if he was correct and if so, who was responsible. Babson's action eventually led to the arrests of nine people for witchcraft in the town. None, however, were tried until the reconstituted court convened in January 1693 and they were acquitted. Gloucester was spared the horror that enveloped Andover and Salem Village by the good fortune of timing. Nonetheless, with nine suspects arrested, Gloucester ranks fourth—after Andover, Salem Village, and Salem Town—in the number of accused residents. At least in part, Gloucester owed the short-circuiting of its own witch hunt to the Andover resistance movement. In early September 1692, new suspects were being arrested and examined daily and the pace of the trials was quickening. The hanging of eight people on September 22 stands out as the single largest mass execution of convicted witches in colonial American history. No one can deny the importance of the writings of Thomas Brattle and Increase Mather in slowing down and eventually halting the trials. Governor Phips must be credited with seeing the error of his initial action in creating the Court of Oyer and Terminer and in allowing it free reign while he was away fighting Indians.

There is, however, strength in numbers. Andover provided the organized opposition that the region needed to put out the blaze that the town had helped to ignite in the first place. The backlash came too late for four of the town's residents—Martha Carrier, Mary Parker, and Samuel Wardwell all died on the gallows, and Ann Foster did not survive the ordeal of nearly five months in jail. Andover paid a terrible price for its involvement in the witch hunt of 1692. Never again did any New England community fall victim to an equivalent disaster.

Appendix A

Accused Witches

Women who were married at the time of the trials are listed under their married names, although their maiden names are provided when known. Women who did not marry until after the trials are listed under their maiden names.

Brief Biographical Sketches

BARKER, ABIGAIL WHEELER
Residence in 1692: Andover, South End
Confessed: Yes
Fate: Tried, acquitted
Born February 2, 1656, Newbury, Massachusetts, daughter of David Wheeler and Sarah Wise. Married May 25, 1686, in Andover to Ebenezer Barker (1651–1747), a son of original Andover proprietors Richard and Joanne Barker. Abigail lived out her life in Andover and died there October 16, 1743.

BARKER, MARY
Residence in 1692: Andover, North End
Confessed: Yes
Fate: Tried, acquitted
Born September 3, 1679, in Andover, daughter of John Barker and Mary Stevens and granddaughter of two original Andover proprietors, Richard Barker and John Stevens. Married her first cousin, William Barker, Jr. (who was also accused) on February 20, 1704. Lived out her life in Andover and died there February 10, 1752.

BARKER, WILLIAM, JR.
Residence in 1692: Andover, North End
Confessed: Yes
Fate: Tried, acquitted
Born in Andover January 22, 1678, son of William Barker and Mary Dix

and grandson of original Andover proprietor Richard Barker. Married his
first cousin, Mary Barker (who was also accused) on February 20, 1704.
Lived out his life in Andover and died there January 16, 1745.

BARKER, WILLIAM, SR.
Residence in 1692: Andover, North End
Confessed: Yes
Fate: Indicted, fled before trial
Born ca. 1645, son of original Andover proprietors Richard and Joanne
Barker. Married February 20, 1676, to Mary Dix (ca. 1655–1744). William
lived out the rest of his life in Andover and died there March 4, 1718.

BRIDGES, MARY, JR.
Residence in 1692: Andover, North End
Confessed: Yes
Fate: Tried, acquitted
Born January 27, 1679, Andover; daughter of John Bridges and Mary Tyler,
each of whom had been married previously. She moved with her parents to
Mendon a few years after the trials and married there December 25, 1705,
to James Godman. Her fate after that is unknown.

BRIDGES, MARY TYLER (POST)
Residence in 1692: Andover, North End
Confessed: Yes
Fate: Tried, acquitted
Born ca. 1644, probably Newport, Rhode Island. Married first November
18, 1662, in Woburn to a widower named Richard Post. Mary and Richard
soon followed her parents to the frontier town of Mendon. Richard Post
was killed there July 14, 1675, at the beginning of King Philip's War and
the rest of the family fled back to Andover and the surrounding area. Mary
remarried March 1, 1678, in Andover to another widower, John Bridges.
Soon after the trials Mary and her husband moved to Mendon (where her
parents had already settled again) and she died there January 7, 1707.

BRIDGES, SARAH
Residence in 1692: Andover, North End
Confessed: Yes
Fate: Tried, acquitted
Born ca. 1675 in Andover, daughter of John Bridges by his first wife, Sarah
How (niece of Francis Dane). Married April 2, 1694, in Andover to Samuel
Preston, Jr. He died April 29, 1717. She remarried October 19, 1722, in

Andover to William Price of Ashford, Connecticut, who died before 1725 when Sarah, as his widow, sold land to Peter Osgood of Salem. Her death date is not known.

BROMAGE, HANNAH (maiden name uncertain)
Residence in 1692: Haverhill
Confessed: No
Fate: Charges dismissed
Her origins are not entirely certain. At time of trials, lived in Haverhill with husband Edward Bromage (or Brumidge). Edward died in Haverhill June 10, 1699. Hannah's date of death is not known. She may have been the same person as Hannah Varnum (or Farnum) who married Abraham Tyler December 26, 1650, in Haverhill. Abraham died in 1673, after which she may have married Edward Bromage/Brumidge.

CARRIER, ANDREW
Residence in 1692: Andover, South End
Confessed: Yes
Fate: Never tried
Born April 7, 1677, in Billerica, son of Thomas and Martha Allen Carrier. Moved with his parents and siblings to Andover by 1689. After the trials, moved with others in his family to Colchester, Connecticut and married there January 11, 1705, to Mary Adams. Died in Colchester July 22, 1749.

CARRIER, MARTHA ALLEN
Residence in 1692: Andover, South End
Confessed: No
Fate: Convicted, executed
Born ca. 1653, probably Andover, daughter of Andrew and Faith Ingalls Allen (original proprietors of Andover). Married May 7, 1674, Billerica, to Thomas Carrier (alias Morgan according to his marriage record, died 1735, Colchester, Connecticut, allegedly aged 109, probably younger). Martha and her husband moved to her hometown of Andover in the mid- to late 1680s where the family was blamed for starting the smallpox outbreak of 1690 which may have killed as many as thirteen people. Martha was hanged for witchcraft in Salem August 19, 1692.

CARRIER, RICHARD
Residence in 1692: Andover, South End
Confessed: Yes
Fate: Indicted, never tried

Born July 19, 1674, Billerica, son of Thomas and Martha Allen Carrier. Moved to Andover with his parents in the mid- to late 1680s. Married July 18, 1694 in Andover to Elizabeth Sessions. Later moved to Colchester, Connecticut, and died there November 17, 1749.

CARRIER, SARAH
Residence in 1692: Andover, South End
Confessed: Yes
Fate: Never tried
Born November 17, 1684, Billerica, daughter of Thomas and Martha Allen Carrier. Moved with parents to Andover soon after. Moved with others in her family to Colchester, Connecticut, a few years after the trials. She married there to John Chapman September 7, 1707, and lived out the rest of her long life in Colchester, dying December 7, 1772. She may have been the last living person accused of witchcraft in 1692.

CARRIER, THOMAS
Residence in 1692: Andover, South End
Confessed: Yes
Fate: Never tried
Born June 18, 1682, Billerica, son of Thomas and Martha Allen Carrier. Moved with parents to Andover a few years later. Married Susannah Johnson June 19, 1705, in Andover. Later moved to Colchester, Connecticut, with other family members and died there July 18, 1739.

CLARK, MARY JOHNSON (DAVIS)
Residence in 1692: Haverhill
Confessed: No
Fate: Never tried
Born ca. 1638, probably Ipswich, a daughter of John and Susan Johnson who had arrived in Massachusetts Bay on the ship *James* in 1635. Married first December 31, 1659, in Andover to Ephraim Davis of Haverhill. He died September 28, 1679. She remarried November 1, 1682, in Haverhill to Edward Clark. At the time of the trials, she was living with her second husband in Haverhill. Her fate after the trials is unknown.

COLSON, MARY DUSTIN
Residence in 1692: Reading
Confessed: Yes
Fate: Never tried
Lived in Reading as a widow at the time of trials. Married September 26,

1698, in Reading to Cornelius Brown. Her first husband, Adam Colson, had died before the trials.

DANE, DELIVERANCE HASELTINE
Residence in 1692: Andover, North End
Confessed: Yes
Fate: Never tried
Born ca. 1654, probably Haverhill, daughter of Robert and Ann Haseltine. Married December 12, 1672, in Andover, to Nathaniel Dane, son of Andover's minister Francis Dane and his wife Elizabeth Ingalls Dane. Lived out her life in Andover and died there June 15, 1735.

DRAPER, JOSEPH
Residence in 1692: Andover, South End
Confessed: Yes
Fate: Never tried
Born July 27, 1671, Concord, Massachusetts, son of Adam and Rebecca Brabrook Draper. Living in Andover at time of trials, possibly as a hired worker. Fate after trials unknown.

EAMES, DANIEL
Residence in 1692: Boxford
Confessed: No
Fate: Charges dismissed
Born ca. 1663, probably in modern-day Boxford, son of Robert and Rebecca Blake Eames. Married April 25, 1683, Andover, to Lydia Wheeler, sister of Abigail Wheeler Barker who was also accused of witchcraft in 1692. Abandoned his wife and children soon after the trials and went to Connecticut. In January 1695, Daniel appeared before the court in Hartford, Connecticut, charged by an unmarried woman named Mary Case of fathering her as-yet-unborn child. The court sentenced Daniel to be whipped and ordered him to return to his wife in Boxford. Apparently, he never followed that order. His fate after that is unknown.

EAMES, REBECCA BLAKE
Residence in 1692: Boxford
Confessed: Yes
Fate: Convicted, reprieved
Born ca. 1641, probably Gloucester, daughter of George Blake. Married ca. 1660 to Robert Eames. Rebecca was a sister of Prudence Blake (died 1689), the first wife of Moses Tyler. Rebecca lived out her life in Boxford and died

there May 8, 1721. Her stone in Mount Vernon Cemetery in Boxford still exists and may be the only one in existence for a person convicted of witchcraft in 1692 that dates from the time of her actual death.

EMERSON, MARTHA TOOTHAKER
Residence in 1692: Haverhill
Confessed: Yes
Fate: Charges dismissed
Born June 25, 1668, Billerica, daughter of Roger and Mary Allen Toothaker (both of whom were also arrested for witchcraft in 1692). Married June 16, 1690, in Haverhill to Joseph Emerson, a cousin of Elizabeth Emerson who may have been raped by Timothy Swan in 1685. Martha lived out her life in Haverhill and died there January 14, 1726.

FARRINGTON, EDWARD
Residence in 1692: Andover, North End
Confessed: Uncertain
Fate: Indicted, fled
Born July 5, 1662, in Lynn, son of John and Elizabeth Knight Farrington. After the early death of John, Elizabeth remarried to Mark Graves and moved with him to Andover. Edward married in Andover April 9, 1690, to Martha Brown. He lived out his life in Andover and died there January 3, 1747.

FAULKNER, ABIGAIL, JR.
Residence in 1692: Andover, North End
Confessed: Yes
Fate: Never tried
Born August 12, 1683, Andover, daughter of Francis and Abigail Dane Faulkner. Married Thomas Lamson of Ipswich in 1708. Supposedly died December 26, 1746, (no primary source found).

FAULKNER, ABIGAIL DANE
Residence in 1692: Andover, North End
Confessed: No
Fate: Convicted, reprieved
Born October 13, 1652, Andover, daughter of the town minister, Francis Dane, and his first wife Elizabeth Ingalls Dane. Married there October 12, 1675, to Francis Faulkner. Lived out her life in Andover and died there February 5, 1730.

FAULKNER, DOROTHY
Residence in 1692: Andover, North End
Confessed: Yes
Fate: Never tried
Born February 15, 1680, Andover, daughter of Francis and Abigail Dane Faulkner. Married Samuel Nurse of Salem Village November 25, 1708, grandson of Rebecca Towne Nurse who was executed for witchcraft July 19, 1692. Died sometime after 1740 (the year she was named in her husband's will), probably in Salem Village.

FOSTER, ANN (maiden name unknown)
Residence in 1692: Andover, South End
Confessed: Yes
Fate: Convicted, reprieved, died in jail
Born ca. 1617, presumably England. Some sources give her maiden name as Alcock, but no proof of this has surfaced. She married in the late 1630s to Andrew Foster, who may have been more than thirty years older than her (the record of his death in Andover, May 7, 1685, indicates that she was 100 years old, but this could be an exaggeration). Ann Foster died in jail December 3, 1692, having been convicted of witchcraft in September but reprieved.

FRYE, EUNICE POTTER
Residence in 1692: Andover, South End
Confessed: Yes
Fate: Tried, acquitted
Born April 2, 1641, Concord, Massachusetts, daughter of Luke and Mary Potter. Married October 4, 1660, in Andover to John Frye. Lived out her life in Andover and died there November 24, 1708.

GREEN, MARY (GREEN)
Residence in 1692: Haverhill
Confessed: No
Fate: Never tried
Married November 4, 1675 (or 1678, sources disagree), in Haverhill, to Peter Green (they may have been cousins). At time of trials, lived in Haverhill with husband. Fate after trials uncertain.

HAWKES, SARAH
Residence in 1692: Andover, South End
Confessed: Yes
Fate: Tried, acquitted

Born June 1, 1671, Lynn, daughter of Adam and Sarah Hooper Hawkes. After Adam's death in 1671, Sarah Hooper Hawkes remarried to Samuel Wardwell in Andover. Sarah Hawkes married Francis Johnson in Andover February 2, 1693. Lived out her life in Andover and died there December 23, 1716.

HOWARD, JOHN
Residence in 1692: Rowley
Confessed: No
Fate: Never tried
One of the most obscure people accused of witchcraft in 1692, he lived in Rowley at time of trials. Fate after trials unknown.

HUTCHINS, FRANCES
Residence in 1692: Haverhill
Confessed: No
Fate: Never tried
Arrived in Massachusetts Bay in 1638 with husband John Hutchins. Some secondary sources given her maiden name as Alcock, but no documentary proof is cited. Lived for a few years in Newbury, then settled in Haverhill, where John Hutchins died in 1685. Frances died there April 5, 1694.

JACKSON, JOHN, JR.
Residence in 1692: Rowley
Confessed: Yes
Fate: Charges dismissed
Born May 22, 1670, Rowley, son of John and Elizabeth Poore Jackson. Lived in Rowley at time of trials. Fate after trials uncertain. May be the John Jackson who died August 19, 1719, in Boston, aged forty-nine. The age fits for John Jackson, Jr. of Rowley.

JACKSON, JOHN, SR.
Residence in 1692: Rowley
Confessed: No
Fate: Charges dismissed
Born ca. 1645, probably in Rowley, son of William Jackson. Brother of Elizabeth Jackson How who was hanged for witchcraft July 19, 1692. Married February 27, 1669, to Elizabeth Poore. He somehow incurred the displeasure of his father who specifically bypassed him in favor of his son, John Jackson, Jr., when he wrote his will in 1688. John Jackson, Sr. died February 23, 1718, in Rowley.

JOHNSON, ABIGAIL
Residence in 1692: Andover, North End
Confessed: Yes
Fate: Never tried
Born March 16, 1681, Andover, daughter of Stephen and Elizabeth Dane Johnson. May have married James Black of Boxford. If so, she died November 24, 1720, in Boxford.

JOHNSON, ELIZABETH, JR.
Residence in 1692: Andover, North End
Confessed: Yes
Fate: Convicted, reprieved
Born ca. 1670, Andover, daughter of Stephen and Elizabeth Dane Johnson. Described by her grandfather, Francis Dane, as "simplish at the best," she apparently lived out her life in Andover unmarried. She was last known to be alive in 1716. May be the "Elizabeth Johnson, single woman" who died January 3, 1747, in Andover.

JOHNSON, ELIZABETH DANE
Residence in 1692: Andover, North End
Confessed: Yes
Fate: Tried, acquitted
Born ca. 1641, probably in Ipswich, daughter of Francis and Elizabeth Ingalls Dane. Married November 5, 1661, Andover, to Stephen Johnson. Stephen died November 30, 1690, in Andover, probably a victim of the smallpox epidemic that was blamed on Martha Carrier. Elizabeth lived out the rest of her life in Andover and died there April 15, 1722.

JOHNSON, REBECCA, JR.
Residence in 1692: Andover, North End
Confessed: Yes
Fate: Charges dismissed
Born ca. 1675, Andover, daughter of Timothy and Rebecca Aslebee Johnson. Married August 7, 1698, to Joseph Ballard, Jr. Lived out her life in Andover and died there February 11, 1740.

JOHNSON, REBECCA ASLEBEE
Residence in 1692: Andover, North End
Confessed: Yes
Fate: Charges dismissed
Born May 6, 1652, Andover, daughter of John and Rebecca Ayer Aslebee.

She was a niece of Mary Ayer Parker who was hanged for witchcraft September 22, 1692. Rebecca married December 15, 1674, in Andover to Timothy Johnson who died March 15, 1688. The town's selectmen gave the widowed Rebecca the responsibility of cleaning Andover's meetinghouse knowing that she needed the income. She was still alive in Andover in 1705 but had died by June 17, 1728 when her brother John Aslebee wrote his will.

JOHNSON, STEPHEN
Residence in 1692: Andover, North End
Confessed: Yes
Fate: Indicted, no trial record
Born December 7, 1679, Andover, son of Stephen and Elizabeth Dane Johnson. Married first before 1709 to Sarah Whitaker. Married second in Haverhill to widow Ruth Kimball. Died January 8, 1769, Goffstown, New Hampshire.

LACEY, MARY, JR.
Residence in 1692: Andover, North End
Confessed: Yes
Fate: Tried, acquitted
Born May 25, 1674, Andover, daughter of Lawrence and Mary Foster Lacey. Married January 23, 1704, to her first cousin, Zerubbabel Kemp, son of her mother's sister Sarah Foster Kemp. They lived in Groton. Mary was still alive in Groton in 1748 (aged 74) when Zerubbabel wrote his will and named her as one of the beneficiaries. How long she lived after that is uncertain.

LACEY, MARY FOSTER
Residence in 1692: Andover, North End
Confessed: Yes
Fate: Convicted, reprieved
Born July 9, 1652, Andover, daughter of Andrew and Ann Foster. Ann was also accused of witchcraft in 1692. Mary married August 5, 1673, Andover, to Lawrence Lacey. Lived the rest of her life in Andover and died there June 18, 1707.

LILLY, JANE
Residence in 1692: Reading
Confessed: No
Fate: Charges dismissed
Her husband was supposedly named George Lilly and he was probably dead by 1692. Jane lived in Reading at time of trials. Fate after trials unknown.

Marston, Mary Osgood
Residence in 1692: Andover, North End
Confessed: Yes
Fate: Tried, acquitted
Born July 5, 1665, Andover, daughter of Christopher Osgood and his first
wife Hannah Belknap. Married May 2, 1689, to John Marston. Died April
5, 1700 in Andover.

Osgood, Mary Clements
Residence in 1692: Andover, North End
Confessed: Yes
Fate: Tried, acquitted
Born ca. 1637, daughter of Robert Clements who lived in Haverhill later
in his life. Married November 15, 1653, in Haverhill to John Osgood
(1630–1693). John and Mary were two of the wealthiest and most promi-
nent people in Andover in 1692, but that did not prevent Mary from being
accused. John died the year after the witch hunt. Mary lived out her life in
Andover and died there October 27, 1710.

Parker, Mary Ayer
Residence in 1692: Andover, North End
Confessed: No
Fate: Convicted, executed
Born ca. 1637, apparently in England, daughter of John Ayer who had settled in Salisbury by 1640 and then later moved on to Haverhill. Mary was
an aunt of Rebecca Aslebee Johnson who was also accused. Mary married
ca. 1653 to Nathan Parker, an original proprietor of Andover, who died in
1685. Mary was hanged for witchcraft September 22, 1692, in Salem.

Parker, Sarah
Residence in 1692: Andover, North End
Confessed: Uncertain
Fate: Never tried
Born April 3, 1670, Andover, daughter of Nathan and Mary Ayer Parker.
She was still living in Andover as a single woman in 1712 (unless she married
a man with the Parker surname) when she sought compensation for her im-
prisonment.

Post, Hannah
Residence in 1692: Boxford
Confessed: Yes

Fate: Tried, acquitted

Born September 13, 1666, Woburn (recorded as Joanna), daughter of Richard and Mary Tyler Post. Resident of Boxford when arrested. Fate after trials unknown.

POST, MARY
Residence in 1692: Rowley
Confessed: Yes
Fate: Convicted, reprieved
Born September 29 1664, Woburn, daughter of Richard and Mary Tyler Post. She was still single and apparently living in Andover in 1710 when she sought and received compensation for her sufferings. Robert Calef had described her and young Elizabeth Johnson as "two of the most senseless and ignorant creatures that could be found" suggesting that she was mentally challenged. Her mother and stepfather (Mary Tyler Post Bridges and John Bridges) had long since moved to Mendon by 1710 and her mother had died in Mendon three years earlier. Mary Post's fate after 1710 is not known.

POST, SUSANNAH
Residence in 1692: Andover, North End
Confessed: Yes
Fate: Tried, acquitted
Born 1662, Woburn, daughter or Richard Post and his first wife, Susannah Sutton and therefore a half-sister of Hannah and Mary Post. Resident of Andover when arrested. Fate after trials unknown.

SADIE/SADY, JOHN
Residence in 1692: Andover, South End
Confessed: Yes
Fate: Never tried
Born ca. 1679, probably Ipswich, son of John and Elizabeth Peters Sadie. Elizabeth moved with her parents, Andrew and Mercy Peters, to Andover after the death of her first husband and remarried there to the widower Walter Wright. The younger John Sadie died unmarried in Andover August 13, 1702, aged about twenty-three.

SALTER, HENRY
Residence in 1692: Andover, South End
Confessed: No
Fate: Charges dismissed
Born ca. 1628. He was a fairly recent arrival in Andover at the time of the

trials, having spent most of his adult life in Charlestown. He had a wife named Hannah, who was probably deceased by 1692. Living in Andover at time of arrest, aged about 64. Fate after trials unknown. Through one of his sons, Richard, who relocated to New Jersey, Henry Salter was a direct ancestor of Abraham Lincoln.

TAYLOR, MARY HARRINGTON
Residence in 1692: Reading
Confessed: Yes
Fate: Tried, acquitted
Born ca. 1652, supposedly a daughter of Richard and Elizabeth Harrington. Married November 21, 1671, Reading, to Seabred Taylor. Lived in Reading at time of trials. Supposedly died in Reading in 1733, not confirmed.

TOOTHAKER, MARGARET
Residence in 1692: Billerica
Confessed: Uncertain
Fate: Never tried
Born January 31, 1683, Billerica, daughter of Roger and Mary Allen Toothaker. Taken captive August 5, 1695, by Native Americans when they attacked her home in Billerica and never seen again.

TOOTHAKER, MARY ALLEN
Residence in 1692: Billerica
Confessed: Yes
Fate: Tried, acquitted
Born mid–1640s, probably Andover, daughter of Andrew and Faith Ingalls Allen, original proprietors of Andover. Married June 9, 1665, in Billerica to Roger Toothaker who was accused of witchcraft along with her. Roger died in jail June 16, 1692.[1] Mary was killed August 5, 1695, in or near her home in Billerica when Native Americans attacked the town.

TYLER, HANNAH
Residence in 1692: Andover, South End
Confessed: Yes
Fate: Tried, acquitted
Born ca. 1679, possibly in Andover, daughter of Hopestill and Mary Lovett Tyler. Married in Andover December 9, 1697, to Robert Buswell. They moved to Preston, Connecticut. Hannah died November 6, 1717, in Canterbury, Connecticut.

TYLER, JOANNA
Residence in 1692: Andover, South End
Confessed: Yes
Fate: Never tried
Born ca. 1681, possibly in Andover, daughter of Hopestill and Mary Lovett
Tyler. Died before 1728 (when her father wrote his will), presumably un-
married.

TYLER, MARTHA
Residence in 1692: Andover, South End
Confessed: Yes
Fate: Never tried
Born ca. 1676, Roxbury, daughter of Hopestill and Mary Lovett Tyler. Mar-
ried April 3, 1700, Preston, Connecticut, to Robert Geer. Died September
18, 1741, Groton, Connecticut.

TYLER, MARY LOVETT
Residence in 1692: Andover, South End
Confessed: Yes
Fate: Tried, acquitted
Born ca. 1652, probably Braintree, Massachusetts, daughter of Daniel and
Joanna Lovett. Married January 20, 1668, Mendon, to Hopestill Tyler. They
relocated to Hopestill's childhood home of Andover during King Philip's
War. After the trials, about 1697, moved to Preston, Connecticut, and lived
out their lives there. Mary died March 3, 1732.

WARDWELL, MERCY
Residence in 1692: Andover, South End
Confessed: Yes
Fate: Tried, acquitted
Born October 3, 1673, Andover, daughter of Samuel and Sarah Hooper
Wardwell. Married August 31, 1697, in Andover to John Wright. Lived out
her life in Andover and died there February 16, 1754.

WARDWELL, SAMUEL
Residence in 1692: Andover, South End
Confessed: Yes (but retracted)
Fate: Convicted, executed
Baptized May 16, 1643, in Boston, son of Thomas and Elizabeth Wardwell,
but probably born in Exeter, New Hampshire. Had a brief marriage in the
later 1660s to an unknown wife by whom he had one son, Thomas. Re-

married January 9, 1673, Andover, to Sarah Hooper Hawkes, widow of Adam Hawkes. Samuel was hanged for witchcraft in Salem, September 22, 1692.

WARDWELL, SARAH HOOPER (HAWKES)
Residence in 1692: Andover, South End
Confessed: Yes
Fate: Convicted, reprieved
Born December 7, 1650, Reading, daughter of William and Elizabeth Hooper. Married first in June 1670, Lynn, to Adam Hawkes, a widower forty-five years her senior. He died in 1671. She married second January 9, 1673, Andover, to Samuel Wardwell. Sarah died before 1710, presumably in Andover.

WILFORD, RUTH
Residence in 1692: Haverhill
Confessed: No
Fate: Never tried
Born May 15, 1672, Bradford, daughter of Gilbert and Mary Dow Wilford. Married June 12, 1694, Haverhill, to Thomas Ayer, nephew of the executed Mary Ayer Parker. Lived out her life in Haverhill and was killed by Indians, August 29, 1708, along with daughter, also named Ruth.

WILSON, SARAH, JR.
Residence in 1692: Andover, South End
Confessed: Yes
Fate: Never tried
Born December 31, 1678, Andover, daughter of Joseph and Sarah Lord Wilson. Married June 17, 1702, in Andover to Jacob Preston. Moved to Ashford, Connecticut. Death date unknown.

WILSON, SARAH LORD
Residence in 1692: Andover, South End
Confessed: Yes
Fate: Never tried
Born ca. 1648, probably Ipswich, daughter of Robert and Mary Lord. Married April 24, 1678, Andover, to Joseph Wilson. Lived out her life in Andover and died there May 21, 1727.

Appendix B

Accusers and Afflicted

Women who were married at the time of the trials are listed under their married names, although their maiden names are provided when known. Women who did not marry until after the trials are listed under their maiden names.

Brief Biographical Sketches

ABBOT, BENJAMIN
Born December 20, 1662, Andover, son of George and Hannah Chandler Abbot and stepson of Francis Dane. Prior to his marriage, he was accused of fathering a daughter by Naomi Hoyt Lovejoy, who was the widow of John Lovejoy, Jr. Benjamin was married in Andover April 22, 1685, to Sarah Farnum. Lived out his life in Andover and died there March 30, 1703.

ABBOT, SARAH FARNUM
Born January 14, 1661, Andover, daughter of Ralph and Elizabeth Holt Farnum. Married April 22, 1685, in Andover to Benjamin Abbot. Lived in Andover until at least 1711 when she became an original member of the South Parish.

BALLARD, ELIZABETH PHELPS
Born ca. 1646, Newbury, daughter of Edward and Elizabeth Adams Phelps. Married February 28, 1666, Andover, to Joseph Ballard. Died July 27, 1692 in Andover, just as accusations there gained steam.

BALLARD, JOSEPH
Born ca. 1644, probably Newbury, son of William and Grace (Lovejoy?) Ballard. Married February 28, 1666, Andover, to Elizabeth Phelps. Her illness prompted him to request the help of the afflicted girls of Salem Village. Joseph remarried in November 1692 (four months after the death of his

wife), lived out the rest of his life in Andover and died there September 29, 1722.

BIXBY, HANNAH CHANDLER

Born early 1650s, probably Andover, daughter of Thomas and Hannah Brewer Chandler. Married December 2, 1674, Andover, to Daniel Bixby. Lived out her life in Andover and died there November 20, 1730.

BRIDGES, JOHN

Born early 1640s, Rowley or Ipswich, son of Edmund and Elizabeth Bridges. Married first December 5, 1666, in Ipswich to Sarah How (died about 1677). Married second March 1, 1678, Andover, to the widow Mary Tyler Post. Testified against Samuel Wardwell and also encouraged his sister-in-law, Mary Lovett Tyler, to confess, but later signed the petitions defending his own wife, Mary Tyler Post Bridges, and his accused daughters and step-daughters. Moved to Mendon with his family after the trials and is assumed to have died there sometime after the death of his wife in 1707.

CHANDLER, BRIDGET HENCHMAN (RICHARDSON)

Born ca. 1640, probably Concord, Massachusetts, daughter of Thomas Henchman. Married first November 28, 1660, Chelmsford, to James Richardson. Married second October 8, 1679, to William Chandler of Andover. She accused Martha Carrier, but signed petition defending suspects in January 1693. Lived out her life in Andover and supposedly died there March 6, 1731, but her death is not recorded in the vital records.

CHANDLER, PHEBE

Born September 17, 1680, Andover, daughter of William and Bridget Henchman (Richardson) Chandler. Married June 14, 1708, to Jonathan Tyler of Boxford. Jonathan and Phebe Tyler were last known to have been living in Boxford in 1727. After that time, they may have gone to modern-day Maine where their son Jonathan (born in 1715) is known to have lived.

CHANDLER, THOMAS

Born ca. 1627, England, son of William and Annis Chandler and stepson of John Dane, the father of Francis Dane. Arrived in Massachusetts Bay with parents 1637. Married before 1651 to Hannah Brewer. Testified against Samuel Wardwell but switched sides and signed petitions defending suspects in October 1692 and January 1693. Lived out his life in Andover and died there January 15, 1703.

FARNUM, JOHN
Born April 1, 1664, Andover, son of Ralph and Elizabeth Holt Farnum. Married there April 10, 1684, to Elizabeth Parker (daughter of Mary Ayer Parker who was to be hanged for witchcraft in 1692). John lived out his life in Andover and died there January 10, 1729.

FARNUM, RALPH, JR.
Born June 1, 1662, Andover, son of Ralph Farnum and Elizabeth Holt. Married there October 9, 1685, to Sarah Sterling. Ralph lived in Andover at least until April 13, 1732, when his wife Sarah died. Soon after her death, he moved to Rumford, New Hampshire, and died there January 3, 1738.

FARNUM, RALPH, SR.
Baptized August 4, 1633, Rochester, County Kent, England, son of Ralph and Alice Farnum. Accompanied his parents to Massachusetts Bay in 1635 on the ship *James*. The Farnums settled in Ipswich after their arrival. After the death of the elder Ralph, Alice remarried Solomon Martin and moved with him to Andover. The younger Ralph married October 26, 1657, in Andover to Elizabeth Holt. He died January 8, 1693, in Andover, the day after the acquittal of Abigail Wheeler Barker who had been accused of afflicting him.

FARNUM, SAMUEL
Born ca. 1665, Andover, son of Ralph Farnum and Elizabeth Holt. Married January 4, 1698, Andover, to Hannah Holt. Samuel lived out his life in Andover and died there December 20, 1754, aged about eighty-nine.

FOSTER, ANDREW
Born ca. 1640, son of Andrew and Ann Foster, original proprietors of Andover. Married June 7, 1662, in Andover, to Mary Russ. Andrew died shortly before June 14, 1697, Andover.

FOSTER, EPHRAIM
Born 1657, Ipswich, son of Abraham and Lydia Burbank Foster. Married ca. 1677 to Hannah Eames. Lived out his life in Andover and died there September 21, 1746.

FOSTER, HANNAH EAMES
Born December 18, 1661, Andover, daughter of Robert and Rebecca Blake Eames. Rebecca was convicted of witchcraft in 1692, but reprieved. Hannah married ca. 1677 to Ephraim Foster. Lived out her life in Andover and died there July 8, 1731.

FOSTER, ROSE
Born May 9, 1679, Andover, daughter of Ephraim and Hannah Eames Foster. Died February 25, 1693, aged only thirteen, less than a month after the reprieve of the last of the convicted witches by Governor Phips.

MARSHALL, MARY SWAIN
Born ca. 1645, Charlestown, daughter of Jeremiah and Mary Swain. Married ca. 1665 to Edward Marshall, who died August 3, 1692, in Reading. Lived in Reading at time of trials. Fate after trials unknown.

MARTIN, ABIGAIL
Born March 29, 1676, Andover, daughter of Samuel and Abigail Norton Martin. Married June 28, 1702, in Ipswich to John Safford and later moved with him to Lisbon, Connecticut. Died in Lisbon March 20, 1768, possibly the last of the accusers of 1692.

MARTIN, SAMUEL
Born April 16, 1645, Gloucester, son of Solomon and Mary Pindar Martin. Mary died in 1648 and Solomon remarried to Alice Farnum, widow of Ralph Farnum. Samuel Martin was thus a stepbrother of Ralph Farnum (born 1633). The family moved to Andover in 1652. Solomon eventually left the family and Samuel was placed under the guardianship of Nathan Parker in Andover. Samuel married March 30, 1676, to Abigail Norton. He filed complaints against suspects in late August 1692, but changed his mind and signed petitions supporting the accused. Died November 16, 1696, in Andover.

PHELPS, SARAH
Born October 10, 1682, Andover, daughter of Samuel and Sarah Chandler Phelps. Married February 6, 1720, in Andover to Samuel Field. Sarah was thirty-seven when married, unusually late for a first marriage for a woman. Nothing further known.

PRESTON, SAMUEL
Born ca. 1651, probably Ipswich, son of Roger and Martha Preston. Roger died in 1666 and Martha remarried the widower Nicholas Holt of Andover. Samuel married May 27, 1672, to Susanne Gutterson. Samuel lived in Andover until at least 1713 when he married his second wife, the widow Mary Blodgett. Date of death unknown.

SPRAGUE, MARTHA
Born ca. 1676, Malden, daughter of Phineas and Sarah Hasey Sprague. After

the death of her father in January 1691, her mother remarried the widower Moses Tyler of Boxford and moved there. Martha probably married first before the end of 1692 to stepbrother Joseph Tyler. He died in 1699. Married second June 5, 1701, in Andover to Richard Friend of Salem. He died in 1706. Married third November 22, 1714, in Andover to Isaac Mirick (or Merrick) and went to live in Newbury. She outlived Isaac also, dying as his widow in Newbury about 1736. Despite three marriages, she had no children.

STEVENS, EPHRAIM
Born ca. 1648, Andover, son of John and Elizabeth Stevens. Married October 11, 1680, Andover, to Sarah Abbot. Summoned to bear witness against Daniel Eames, but his testimony does not survive. He later switched sides and signed petitions on behalf of the accused. Lived out his life in Andover and died there June 26, 1718.

SWAIN, JEREMIAH
Born March 1, 1643, Boston, son of Jeremiah and Mary Swain. Married November 5, 1664, Reading, to Mary Smith who died in 1677. Jeremiah lived out his life in the part of Reading that became Wakefield. Died August 13, 1710 in Wakefield.

SWAN, JOHN
Born August 1, 1669, Haverhill, son of Robert and Elizabeth Acie Swan. Married August 1, 1699, in Haverhill to Susanna Wood, a widow. Moved to Stonington, Connecticut, and died there May 1, 1743.

SWAN, ROBERT
Born May 30, 1657, Haverhill, son of Robert and Elizabeth Acie Swan. Married there April 20, 1685, to Elizabeth Story. Was living in Andover in 1692. Eventually moved to Methuen where he died in 1747.

SWAN, TIMOTHY
Born March 12, 1663, Haverhill, son of Robert and Elizabeth Acie Swan. Named by Elizabeth Emerson as the father of her illegitimate daughter when she gave birth in Andover on April 10, 1686. Emerson also accused Swan of raping her. Swan moved with his brothers to Andover and fell ill in 1692, prompting numerous witchcraft accusations. Died February 2, 1693, in Andover, shortly after Governor Phips reprieved the last convicted suspects.

TOOTHAKER, ALLEN
Born September 17, 1670, Billerica, son of Roger and Mary Allen Toothaker

(both of whom were accused in 1692). He was the only member of the heavily persecuted Ingalls clan to act as an accuser (other than some of the suspects). He was living in Andover in 1692. Fate after trials unknown.

TYLER, JOSEPH

Born September 18, 1671, Rowley Village (later Boxford), son of Moses and Prudence Blake Tyler. Probably married late in 1692 to his stepsister Martha Sprague. There is no question that he had a wife named Martha, but the marriage was unrecorded. He became involved in trade with the West Indies along with a stepbrother (and possible brother-in-law) Phineas Sprague, Jr. Joseph died in 1699, possibly in the West Indies.

TYLER, MOSES

Born ca. 1642, probably Newport, Rhode Island. Married first July 6, 1666, in Andover, to Prudence Blake. He and Prudence remained near Andover, in what was then Rowley Village, while the rest of the Tyler family moved to the frontier community of Mendon (only to return during King Philip's War a decade later). Moses rose to prominence in Rowley Village (later Boxford) and served as a selectman in Boxford in 1691. Prudence died March 9, 1689. Moses remarried in early 1691 to Sarah Hasey Sprague, the widow of Phineas Sprague of Malden. Her children moved with her to Boxford, creating a blended family of twenty children. Sarah died in 1718 and Moses married third to a widow named Martha Fisk. Moses lived out his life in Boxford and Andover and died October 2, 1727. His death was recorded in Andover.

Appendix C

Other Significant Personages

Brief Biographical Sketches

BALLARD, JOHN
Born January 17, 1653, Andover, son of William and Grace (Lovejoy?) Ballard (original proprietors of Andover). Married November 16, 1681 to Rebecca Hooper (sister of Sarah Hooper Wardwell). Served as constable of South End during witchcraft trials. Lived out his life in Andover and died there December 18, 1715 in the same epidemic (confined to one household) that claimed the life of his wife and three youngest daughters.

BARNARD, THOMAS
Born 1657, Hartford, Connecticut, son of Francis and Hannah Merrill Barnard. Moved with his parents to Hadley as a small child and grew up there. Attended Harvard University in the late 1670s, where he was a classmate of Cotton Mather. Became Andover's junior minister in 1681 with the intent that he would eventually succeed Francis Dane, the town's established pastor. Married first December 14, 1686 to Elizabeth Price of Salem. Elizabeth died October 30, 1693 and Thomas married second April 28, 1696 to a widow named Abigail Bull. She died August 13, 1702. Thomas married third July 20, 1704 to the widow Lydia Goffe. He lived out his life in Andover, becoming the sole pastor when Francis Dane died in 1697. He had joined Dane in leading the opposition to the witchcraft trials in the fall of 1692. When Andover divided into two parishes in 1709, he remained with the North Parish, which was the oldest part of town. Thomas died October 13, 1718.

BRADSTREET, DUDLEY
Born ca. 1648, Andover, son of Simon and Anne Dudley Bradstreet (original

proprietors of Andover). Married November 12, 1673, Andover, to the widow Ann Wood Price. He served as Justice of the Peace as well as a selectman in 1692, conducted a few examinations, and signed arrest warrants until refusing to sign any more after the touch test of September 7. He and his wife were then complained of by the afflicted and they fled to the Piscataqua region of present-day New Hampshire for safety. Died November 13, 1702, Andover.

DANE, FRANCIS
Born 1615, probably Bishop's Stortford, Hertfordshire, England, son of John and Frances Dane. Came to Massachusetts Bay Colony in 1636. In 1648, he became the second minister of Andover and spent the rest of his life there. He married first to Elizabeth Ingalls, who was the mother of all his children. She died in 1676. He married second to a widow named Mary Thomas, who died in 1689. His third wife was his stepsister, the widow Hannah Chandler Abbot, whom he married in 1690. In 1692, Dane was a leading opponent of the witchcraft trials. He had also defended John Godfrey three decades earlier when Godfrey was accused of witchcraft in Andover. Francis died in Andover February 17, 1697.

DANE, HANNAH CHANDLER (ABBOT)
Born in England ca. 1629, daughter of William and Annis Chandler. Came to Massachusetts Bay with her parents in 1637. Her father died in 1641 and her mother remarried to John Dane, father of Francis Dane. Hannah married to George Abbot, an original proprietor of Andover, in 1647. George died late in 1681 and in 1690, she became the third wife of her stepbrother, Francis Dane. She and several of her children joined her husband in the growing opposition to the witchcraft trials in the fall of 1692, but one of her sons (Benjamin Abbot) had been an accuser of Martha Carrier. Hannah outlived Francis and died June 11, 1711 in Andover.

Appendix D

The Resisters and Their Families

Twenty-six Andover residents, all men, signed the petition of October 18, 1692, that attacked those who had accused people of witchcraft, describing them as "distempered." This same petition questioned the guilt of any of the suspects still in custody. On January 3, 1693, twelve of these same men joined forty-three other residents of both genders in affixing their signatures to another document defending the suspects. In total, sixty-nine townspeople signed at least one of these two petitions. The town had also produced two shorter defense documents, signed only by husbands and fathers of suspects. Three of the husbands who signed these two items did not join their neighbors in endorsing the larger petitions, perhaps feeling they had already taken enough of a risk. In any event, the total number of Andover residents who publicly defied the witch hunters can be set at seventy-two. The stalwart minister Francis Dane signed both of the larger documents and wrote a letter of his own in early January asserting the innocence of the suspects from his town. The pattern of extensive family connections, far stronger among the accused in Andover than in Salem Village or any other community ensnared in the tragedy of 1692, manifested itself just as clearly among those who rose to the defense of the suspects. Some of the families involved in the resistance had seen numerous relatives hauled away to jail on charges of dabbling in sorcery.

Because of the family orientation of the Andover resistance, the most logical approach to an examination of those who involved themselves is by kinship network. Some of the witch hunt opponents were associated with more than one such group and will be noted as part of each one. Not surprisingly, the most persecuted family also produced one of the largest groups of resisters.

THE EXTENDED INGALLS CLAN

This family descended from long-deceased immigrants Edmund and Ann Ingalls, early settlers of the town of Lynn. No fewer than fifteen of their direct descendants, along with two others who had married into the family, had found themselves charged with witchcraft in 1692. Martha Allen Carrier had already died at the end of a rope, and Roger Toothaker, the husband of her sister Mary, had died in jail on June 16. Another family member, Abigail Dane Faulkner, lived under a sentence of death which could be carried out as soon as her baby was born. Her father, Francis Dane, led the family's opposition to the trials, signing the petitions of October 18 and January 3, as well as writing his own letter criticizing the proceedings. His son Nathaniel, husband of the jailed Deliverance Haseltine Dane, also signed the petition of October 18 and the two shorter documents. Nathaniel did not sign the petition of January 3—undoubtedly because his wife was among the ones specifically named in that petition. Both of Francis Dane's other children who lived in Andover and were not in jail—Phebe Dane Robinson and Francis Dane, Jr.—endorsed the January petition along with their respective spouses, Joseph Robinson and Hannah Poor Dane. Robinson was also a half-brother of Francis Faulkner, the husband of the condemned Abigail. The minister's own third wife, Hannah Chandler (Abbot) Dane, likewise endorsed the January 3 document, meaning that a total of seven members of the Dane branch of the extended Ingalls clan penned their opposition to the witch hunt. The Allen branch of the family (the descendants of Faith Ingalls Allen) did not rise to the occasion as much—only Samuel Holt, the husband of Sarah Allen Holt (sister of the executed Martha Carrier), signed the petitions. Holt was one of only twelve to sign both of the more broadly encompassing petitions against the proceedings. In addition, a branch of the family not directly touched by the witch hunt joined the opposition to it. Sixty-five-year-old Henry Ingalls, a brother to the aged pastor's first wife Elizabeth and also to the late Faith Ingalls Allen, signed the petition of January 3 in support of his many jailed nieces and nephews. Three of his sons—Samuel, John, and Henry, Jr.—joined their father in defending their cousins as did Joseph Stevens (the husband of Henry, Sr.'s daughter Mary). The fact that Henry, Sr.'s immediate family had emerged unscathed from the summer's accusations appears nothing short of miraculous. In addition, the elder Henry's first wife Mary (the mother of all of his children, who had died in 1686) had been the sister of John Osgood, whose wife Mary's arrest inspired other resisters. Having seen so many family members jailed (and one, Martha Carrier, hanged), they unsurprisingly came to oppose the witch hunt. In all, twelve members of the extended Ingalls clan signed at least one petition defending the suspects—nearly matching the total of seventeen who had been accused.

Two other signers had less direct connections to the family. Joseph Marble, a resident of Andover since at least the early 1670s, had married Mary Faulkner in 1671. She was a sister of Francis Faulkner, the husband of the convicted Abigail Dane Faulkner. Joseph signed the petition of October 18. Another signer on that date, Stephen Barnard (not related to the minister Thomas Barnard), was the only son of original proprietor Robert Barnard to remain in Andover after his parents moved to Nantucket in 1667. He had married Rebecca Howe from Ipswich, a niece of Reverend Dane and thus a cousin of his accused daughters. She was also a sister-in-law of the executed Elizabeth Jackson Howe. Even though these last two signers lacked direct connections to the Ingalls clan, they did have ties to certain members of the family who had been jailed on sorcery charges.

Two of the family members most directly affected surprisingly did not endorse any of the petitions. Francis Faulkner, the husband of the condemned Abigail and father of her imprisoned daughters, did not sign. Neither did Thomas Carrier, the widower of the executed Martha, who had four children awaiting trial. Both men did take action to secure the release of some accused children before the petitions were signed. The absence of Faulkner's name from the petitions may be explained by his wife's own petition for a pardon in December. She noted in the document that her husband had suffered a relapse of his emotional collapse of five years earlier. The impairments he dealt with may have rendered him incapable of taking further action at that time. As for Thomas Carrier, his reputation in Andover was hardly sterling—those who circulated the petitions may not have approached him for a signature, thinking he might do the cause more harm than good. Carrier may have realized this himself. Despite that limited participation of these men who were husbands and fathers to suspects, the extended Ingalls clan showed exemplary courage in rallying behind their accused kin.

THE JOHN AND MARY OSGOOD FAMILY

The fact that John Osgood, the husband of Mary (arrested on the occasion of the touch test), his sons Timothy and Samuel, and his nephew Hooker Osgood all signed the petition of October 18 was previously noted. Hooker was the only repeat signer of January 3—obviously because Mary was among the suspects specifically named in that document and the others were her immediate family. These four men did not stand alone in their family in defending Mary and the others, though. Mary, the deceased wife of Henry Ingalls, Sr., had been John Osgood's sister—and therefore his three sons who signed the petition of January 3 were Osgood's nephews. The Ingalls brothers also had a brother-in-law who endorsed the document—Joseph Stevens, who had married their sister Mary. In addition, Daniel Poor, James Frye, and selectman John Aslebee (the husbands of John and Mary Osgood's daughters Mehitabel, Lydia, and Mary, respectively) added their names to the resisters who signed on in January.[2] Altogether twelve petition signers could be considered members of the John and Mary Osgood clan even though five of them (Henry Ingalls, Sr., his children, and his son-in-law) also counted themselves part of the Ingalls kinship network. The fact is, Henry Ingalls's children knew cousins on both sides of their family who awaited their fates on witchcraft charges. For them, to ignore the resistance to the witch hunt must have been unthinkable by the time the trials were set to resume. Their uncles had led the charge from the beginning, with John Osgood's name appearing first on both of the shorter petitions, and Francis Dane writing his own letter in addition to signing both of the larger documents. The two family groups had shown a sense of unity even before the formal opposition began, with Mary Clements Osgood vouching for the innocence of Francis Dane even as she incriminated herself after her arrest. The accusers had aimed too high in attacking this prominent woman, and the rise of the backlash against the witch hunt had demonstrated that. Her powerful relatives were not about to sit idly by while she went to the gallows.

CHRISTOPHER OSGOOD AND HIS CONNECTIONS

Christopher Osgood also signed the petition of October 18, as well as both shorter petitions. His relationship to John Osgood was not at all close, and he had his own reasons for signing—his oldest daughter Mary Osgood Marston had been arrested. Despite having the same surname, Christopher was not really a member of the John and Mary Osgood family and his connections to the witch hunt differ from theirs. His jailed daughter's husband John Marston joined him in signing the first of the short petitions, but another witch defender in Andover had two collateral connections with Christopher. This was Joseph Wilson, who signed both short petitions and the October 18 document on behalf of his wife, Sarah Lord Wilson, and his daughter, also named Sarah. Joseph was not a native of Andover, having been born in Boston in 1643 to William and Patience Wilson. His older brother Sherburn had married Abigail Osgood (an older sister of Christopher) in Andover in 1659. Joseph followed him there and in 1670, married Mary Lovejoy, a niece of his brother's wife (her parents were John Lovejoy and Mary Osgood, the latter being the eldest sister of Christopher and Abigail). Sherburn and Abigail eventually left Andover for Ipswich, but Joseph stayed around, even after the early death of his wife in 1677. His second wife, whom he married in 1678, was Sarah Lord. Sarah, like Joseph, was not a native of Andover, having been born in Ipswich in 1648 to Robert and Mary Lord. This marriage created another connection between Joseph Wilson and Christopher Osgood—Sarah Lord's sister Susannah had been married in 1674 to Christopher's brother, Thomas Osgood. Thomas, surprisingly, declined to involve himself, even though his niece (Christopher's daughter Mary Osgood Marston) and his wife's sister and niece (young Sarah Lord Wilson) all faced charges. When considering Christopher Osgood and his involvement in resisting the witch hunt (aside from the obvious fact of the accusation of his daughter), he had a closer connection to the Wilson women than to Mary Clements Osgood. In another sense, when considering prominent Andover families, Christopher (who had already served the town as a selectman and militia captain) might more properly be considered a member of the Barker family since his second wife Hannah Barker Osgood (who had died in 1687) had been a daughter of the original town proprietor Richard Barker. The Barkers had also seen family members persecuted in the witch hunt, and some of them had also engaged in the growing opposition.

The Barker/Stevens Network
The families of Barker and Stevens—both descendants of original proprietors of Andover—established a pattern of frequent intermarriage early in the town's history that portended marriages between cousins in later generations.[3] Richard Barker and his wife Joanne had obtained seven acres in the first land distribution in Andover, while John Stevens and his wife Elizabeth, who were more than a decade older, received eight. Joanne Barker and John Stevens were both dead by the time of the witch hunt of 1692, but Richard Barker and Elizabeth Stevens, aged seventy and seventy-nine, respectively, lived to see it—though they may have regretted that fact before the matter ended. The first marriages between the two families involved two of each couple's children. The Barkers' oldest son John, born in 1643, was married July 6, 1670 to Mary Stevens, aged about twenty-one. Mary's oldest brother, John Stevens, Jr., was married at that time to Hannah Barnard (daughter of

the original proprietor Robert, not the family of the Reverend Thomas Barnard). After Hannah died in 1675, the younger John Stevens remarried Esther Barker, a sister of John Barker. The elder Stevens had already been dead for several years by that time, having died at age fifty-seven in 1662. The second John Stevens did not live to see the witch hunt, either, dying in Casco Bay in modern-day Maine in 1689 while serving in the militia. His mother and several siblings remained alive in 1692, and some of them joined their Barker kindred in fighting the witch hunt.

Four members of the Barker clan had fallen under suspicion during the second phase of Andover's witch hunt. William Barker, Sr., aged forty-seven, the second son of Richard and Joanne, was named on a complaint filed on August 25 by Moses Tyler and Samuel Martin. The name of William's thirteen-year-old niece Mary Barker, a daughter of John Barker and Mary Stevens, appeared on the same complaint. Both of these suspects had confessed, apparently thinking it was their ticket to survival. William Barker's fourteen-year-old son William, Jr. had followed his family members to jail just a few days later, and then finally a third Barker brother, Ebenezer, had seen his wife Abigail Wheeler Barker arrested on the occasion of the touch test. No one bearing the Stevens name had been arrested, but this family could not have been unaffected considering their growing ties to the Barkers.

Ebenezer Barker signed both short petitions and the document of October 18. His oldest brother John, somewhat surprisingly, did not sign the latter although he did participate in bailing out some of the accused children in that month and signed the later petition on January 3. Two brothers-in-law of the Barkers also entered their names in defense of the suspects. Christopher Osgood, whose late second wife Hannah had been a sister of Ebenezer, John, and the accused William, signed the petition of October 18 in addition to the two short petitions. An additional signer of the January document, John Abbot (a selectman at the time), had in 1673 married another Barker sister, Sarah—coincidentally the "maid Barker" spoken of by Samuel Wardwell as having "slighted his love" twenty years earlier. As will be shown, John Abbot's own birth family played a major role, but his ties to the Barkers must also have influenced him.

Some members of the Barker family chose not to involve themselves in the resistance though. The aging Richard Barker himself did not sign, but he may not have been well—he was to die on March 18, 1693. None of the three youngest Barker sons—Richard, Jr., Stephen, and Benjamin, all under the age of forty—endorsed the documents, either, but some collateral relatives did.

Two other names appearing on the petition of October 18 were those of Joseph and Ephraim Stevens, brothers of Mary Stevens Barker, the mother of the accused child Mary Barker. Joseph, as has already been noted, had married into the heavily persecuted Ingalls family so he possessed a double dose of motivation to oppose the witch hunt. Ephraim Stevens had been quoted by Samuel Farnum on August 13 as a witness against suspect Daniel Eames of Boxford, but Ephraim did not testify against Eames himself. Ephraim signed again in January, joined this time by another brother, Benjamin Stevens, along with an Elizabeth Stevens whose identity is uncertain. Elizabeth may have been their widowed mother who, as the grandmother of suspect Mary Barker, had unquestioned reasons to support the resistance movement. This Elizabeth Stevens may also have been Elizabeth Abbot Stevens, the young wife of their nephew Nathan Stevens (son of their deceased oldest brother John). The younger Elizabeth was also a sister of selectman John Abbot. Altogether, eight members of the increasingly connected Barker/Stevens clan endorsed the resistance to the witch hunt of 1692. The Barkers had seen several relatives arrested. Of those, only the youthful Mary Barker had any genetic connection to the Stevens clan but that, along with additional marital ties to others involved in the opposition to the accusations, served as reason enough for some in the family to enlist in the fight. Another possible motivation can never be ruled out: some of them, possibly inspired in part by sermons of their resistance-leading ministers, may have simply come to believe standing up for their accused neighbors was the right thing to do. They would not have been alone in that regard. As with the Barkers, some of the Stevenses also ignored the issue at least in the public forum. Some families, with ties to accused and accusers, were even more divided.

The Hooper/Ballard/Marshall/Russell Network

Sarah Hooper (Hawkes) Wardwell lost her husband Samuel to the witchcraft persecution on September 22, 1692. She and her two oldest daughters, Sarah Hawkes and Mercy Wardwell, still awaited trial. All had acknowledged guilt, undoubtedly believing that their lives would be spared if they did, but they now knew that the previous court had sentenced five other confessors to death. By the same token, Samuel Wardwell had gone to his execution only after retracting his confession. This bereaved widow and her two daughters must have been as confused about their possible fates as any of the suspects remaining in jail.

Though not a native of Andover, Sarah Wardwell had an extensive kin network in town by 1692. As noted previously, her younger sisters Rebecca and Hannah had followed her to Andover from their previous home in Reading a decade after her own marriage and married the Ballard brothers, John and William, respectively. By 1692, Sarah's two youngest brothers, Thomas and John Hooper (aged twenty-four and twenty-two, respectively), had taken up residence in town. Both were still bachelors and may have resided together in the town's South End. The Hoopers also had cousins in Andover. The will of their father, William Hooper (who died December 5, 1678 in Reading), mentioned a "brother" named Thomas Marshall. Marshall, slightly older than Hooper, had been born in 1613 and may have come to the New World in his company; their exact relationship has never been determined. William's wife Elizabeth may have been a sister of Thomas, Thomas's wife Joanna may have been a sister of William, or Elizabeth and Joanna may have been sisters. Any of those connections would have prompted William Hooper to refer to Thomas Marshall as a "brother" in that era. Regardless of what the connection was, Thomas Marshall had a daughter named Mary residing in Andover in 1692, aged fifty. She and her husband Robert Russell lived in the town's South End.

Considering the situation of Sarah Wardwell and her daughters, an obvious expectation would have been that her relatives there would have lined up to defend the accused. There were, however, reasons that this family group was not entirely united on this matter. The Ballard husbands of Rebecca and Hannah Hooper were brothers of Joseph Ballard, whose wife had died after allegedly suffering at the hands of witches the previous summer. Rebecca's husband, John Ballard, had put the idea of witchcraft in Joseph's head after a conversation with Samuel Wardwell. As South End constable, John had also arrested numerous suspects. Events in the Hoopers' original hometown of Reading had raised suspicion of witchcraft there as well. Another Hooper brother, William Hooper, Jr., had died in Reading on August 8, 1692, aged only thirty-three. Likewise, Edward Marshall, a brother of Mary Marshall Russell, died five days before his cousin William. On September 5 Edward's widow, Mary Swain Marshall, accused three Reading women, Jane Lilly, Mary Coulson, and Mary (sometimes written as Hannah) Taylor, of bewitching her and of causing the deaths of her husband and William Hooper by witchcraft. Samuel Wardwell himself had accused Lilly and Taylor during his own confession four days earlier.

This kinship group had a complex association with the witch hunt exceeded only by that of the descendants of Job and Mary Tyler. Not surprisingly, some supported the suspects and others did not. No one from this family signed the petition of October 18 or either of the short petitions.

Some of them did endorse the document circulated in early January. William Ballard, the only Ballard brother who had not played a role in the witch hunt, signed on behalf of his wife Hannah's sister and nieces. Somewhat surprisingly, Hannah did not join him, but the two of them may have felt William's signature was sufficient. Neither John nor Rebecca Hooper Ballard signed, despite the fact that the oldest Wardwell son, Samuel, Jr., had been placed in their care. Joseph Ballard, the only Ballard brother not married to a Hooper, also ignored the petition. He and John, having played such a major role in touching off the town's witch hunt, may have been among those who still felt that it was justified. Joseph had, after all, lost his wife—although he had not spent much time mourning, having remarried the twice-widowed Rebecca Rea (Stevens) Orne on November 15. Rebecca Hooper Ballard, regardless of her personal feelings, would have been unlikely to defy her husband on the matter.[4]

There was, however, a younger member of the Ballard family who did defend the accused. Oliver Holt, aged only twenty-one, was a nephew of the three Ballard brothers. His mother was their sister, Sarah Ballard Holt. It is not clear which family connection influenced him. He was not genetically related to the Hooper family that his uncles had married into. His father Henry Holt was a brother to Samuel Holt and James Holt who had married the Allen sisters. Samuel had signed the petition of January 3 also (James had died of smallpox in 1690). Neither of young Oliver Holt's parents signed any petitions, so it may be that he was simply an idealistic young man who felt compelled to defend the suspects. A surprising number of them, after all, were his contemporaries. Some of the Hooper relatives of Sarah Wardwell in Andover also supported the suspects. Her two young brothers—Thomas and John—endorsed the petition, a hint that they did not take seriously the allegation that witchcraft had caused the death of their brother William five months earlier in Reading. Finally, the Hoopers' cousin Mary Marshall Russell, her husband Robert, and their twenty-five-year-old bachelor son James defended the suspects, including their Wardwell and Hawkes relatives. This suggests that they doubted the role of witchcraft in the death of Mary's brother Edward Marshall the previous August—despite the protests of Edward's widow to the contrary. Family groups did not necessarily unify in their reactions to a series of tragedies. Joseph Ballard apparently had no problem believing that witchcraft had sickened and then killed his wife once the idea had been put in his mind. Six months later, he apparently still clung to that idea. His brother John, who suggested it to him, must not have let go of it either, and his wife Rebecca, even though her sister and two nieces languished in jail, probably would not have disagreed with him publicly. It is also possible that she genuinely believed the charges herself—after all, William Hooper had been her brother and her since-executed brother-in-law Samuel Wardwell had attributed William's death to witchcraft in court. But the younger Hoopers, William Ballard, and the Russell family defied their kin and defended the suspects. Other families faced similar divisions.

The Tyler Family

The long and troubled history of the descendants of Job and Mary Tyler played itself out again in Andover as it had so often over the previous three decades. This complex blended kin network became heavily involved in the witch hunt as accused and accusers, as has already been shown. Divided during the time of the arrests, this family unsurprisingly did not come together to join the resistance later in the year. The two adult males in the family most directly touched by the arrests did take action. Others in the family kept their distance. Hopestill Tyler and John Bridges, the men in the family whose respective wives (Mary Lovett Tyler and Mary Tyler Post Bridges) remained confined, signed both of the shorter petitions. Hopestill took it a step further, endorsing the petition of October 18 that denounced the accusers as "distempered." In doing so, he maligned his brother Moses's stepdaughter Martha Sprague, who had taken on the leading role among the afflicted girls in the town (even though she actually lived in neighboring Boxford). This was risky—Martha had showed no hesitation in attacking her stepfather's family whether Moses himself approved of it or not (which is unlikely). As a resident of Boxford, Moses Tyler did not have the opportunity to sign any of the petitions that circulated among those living in Andover, so his sentiments on the matter by that time are not discernible. John Bridges actually had a mixed record during the witch hunt. On September 14, he had testified against Samuel Wardwell, elaborating on the accused wizard's success as a fortune teller. He had also previously urged Hopestill's wife Mary to confess after the touch test, but it is possible that his reason for that was that he believed, like others in Andover, that admitting guilt would save his sister-in-law's life. By October he realized, as other Andover residents did, that admitting guilt did not guarantee mercy by the court. He signed the short petitions not only on behalf of his wife, but also for his daughter and stepdaughters.

Only one other Tyler household claimed residence in Andover in 1692—that of John and Hannah Parker Tyler. John, the third son of Job and Mary, was more than a decade younger than his oldest brother Moses and about eight years younger than Hopestill. John and his wife had arguably been touched by the witch hunt more than any other members of the Tyler family—Hannah's mother, Mary Ayer Parker, had already been hanged, and her younger sister Sarah had been arrested. This was in addition to the sister, sister-in-law, and numerous nieces of John who were accused. Despite all of these connections, John Tyler did not sign on to the defense of the suspects. On January 3, Hannah did not sign, either, even though the petition presented that day included women as signers. For John and Hannah, discretion may have been the better part of valor. They had four children ranging in age from eight months to nine years by that time, and both of them could easily have fallen under suspicion. John may not have entirely trusted his brother Moses in any event, even though there is no evidence that Moses ever filed a complaint against any of his own family. John had married into the very family that Moses stole Hopestill's indenture from in 1662. Some lingering hostility may have remained, and even if Moses himself never would have acted on it, his son Joseph (enthralled by his bewitched stepsister) might have. John Tyler did not want to follow the path of his other brother Hopestill and possibly see his own wife arrested. For John and Hannah, it made sense to play it safe.

The Peters/Wright/Sadie Network

Thirteen-year-old John Sadie, one of many youthful suspects from Andover, was probably among those taken into custody the day of the touch test. He may also have acted the part of a witch "victim" at one point, since Mary Osgood admitted to afflicting him in her confession of September 8. Unlike most of the other accused children, he was the only one in his family to fall under suspicion. This did not stop them from turning out in large numbers to support him and the other suspects. His mother was Elizabeth Peters, born in 1662 in Ipswich to Andrew and Mercy Peters. She married at the unusually early age of sixteen, and John (named for his father) was born the next year. Another son, Samuel Sadie, followed in 1681. The elder John Sadie soon died, and the young widow Elizabeth accompanied her parents and siblings to Andover where in 1684 she remarried a widower named Walter Wright.[5] By 1692, the Wrights had two daughters of their own, but the intervening years had seen a series of tragedies in Elizabeth's birth family.

If any couple might have felt they had reason to believe themselves under supernatural assault in 1692, it was Andrew and Mercy Peters, who were in their mid-fifties. On August 14, 1689, their two oldest sons (John and Andrew, aged twenty-nine and twenty-five, respectively) were ambushed and killed by a war party of Native Americans who were on their way to raid neighboring Haverhill. These men both left widows and small children behind. Then, in December 1690, their twenty-year-old daughter Mercy and husband John Allen, having previously lost two infant sons, died in the smallpox epidemic. They left behind a three-month-old daughter named Hannah. Despite these losses, Andrew and his wife Mercy did not accuse anyone of witchcraft in 1692. Andrew (a distiller), though a comparatively recent arrival in the town, was growing in influence (he was named a selectman for the first time in March 1693). Had he or his wife chosen to accuse anyone of sorcery, the charge would have stuck. But they went about their business until their young grandson John Sadie suddenly found himself accused. As previously noted, the witch hunters showed an incredible capacity for attacking families who were already suffering for one reason or another (like the Foster/Lacey women).

The family wasted no time in coming to the teenage boy's aid. His stepfather Walter Wright, supported by Francis Faulkner, bailed him out in early October. Wright also affixed his signature to the petition that denounced the accusers as "distempered" while declaring the likely innocence of the suspects on October 18. Young Sadie's grandfather, Andrew Peters, also endorsed it. The two of them unhesitatingly signed the January petition as well, joined this time by some women in the family. Elizabeth Peters (Sadie) Wright, young John's mother, signed along with Mary Edwards Peters, the widow of the slain John Peters. The husband of a Peters daughter (Thomas Chandler, Jr. who had married Mary Peters) signed on as a defender of the suspects. Finally, the two youngest Peters sons (William and Samuel), both less than a decade older than their accused nephew, endorsed the January document defending the suspects. Samuel, aged seventeen at the time, was the youngest person known to have signed any of the documents from Andover that supported those jailed for witchcraft. The family's stance may have contributed to the choice of Andrew Peters as a selectman in March 1693. By that time the discrediting of the witch hunt was well under way.

THE JOHNSONS—RELATED TO SUSPECTS BY MARRIAGE

The Johnson family of Andover had the misfortune to be related by marriage to two accused witches, although some of their own also fell victim to accusation during the summer of 1692. The progenitors, John and Susan Johnson, were not among the earliest settlers in Andover, but they had arrived there about 1659, nearly a quarter of a century after having arrived in

Massachusetts Bay on the ship *James* in 1635. Their two oldest children, Elizabeth and Thomas, had been born in England. Seven more were born in the years after their arrival. Though John and Susan lived to be quite elderly (Susan died in 1683 in Andover and John outlived her, dying by 1688), some of their children were not so lucky. Their daughter Susannah, first wife of the aforementioned Walter Wright, died just months before her husband's second marriage to the widowed Elizabeth Peters Sadie in 1684. Son Stephen, born about 1640, who married Francis Dane's daughter Elizabeth, died November 30, 1690 (during the smallpox epidemic). Stephen and Elizabeth had lost several children in infancy, but at least four survived their father. Stephen's brother Timothy, who had married Rebecca Aslebee in 1674, died March 15, 1688 in Andover, aged about forty-four, leaving his widow with eight children ranging in age from four months to thirteen years. The town's selectmen, knowing the widow needed income, gave her the responsibility of cleaning the meetinghouse. But in 1692, both of these widows found themselves jailed on witchcraft charges. Three of Elizabeth Dane Johnson's children went to jail with her, as did Rebecca Aslebee Johnson's oldest daughter, also named Rebecca. The attacks on this family did not stop with those living in Andover. A daughter of John and Susan Johnson, Mary Johnson (Davis) Clark, residing in Haverhill, was jailed in early August, even before her mentally challenged niece, young Elizabeth Johnson. Unlike her Andover relatives, Mary did not confess.

With so many of their kin jailed, the Johnsons could hardly sit idly by. Francis Johnson, aged about twenty-five, the eldest son of the deceased Stephen Johnson, bailed out his two young siblings Stephen and Abigail and his even younger cousin Sarah Carrier on October 6. He was joined in this action by Walter Wright, the husband of his late aunt Susannah, and Thomas Carrier. Wright also bailed out his stepson John Sadie, and although he had remarried after Susannah's death, he had not turned his back on her family. As noted previously, Wright signed the petition of October 18. He was joined in this by the oldest Johnson son, Thomas Johnson, who was nearing the age of sixty by that time. Thomas undoubtedly felt some degree of responsibility for the widows of his brothers and for their jailed children. He was also concerned about his sister Mary from Haverhill. Mary's oldest son, Ephraim Davis, Jr., endorsed the petition on behalf of his mother and his other imprisoned relatives. Wright and Thomas Johnson signed again in January, and this time his wife Mary Holt Johnson (a sister of the Holts who married the Allen sisters) and their second son Thomas Johnson, Jr. (a twenty-two-year-old bachelor) endorsed along with them.

A notable non-signer was Thomas and Mary's eldest son John Johnson, aged twenty-five. Three years earlier, John had married Eleanor Ballard, a daughter of Joseph and Elizabeth Phelps Ballard. Having recently seen his mother-in-law die of alleged witchcraft, young John may not have cared to offend his wife and father-in-law. Thomas Johnson, Sr. also had another surviving brother—the youngest, William Johnson, about thirty-nine at the time. He had married Sarah Lovejoy, a daughter of original Andover proprietor John Lovejoy who had died in 1690. As noted earlier, it is highly probable that the Ballard brothers' still-living mother Grace Ballard was a sister of John Lovejoy. Those Johnsons who had married into the family of the man who first brought the afflicted girls of Salem to Andover probably felt they had to tread lightly.

The Ayer/Parker/Aslebee Connection

John Ayer, apparently a widower, left England with seven children in the late 1630s. It is also possible that his wife, whose name is unknown, died on the voyage or soon after arrival. The Ayers first settled in the town of Salisbury where John married a second wife whose name was Hannah. By 1645, they had relocated to the newly formed town of Haverhill. Two of John's daughters married original proprietors of Andover. In 1648 Rebecca married John Aslebee. The ill-fated Mary married Nathan Parker. By the time the resistance to the witch hunt began organizing in Andover, Mary had already been hanged. She was not, however, the only member of the family to have been accused. Her daughter Sarah had been arrested at about the same time she had. Two of Rebecca Ayer Aslebee's daughters, Rebecca Aslebee Johnson of Andover and Sarah Aslebee Cole, also languished in jail, along with a seventeen-year-old granddaughter Rebecca Johnson (the third consecutive Rebecca in the lineage). As was the case with other families, some members of this clan came to the aid of their arrested relatives— though the numbers were limited in this instance. John Aslebee, Jr. who was serving the town that year as a selectman, signed the petitions of October 18 and January 3, undoubtedly out of concern for his sisters and his niece in addition to his mother-in-law Mary Clements Osgood. The only Parker who signed was Stephen Parker, who was not one of the sons of the executed Mary Ayer Parker. He was a son of Joseph Parker, a brother of Mary's husband Nathan Parker. Joseph's wife also happened to be named Mary, which caused some confusion even during the examinations. Mary Ayer Parker stated when she was examined that there was another of her name in Andover. Six weeks after her death, her own sons John (who was almost forty) and Joseph Parker (aged only twenty-three, probably named for his uncle Joseph) petitioned the governor for restitution, claiming Sheriff George Corwin had seized property that was actually theirs.[6] These brothers and their other siblings might have been too preoccupied with reclaiming their estate to concern themselves with the fates of the other accused witches. Their mother was already dead. Their sister Sarah may or may not have been in jail.

The Parkers had other concerns related to the witch hunt. Nathan Parker, late husband of the executed Mary, had been at the center of the Tyler family's dispute with Thomas Chandler over Hopestill Tyler's apprenticeship thirty years earlier. Feelings between the two families may have still been uneasy, and this would only have worsened with Martha Sprague's role in the conviction of Mary in September. Martha, probably married to her step-brother Joseph Tyler by that time, stood ready to testify in the newly con-stituted court. It is, as noted previously, doubtful that she acted as a mere puppet of her stepfather Moses Tyler, but the Parkers could not have known that. Their own safety had to be their top priority. It is true that ten years earlier Hannah Parker, a daughter of Nathan and Mary, had married John Tyler, Moses's brother. But despite the persecutions of their own relatives neither John nor Hannah Parker Tyler signed any petitions. They may have simply regarded it as too risky with so many Tylers already jailed.

THE FRYE FAMILY

John Frye, Sr., aged ninety-one in 1692, was the oldest living original pro-prietor of Andover. His daughter in-law, Eunice Potter Frye stood accused of sorcery. Eunice's husband, John Frye, Jr., signed both of the so-called short petitions. His brother James (also a son-in-law of the accused Mary Clements Osgood) signed the petitions of October 18 and January 3, and their ancient father signed the later one. Oddly, their other two brothers (Samuel and Benjamin) did not join this fight on their sister-in-law's behalf. Samuel Frye's inaction on the petitions is particularly surprising since his wife Mary Aslebee Frye was a sister of the two accused Aslebee sisters—Re-becca Aslebee Johnson and Sarah Aslebee Cole. In fact, Samuel stands out as the only 1692 selectman in Andover not to have signed petitions on be-half of his accused neighbors. This is another example of the fact that fam-ilies were not necessarily united about the witch hunt by the end of 1692 in Andover—though there could have been other reasons for not signing petitions such as fear of being accused. James Frye, as an in-law of the res-olute Osgoods, would have been hard-pressed to ignore the issue. Although it was not a fully unified effort, Eunice Potter Frye did have the support of some of her husband's prominent family.

Not everyone who supported the resistance enjoyed the public support of other family members. Some—particularly those related to suspects—may have had the private encouragement of the closest kin. Those who, from all appearances, acted alone in defending the suspects bear mentioning as well. If anything, they showed more courage than those who acted in concert with other relatives. There was, after all, a risk associated with supporting the accused and some families may have simply decided that only one or two people should take that risk. Other solo actors simply lacked extensive family connections in Andover—from all indications, only residents could sign the petitions generated within the town.

Two Individual Witch Defenders
When looking only at records associated with Andover witchcraft suspects, John Preston seems an unlikely candidate to defend them. His brother Samuel had testified against Martha Carrier that previous summer. These brothers, in their forties at the time of the trials, had actually spent their childhood in Ipswich and then later, Salem Village. After their father, Roger Preston, died in 1666, their widowed mother Martha married Nicholas Holt, the wealthiest original Andover proprietor to settle in the town's South End. This was the beginning of their ties to Andover. John Preston himself married Sarah Gerry Holt in 1687, widow of Nicholas's son John Holt. On January 3, 1693, despite Samuel's testimony against Carrier, John Preston signed the petition defending the accused witches. A look at his family connections outside Andover suggests a motive. His brother Thomas, who still resided in Salem Village, had been married for twenty-three years by 1692 to young Rebecca Nurse, a daughter of the executed Rebecca Nurse. Thomas Preston himself had been one of those who filed the first complaint against the original three suspects of Salem Village in early 1692—Sarah Good, Sarah Osborne, and Tituba. He had obviously never expected the witch hunt to grow to the proportions it did, and it is unlikely his brothers in Andover did either. This family's limited record on the witch hunt was decidedly mixed, but John's decision to defend the suspects may have been partly a result of the execution of Thomas's mother-in-law—a woman who had been considered a virtual Puritan saint.

Another defender of the accused with barely any connections to them was Samuel Blanchard. He was not a young man in 1692; nonetheless, he had arrived in Andover's South End only about a decade earlier. Born in England about 1626, he and several siblings had come to Massachusetts Bay on the ship *Jonathan* in 1639 with their parents, Thomas and Agnes. Samuel had lived most of his life in Charlestown, Massachusetts, but relocated to Andover in the early 1680s. His reason for choosing Andover as a new home is not readily apparent. He had married twice and neither wife had ties to Andover. His second son, Jonathan Blanchard, married Anne Lovejoy, a daughter of original town proprietor John Lovejoy, soon after their arrival in town. Neither he nor any members of his family was touched by the witchcraft accusations in 1692. Nonetheless, he signed the petition of January 3, 1693. Of all of the signers, none had any less obvious concern with the matter than Blanchard. The only conclusion to be drawn from the fact that he chose to endorse the petition is that he must have considered it the right thing to do. He undoubtedly heard the ministers preach in the meetinghouse, and the fact that both defended the accused suggests strongly that they also spoke in opposition to the actions of the witch hunters. In any case Blanchard took a stand—one that may have helped propel him to being named as a town selectman early in 1694. Worthy of note is the fact that his son Jonathan did not join his father in defending the suspects. Jonathan Blanchard had married into the Lovejoy family, and his wife Anne was probably a cousin to the Ballard brothers who had been so instrumental in bringing the witch scare to Andover in the first place.

Appendix E

Defenders Who Acted to Make Amends

Many of the defenders of the witchcraft suspects in Andover had a family connection to one or more of the accused. Other defenders had different reasons to publicly stand up for neighbors accused of pacts with the devil. Some of them had initially participated in the accusations in some way or had close family members who did so. Others had reason to believe that they had neglected their obligations to the community in some way and had thus helped the witch hunt to spiral out of control in Andover and the surrounding area. For them, defending their neighbors was an act of atonement.

Thomas and Elizabeth Price Barnard

Ministers carried influence, and with that influence came responsibility. In all fairness, Thomas Barnard had little reason for guilt (other than possibly ignoring actions of some in his congregation), and his wife Elizabeth had none at all. Previous writers have exaggerated Thomas Barnard's role in promoting the witch hunt in Andover, accusing him of arranging the touch test as well as participating in it. He did lead a prayer at the beginning of the event and on other days, he listened to confessions of suspects. Those actions were nothing extraordinary on his part though—they simply constituted basic responsibilities of a pastor in a time such as 1692. With Francis Dane disavowing the accusations, Barnard may have sensed an opportunity to establish himself once and for all as Andover's primary spiritual leader, but he did not hesitate to stand up for the accused parishioners once the flaws in the process became obvious. He would have been out of step with the era if he did not believe in witchcraft at all, but clear evidence exists that he did not unconditionally accept the validity of spectral evidence—as Samuel Parris, Nicholas Noyes, and John Hale did. Barnard's signature appears only after that of Francis Dane on the document of October 18, and he defended his flock once again on January 3, along with the older clergyman. As was the case with Dane, Barnard's wife Elizabeth signed along with her husband. Taking this stance did carry certain risks—a minister had been among the ones hanged in the summer. Unlike Francis Dane, the Barnards had no close relatives in the jail in Salem, so they lacked Dane's personal stake in the affair. They simply took what was, in their minds, the ethical path. Barnard remained in Andover for the remaining quarter of a century of his life after the trials of 1692 and died as a highly regarded figure in town.

Dudley and Ann Wood Bradstreet

By early 1693, Dudley Bradstreet must have borne a heavy load of guilt about the witch hunt in Andover. As justice of the peace, he filled out numerous arrest warrants and conducted at least three preliminary examinations throughout the months of July and August. On the day of the infamous touch test (which he, as a town selectman, undoubtedly helped to organize) he filled out the warrants for those accused by the afflicted. Having grown skeptical of the whole process, he refused to sign any more such warrants after the test. The horror struck home when this refusal prompted the accusers to cry out on him and his wife Ann. The two of them, knowing the fate that had befallen the others regardless of rank, promptly fled town. After a few months in isolation, apparently in the Piscataqua area of modern-day New Hampshire, the couple felt compelled to return home and join the resistance.

Dudley Bradstreet, aged about forty-four in 1692, had resided in Andover all of his life. His father, Simon Bradstreet, had received twenty acres in the original land allotment in town, a total equaled only by the long-dead John Osgood, Sr., the father of the John Osgood whose wife Mary had been arrested as a result of the touch test. By 1692, Dudley Bradstreet had served numerous terms as an Andover selectman beginning when he was in his early twenties and had also taken on the role of town clerk at times. As one of Andover's most influential citizens, he felt a great deal of responsibility to the town and took on the job of examining a few witchcraft suspects before they were carted off to Salem to be jailed. In some cases, he became the first to hear the confessions. There is no reason to doubt that in the early stages of the town's witch hunt, Bradstreet believed in what he was doing.

The eventual arrests of some of Andover's more prominent citizens must have given him pause—he would have been every bit as class conscious as anyone else of the era. Once he balked at issuing any more warrants and found himself and his wife accused, he fled for safety along with her. If the likes of Mary Clements Osgood could be arrested, so could the Bradstreets. It may also be that by the time someone voiced suspicions of Dudley and Ann Bradstreet, the trials of certain confessors had already begun. Mary Osgood had acknowledged guilt before any confessors had been tried. The Bradstreets had the benefit of knowing confessions would not save them while they were still free. They made the most of it and escaped the area. They did not, however, stay away.

Dudley Bradstreet's signature appears first on the document supporting the accused on January 3, 1693—ahead of the ministers. It is possible that he even partially wrote it. With influence comes responsibility, and though he had fled his lifelong home for a time, he rose to shoulder that obligation upon returning to the town. His wife Ann signed along with him. Having initially played in important role in enabling the witch hunt, Dudley Bradstreet now stood up for some of the very people he arrested and his wife Ann also lived up to the responsibility of the family's position of power in the town.

The Chandler/Abbot Connection

The families of two original Andover proprietors—Thomas Chandler and George Abbot—established a marital alliance similar to that of the Barker and Stevens clans. Neither of these men started with as much land as Richard Barker or John Stevens in the original allotment—Chandler got five acres and Abbot four. Nonetheless, both families established themselves as prominent residents in the town well in advance of 1692. In the case of Chandler, his influence helped him keep the upper hand throughout his years of disputes with Job Tyler. Thomas, born about 1627 to immigrants William and Annis Chandler, arrived in the Massachusetts Bay colony with them in 1637 when they settled in Roxbury. Among his younger siblings were Hannah and William Chandler, who also spent their adult lives in Andover. The elder William Chandler died in Roxbury in early 1642, and the next year, Annis married John Dane, the father of Andover's future minister Francis Dane. The three Chandlers were thus, as previously noted, stepsiblings to their town's longtime pastor. The younger William Chandler's first wife had been Mary Dane, the daughter of Francis's elder brother John Dane, who had lived in Ipswich. Hannah Chandler married George Abbot around the time of the founding of Andover, the first connection between the Chandler and Abbot families. She remained a widow for eight years after George's death in early 1682 before marrying her twice-widowed stepbrother Francis Dane.

Despite their extensive marital ties to the Danes, some of the Chandlers, at least initially, played a role in the witchcraft persecution. Thomas Chandler himself deposed against Samuel Wardwell, saying, "I have often hard Samuel Wardle of Andovr till yung person thire fortine and he was much addicted to that and mayd sport of it and farther saith not."[7] Thomas's daughter Hannah Chandler Bixby also claimed affliction, but the most active member of the family in complaining of abuse by witches was Sarah Phelps (Thomas's granddaughter by his daughter Sarah Chandler Phelps). It is noteworthy that the younger Sarah Phelps was also a niece of Elizabeth Phelps Ballard, whose illness had prompted her husband to invite the witch finders to Andover in the first place. Among those complained of by Bixby and Phelps were some of Francis Dane's own family, particularly Abigail Dane Faulkner and young Elizabeth Johnson. Some of William Chandler's family also joined the act. His first wife Mary Dane had died in 1679, and he had remarried the widow Bridget Henchman Richardson later that same year. His first child by Bridget was Phebe Chandler, who was twelve years old by the time of the witch hunt. Phebe and her mother both joined the chorus of those accusing Martha Carrier that summer. Even Hannah's family got involved, despite the fact she had been married to Francis Dane for two years by that time. Her son Benjamin Abbot blamed Martha Carrier's alleged sorcery for an affliction he suffered, and his wife Sarah Farnum Abbot backed up his allegation.

By October, at least some of the prolific Chandler/Abbot family had changed their minds about the witch hunt. The Chandler brothers, Thomas and William, both signed the petition of October 18, denouncing the accusers as "distempered persons" even though they maligned some of the own female family members by doing so. Thomas's son, Thomas Chandler, Jr. joined his father and uncle in endorsing the document, and one of his Abbot cousins—William Abbot—affixed his name to it too. It is also noteworthy that one of the signers from the Stevens family—Ephraim Stevens, an uncle of the accused Mary Barker—was married to William Abbot's sister Sarah. As relatives by marriage of the venerable Francis Dane, this clan's change of heart comes as no surprise. Some of them may have agreed with the minister all along and not had the courage to say so before. The elder Thomas Chandler came to oppose the witch hunt even though no fewer than ten of the accused were related to his old adversary, Job Tyler. His brother William agreed with him. By early January, more of the family grew emboldened enough to state their opposition publicly. Hannah Chandler (Abbot) Dane took advantage of the fact that women were offered the opportunity to sign the petition of January 3, 1693, joining her husband and brothers in taking that action. Her son William signed again, but this time two more Abbot sons—John and George, Jr.—inscribed their names to the defense of the remaining witchcraft suspects.[8] Tellingly, their brother Benjamin did not join them. Aside from his testimony against Martha Carrier, he may have still believed in the guilt of some of the other suspects. Some members of his wife's family, the Farnums, had deposed against others of the accused, and no one named Farnum signed any petitions defending suspects. Perhaps Benjamin identified more with his wife's relatives than his birth family by that time. His inaction raises doubt that everyone in this extended family had come to question the witch hunt.

Others in the Chandler/Abbot family stood with the resisters. Bridget Henchman (Richardson) Chandler, despite having earlier corroborated her daughter Phebe's claim of affliction by Martha Carrier that summer, backed her husband William in defending the remaining suspects. Bridget, unlike Benjamin Abbot, may not have believed that anyone other than Martha Carrier was guilty. Bridget's stepson, William Chandler, Jr. (whose late mother Mary had been Francis Dane's niece), joined his kin network in affirming the petition, as did John Chandler, another of the elder Thomas Chandler's sons. John served the town of Andover as a selectman during that fateful year. Thomas's wife, Hannah Brewer Chandler, may or may not have signed. There was a signer named Hannah Chandler, but that was also the given name of son John's wife. As with the Abbots, not all of Thomas Chandler's children took up the cause. Not surprisingly, Hannah Chandler Bixby and her husband Daniel did not defend the suspects. Neither did Sarah Phelps's parents, Sarah Chandler Phelps and her husband Samuel. Thomas also had a son named William who did not sign—again, other connections of his may have played a role in that. This William Chandler's wife Eleanor was also a Phelps—another sibling of the "bewitched to death" Elizabeth Phelps Ballard.

Despite this lack of unity, the extended Chandler/Abbot clan contributed ten signers of petitions defending the accused residents of Andover—eleven if one counts Francis Dane as a member of this family group and twelve if the Abbots' brother-in-law Ephraim Stevens (husband of their sister Sarah) is included. This was a complete about-face for this prominent Andover clan, four of whose members (Hannah Chandler Bixby, Sarah Phelps, Phebe Chandler, and Benjamin Abbot) had acted the part of witch "victims" in previous months with the support of two others (Thomas Chandler and his sister-in-law Bridget) who were now defending their accused neighbors. Though the family lacked complete cohesion on the subject of the trials by the time they resumed, they had contributed enough to lend a powerful voice to the opposition. The actions of those who did defend the accused speak volumes since they had no close family ties to any of them. The defenders did have each other and they also had the strength of the family's longstanding influence in Andover. There was another defender who had no such network.

Samuel Martin

The most surprising name found on the petition of October 18 is that of Samuel Martin. He had joined Moses Tyler in filing against at least five suspects at the end of August. He probably signed on to at least some of the other complaints that have not survived, as his daughter Abigail accused additional suspects of afflicting her. It is hard to ascribe Martin's endorsement of this document to anything other than a change of heart on the matter— after all, by signing it, he was describing his own daughter as "distempered." He may also have been taking a greater risk than any other resister—the experience of Mary Warren in the Salem courtroom six months earlier had demonstrated what could happen to turncoats. In addition to imperiling his own freedom, his reversal could have endangered his daughter. Despite this, he also signed the petition of January 3, 1693—just as the trials were about to resume. There is no certainty that father and daughter agreed on the matter by that time—Abigail Martin's name appeared among those allegedly afflicted by accused witches in the accounts of several trials. Unlike her contemporaries Martha Sprague and Rose Foster, though, Abigail was never listed as having appeared as a witness before the new court. The use of her name probably carried over from the earlier examinations and trials. Father and daughter, weighted down by the guilt of their earlier actions, may have wished to atone for what they had done. Samuel's signing of the petitions stood out as the most obvious method. In doing so, he may have risked the wrath of his fellow accuser Moses Tyler, but the latter's own feelings on the matter at that point cannot be ascertained. Tyler knew that his sister, his sister-in-law, and several nieces might not survive the trials by that time. The fact that he did not sign either petition means nothing—he resided in Boxford, not Andover. Unlike Abigail Martin, though, Martha

Sprague (alias Tyler as the 1693 documents designated her) continued offering evidence before the new court. But if she was, in fact, married to her stepbrother Joseph Tyler by that time (and there is every reason to believe she was), Moses's influence over her would have lessened significantly—if he ever had much to begin with. In 1693, young Joseph Tyler—not his father Moses—was the most significant male figure in the life of the supposedly bewitched Martha. If anyone would lash out at the Martins (father and daughter), Joseph and Martha would have been the most likely candidates. Neither did. Joseph's name did not appear in any 1693 trial documents. Martha bore witness against many she had already accused, but no one new. Neither Samuel Martin nor his daughter Abigail paid any obvious price for the father's change of heart, but neither of them could have known at the time that it would turn out that way.

Appendix F

Suspects with No Kin or Local Supporters

Significant opposition to the witch persecution had taken root in Andover by the fourth of January, the day the new court first convened. The town did not unify entirely on the matter, though. While many of the suspects saw large contingents of family members rally around them, others experienced no public support from relatives at all. Some of them simply had very few, if any, kin in town.

The widower Henry Salter, aged about sixty-five, lived alone or perhaps with some servants in the South End. He had only relocated to Andover a few years before 1692 so he lacked roots in the town. He was not alone in this among those accused of witchcraft.

Edward Farrington, a much younger man (only thirty when accused in 1692) was a native of the town of Lynn. His widowed mother, Elizabeth Knight Farrington, had married Mark Graves of Andover when Edward was a child and this suspected wizard's only relatives in town were some of his stepfather's children by his first wife. One of Farrington's stepsisters, Dorcas Graves, was married to George Abbot, Jr., the son of original town proprietor George Abbot. This stepbrother-in-law was the only person who could be considered "family" to Edward Farrington who signed a petition—the one presented on January 3. Farrington's plight may have been a contributing factor to Abbot's choice to defend the suspects, but so many of the extended Chandler/Abbot clan endorsed the petitions that they undoubtedly had other motives. Edward Farrington was not quite an "Andover orphan" but he was close.

A suspect who genuinely did stand alone in Andover (in terms of family) was Joseph Draper, aged twenty-one. He apparently worked for some of the members of the Hooper family, but he is not known to have had any relatives in town.

Other accused witches did have next of kin in town, but their relatives did not join the resistance. One example that stands out is the family of the Foster/Lacey women. Ann Foster had a total of five children—three daughters and two sons. Mary Foster Lacey, of course, was jailed along with her mother. Hannah Foster Stone had been murdered three years before the witch hunt. The other daughter, Sarah Foster, had moved with her husband Samuel Kemp to Groton by the mid-1680s. Both of Ann's sons remained in Andover, however. Andrew Foster, aged about fifty-two, remained near his mother's home in the South End, having married Mary Russe, a daughter of original Andover proprietors John and Margaret Russe. The younger son Abraham Foster had married to another Foster (Esther Foster from Chelmsford), who may or may not have been related. He, like his jailed sister Mary, had moved to the North End as an adult. Both brothers looked on helplessly as their mother, sister, and niece were not only arrested on witchcraft charges in the summer of 1692 but also confessed to everything they were accused of and fueled the flames of the witch hunt by doing so. The family had already endured the devastating murder of another sister three years earlier. The witch hunters showed an amazing propensity for "kicking people when they were down" so to speak.

Surprisingly, neither of these men signed any petitions defending the accused that fall or winter after the suspension of legal action against the suspects. Ann Foster died in jail on December 3, but she had still been alive at the time of the petition of October 18. The elder Mary Lacey remained in jail, her namesake daughter having been bailed out by the surprising benevolence of Francis Faulkner and John Barker. These two men—whose families had been so adversely affected by the distraught girl's efforts to transform herself from suspect to victim—did more for her than any of her own family did. It may be, of course, that the Foster brothers regarded any efforts on their part as useless. The mother and sister (Ann Foster and the elder Mary Lacey) not only remained in jail—they had already been sentenced to death. Young Mary Lacey still faced the possibility of a trial, but her uncles may not have felt inclined to assist her—she had, after all, betrayed her own mother and grandmother. Even Lawrence Lacey, the husband of the elder Mary and father of the younger Mary, took no public action. The cousin (John Stone) who aided the latter Mary when she had run away from home the previous year did not come to her assistance this time. He and his gravely wounded brother Simon were the only grandsons of Ann Foster who had reached adulthood by 1692. Ultimately, the only public action any man in this family took to aid the persecuted women was when Abraham Foster paid to retrieve Ann's body after her death in December. It may be that the entire clan was simply shell-shocked by the end of 1692—they had endured one tragedy after another for the previous three years. Yet by way of comparison, the Peters clan had suffered nearly as much, losing two sons in an Indian attack in 1689 and a daughter to smallpox in 1690. They still rallied in large numbers for their youthful family member John Sadie and the other suspects. At that point in time, though, the Foster clan's reputation in Andover was less than sterling. The men in the family may have reasoned that their involvement in the resistance would not help.

This family was not the only Foster clan in Andover associated with the witch hunt in 1692. Their distant relative Ephraim Foster (identified as such by DNA testing of descendants) served as constable of the North End that year and had, in fact, arrested the two Mary Laceys in July. Ephraim became an active accuser in late August when his oldest daughter Rose began experiencing fits. Despite that fact, he could have signed on to the resistance later that year. He had reasons—his mother-in-law, Rebecca Blake Eames, and her son Daniel were both among those accused, and Rebecca had already been convicted. Ephraim's fellow accuser Samuel Martin stepped up to defend the suspects at that point even though none of his own family had fallen under suspicion. Ephraim, however, did not take that step. His name does not appear on any petition. Having found material evidence in the Lacey home and having seen the afflictions suffered by his daughter Rose, he may still have believed in the guilt of the suspects (or at least most of them). There is no evidence that he or his daughter Rose played any role in the arrest of the Eames relatives, but he did nothing to help them.

Accusers who joined the resistance were the exception—not the norm. The extended Chandler/Abbot clan stands out as the most obvious example of a family group with some members who accused suspects but then later rallied behind the accused in large numbers. Samuel Martin's change of heart showed even more courage—he did not have the backing of an extended kin network. His genetic family, aside from his children, was limited. He had actually been born in Gloucester in 1645, a son of Solomon and Mary Pindar Martin. His only full sibling was a younger sister named Mary, who may have died young. Mary Pindar Martin died in 1648 and Solomon remarried Alice Farnum of Ipswich. Alice, twelve years older than her second husband Solomon, did not have children by him. Therefore, the home young Samuel Martin grew up in consisted primarily of Farnums—his stepmother's five children by her first husband, Ralph Farnum. The youngest of these Farnums, John, was five years older than Samuel Martin and so not surprisingly, some of them married and began having families while their younger stepbrother was still a child. The family relocated to Andover by 1652 and had established itself primarily in the North End by 1692. Some of the Farnums played minor roles in the accusations, but none involved themselves as thoroughly as their stepbrother Samuel did. Sarah Farnum Abbot (oldest daughter of Ralph Farnum, Sr., the son of Alice) joined her husband Benjamin Abbot in testifying against Martha Carrier in early August. Two of Sarah's brothers, Ralph, Jr. and John, were also summoned to depose against Carrier although if either did, the testimony does not survive. A third Farnum brother—Samuel—testified against Daniel Eames. Abigail Martin identified another John Farnum (John Farnum, Jr., twenty-year-old cousin of the aforementioned Farnums and son of John, Sr.) as one of the many young people in Andover whose fortune was told by Samuel Wardwell. Wardwell's predictions had not been positive—young Farnum was to be crossed in love, be shot with a gun, and fall from a horse. All of these, according to Abigail Martin, came true.[9] Finally, the name Ralph Farnum, Sr. (who was aged almost sixty) appeared in the trial record of Abigail Wheeler Barker before the reconstituted court on January 7, 1693. The document identified Farnum as Barker's primary victim, though it does not indicate if he testified or not. It is doubtful that he did—he died the next day.

Not surprisingly, the Farnum family did not join the resistance against the witchcraft trials. Samuel Martin defied the only real family he had in Andover by endorsing documents defending the suspects. Martin had also played a larger role in the persecution than any of the Farnums and had more to atone for. Benjamin Abbot, married to Sarah Farnum, did not join others in the extended Chandler/Abbot clan who did defend the accused. One Farnum family member who did sign on to the resistance was Daniel Poor, Jr. whose mother Sarah was the oldest daughter of Alice Farnum Martin. Daniel, as noted previously, had married a daughter of the jailed Mary Clements Osgood, so he faced intense pressure from the other direction. Most of the other Farnums lacked connections to suspects. Therefore, their decision to stay out of the resistance should surprise no one. The one Farnum who did have a close tie to some of the accused was John Farnum (the aforementioned son of Ralph, Sr.). He had been married in 1684 to Elizabeth Parker, whose mother (Mary Ayer Parker) had been hanged on September 22 and whose sister Sarah remained under suspicion. It should be noted that none of Mary's children signed the petitions. Her two adult sons,

John and Joseph, took action to reclaim some items that had been seized from her estate, but they did not endorse the documents defending the other accused.

Other families played no role in defending the suspects. Members of the Phelps family had lived in Andover since 1661 when Edward and Elizabeth Adams Phelps, both in their thirties, purchased land in the town from none other than John Godfrey, who had already faced one charge of witchcraft and was soon to be accused again. Edward and Elizabeth brought four children with them to their new home and their youngest, Edward Phelps, Jr., was born about two years after their arrival. Edward Phelps, Sr. outlived one son, John Phelps, who was killed during King Philip's War in 1677, aged about twenty. Two of their surviving children—Samuel and Elinor—married into the Chandler family. Their respective spouses were Sarah and William Chandler, both of them children of the prominent Thomas and Hannah Brewer Chandler. Another Phelps daughter was the ill-fated Elizabeth Phelps, who had married Joseph Ballard in 1668. It was Elizabeth's illness that brought the witch hunters to Andover in the summer of 1692, with two of the afflicted girls from Salem Village having been summoned by her husband. Two weeks after the death of Elizabeth Ballard on July 27, her ten-year-old niece Sarah Phelps (daughter of Samuel and Sarah Chandler Phelps) began accusing people of witchcraft—probably scared into believing herself bewitched after the death of her aunt. A few of her Chandler relatives joined young Sarah in complaining of bewitchment though none of them ever became leading accusers.

The fact that many in the Chandler family eventually defended the suspects did not influence the Phelps clan, not even those who were related to them by blood or marriage. The father, Edward, died three years before the witch hunt, but his wife, the elder Elizabeth Phelps, remained alive and was sixty-five at the time (she did not die until 1718 at the age of ninety-one). The death of the younger Elizabeth, aged about forty-six in 1692, would have devastated her mother and siblings. Only the young Sarah became an active accuser after Elizabeth's death (although her father Samuel Phelps may have filed complaints on her behalf). When public opinion began turning away from the witch hunt in the fall, several of the Chandlers and their Abbot cousins joined the resistance. The Phelps family did not—and the Chandlers that had intermarried with them (Sarah Chandler Phelps and William Chandler) avoided the matter as well. At least some in the family probably did genuinely believe that witchcraft was the cause of the death of Elizabeth Phelps Ballard. They may also have feared that the witches, if not stopped, would kill little Sarah too. They were not the only family worried about the health of a supposedly bewitched relative.

Sarah Phelps's symptoms, whatever they were, may have been entirely psychosomatic in nature, brought on by the illness and death of her aunt. In contrast, thirty-year-old Timothy Swan had been genuinely physically ill since the summer if not longer. Given his reputation, it may be that the only people in Andover who cared about him were his brothers, Robert and John. Robert, five years older than Timothy, had been married for about a decade and had four young children, including an infant son named for his gravely ill brother. John and Samuel Swan, bachelors like Timothy, were only twenty-four and twenty, respectively. Robert and John had joined forces the previous August to file a complaint against Mary Johnson (Davis) Clark of Haverhill, accusing her of bewitching Timothy. None of the Swan brothers changed their minds by the fall of 1692 when others were turning against the witch hunt. They probably still believed that Timothy was slowly being tortured to death by acts of sorcery on the part of those who had confessed to afflicting him and others still at large. After all, Ann Foster, the first to admit to hurting Timothy, had claimed that there were 305 witches in the region altogether. Barely half that number had been taken into custody. There must have been others that Timothy and his brothers suspected, but by the fall of 1692, they had no means to pursue further actions against new suspects. They had to wait for the new court to convene before they could resume the fight, and they were not about to defend those they believed responsible for Timothy's continually worsening health. They could not have been ignorant of the general disdain for Timothy in the town, and to some degree, the defense of the suspects by their neighbors may have been interpreted as an indifference to their brother's eventual fate.

There were those in Andover who managed to emerge from the disaster of 1692 practically unscathed. One such family was the Lovejoys. Their progenitor, John Lovejoy, arrived in Massachusetts in 1638 at the age of only sixteen. He and his sister Grace (two years older) came as servants in the household of John Stevens, one of the original proprietors of Andover. After his term as a servant had ended, Lovejoy was married in Ipswich in 1651 to Mary Osgood, an older half-sister of Christopher Osgood. Mary, the mother of all of the Lovejoy children, died in 1675. (A year later John remarried the widow Hannah Pritchard, whose husband William had been killed in

King Philip's War the previous year.) John and Mary Osgood Lovejoy were the parents of twelve children. Three of them—Mary (who married Joseph Wilson), John, Jr. (who had married Naomi Hoyt of Amesbury), and Benjamin (a bachelor) died before 1692, the latter a casualty of the fighting that began in 1689. The elder John Lovejoy died in 1690, leaving nine children, all of whom were living in Andover two years later. Given the family's size (there were also several teenage grandchildren by 1692), one would think they would have been somehow touched by the witch hunt. Other than a few distant connections through marriage though, the Lovejoys hardly felt any impact.

As noted previously, the widow Grace Ballard (mother of the brothers John and Joseph Ballard) was probably John Lovejoy's sister Grace, who had come to Massachusetts with him in 1638. The age fits—Grace Lovejoy, born in 1620, was three years younger than the Ballards' father William, who was born about 1617. No Lovejoys ever involved themselves in the accusations, but they would certainly have known of the illness and death of Elizabeth Phelps Ballard. John Lovejoy's wife Mary was an aunt of the accused Mary Osgood Marston and so the second-generation Lovejoys were her cousins.

Some defenders of the suspects were, in fact, no more closely related to them than cousins, but when considering the vast kinship networks in Andover at the time, it is clear that not all cousins of alleged witches rallied to the resistance. Mary Lovejoy Wilson's husband Joseph had remarried Sarah Lord after Mary's death, and his second wife and their daughter were among the accused—but that was a connection only by marriage. Sarah Lovejoy had married William Johnson, whose sister Mary Johnson (Davis) Clark had been accused by the Swan family. On the other side of the matter, the oldest Lovejoy son (William Lovejoy) married Mary Farnum, a sister of the three Farnum siblings summoned to testify against Martha Carrier in August, and of Samuel Farnum, who deposed against Daniel Eames. The Lovejoy family did have a few connections by marriage and genes to people touched by the witch hunt, both accusers and accused. But no one named Lovejoy was accused, nor was any woman whose birth name was Lovejoy. No one in the family acted as an accuser, either. As large as the family was, that level of separation from the madness that swirled around them during the summer of 1692 seems remarkable.

Notes

Introduction

1. Mary Beth Norton, *In the Devil's Snare: The Salem Witchcraft Crisis of 1692* (New York: Alfred A. Knopf, 2002). Norton describes the role played in the trials by several residents of the embattled frontier region (some of whom had fled to the relatively safer confines of Essex County), including afflicted servant girl Mercy Lewis, confessed witch Abigail Hobbs, and convicted wizard George Burroughs.

2. Officially, Essex County contained seventeen separate towns because Salem Village (later Danvers), where the witchcraft accusations first began, was not a truly independent town. Officially, it was still part of the larger town of Salem. However, Salem Village had been granted an independence of sorts from the town by being allowed to form its own church, and culturally, there is no question that it had established itself as a distinct community by 1692. For that reason, it is identified as a town here despite the fact that it did not formally separate from Salem for another sixty years.

3. Paul Boyer and Stephen Nissenbaum, *Salem Possessed: The Social Origins of Witchcraft* (Cambridge, MA: Harvard University Press, 1974), pinpointed the specific residences of fourteen of them and revealed that twelve of the fourteen lived in the eastern half of the village. The authors further stress the geographic divide by noting that thirty of thirty-two adults in the village who testified against accused witches lived on the west side of the village, while twenty-four out of twenty-nine who defended a suspect or formally expressed skepticism about the trials resided on the east side. This perception of an east-west dichotomy in Salem Village in 1692 is not without critics, however. *William and Mary Quarterly* dedicated two-thirds of its July 2008 issue to a reassessment of *Salem Possessed*, with nine articles on the 1974 monograph, including an entry by Boyer and Nissenbaum themselves. The other writers offered criticism and praise of the book, often in the same essays. Historian Benjamin C. Ray emerges as the harshest critic of the geographic divide, noting that when looking at the accusers, Boyer and Nissenbaum discounted the afflicted girls themselves, focusing only on the adults who actually filed formal complaints. Ray also points out that the joint authors of the earlier work did not include those in the village who straddled the issue (joining in accusations against some village suspects while signing petitions on behalf of others). He further takes the earlier authors to task for placing a supposedly arbitrary dividing line between east and west, arguing that shifting it only slightly eastward would change the statistics significantly, and offers several maps of his own to demonstrate his point (Benjamin C. Ray, "The Geography of Witchcraft Accusations in 1692 in Salem Village," *William and Mary Quarterly* 65, no. 3 [July 2008], 449–478). Ray published his own monograph in 2015: *Satan and Salem: The Witch-Hunt Crisis of 1692* (Charlottesville: University of Virginia Press,

254	Notes

2015). In that work, he softened his critique of Boyer and Nissenbaum somewhat, noting
that thirty-two accusers lived on the west side of the village and twenty-five on the east side,
a statistically insignificant difference. He did note that most of those accused resided in the
eastern half of the village though and he did agree with the authors of *Salem Possessed* about
the dispute over Samuel Parris and its role in the witch trials (188–189).
4. The numbers vary a bit from study to study because there is some uncertainty about where
some of those accused actually resided.
5. Charles W. Upham, *Salem Witchcraft* (Boston: Wiggin and Lunt, 186; reprint Mineola,
NY: Dover, 2000), 481.
6. Marion L. Starkey, *The Devil in Massachusetts: A Modern Enquiry into the Salem Witch
Trials* (New York: Alfred A. Knopf, 1949), 180–182. In summing up subsequent events in
Andover, however, Starkey gives the impression that the events over nearly two months happened within a period of just a few days, and she attributes the accusations there primarily
to the Salem Village girls without exploring in detail any of the dynamics within Andover
itself.
7. Norton, *In the Devil's Snare*, 264. The statement that Andover habitually resolved its own
issues is belied by incidents in the 1680s that were taken to the General Court in Boston.
8. Enders A. Robinson, *Salem Witchcraft and Hawthorne's House of the Seven Gables* (Bowie,
MD: Heritage Books, 1992), 173–176.
9. Robinson, 174–175.

CHAPTER ONE: THE EVIL HAND IS UPON THEM

1. John P. Demos, *Entertaining Satan: Witchcraft and the Culture of Early New England* (New
York: Oxford University Press, 1982).
2. There is no known record of the execution of Mary Sanford of Hartford who was convicted
of witchcraft and sentenced to be hanged, but it is assumed that the sentence was carried
out.
3. Demos, 352.
4. Boyer and Nissenbaum, 173 (quoting Parris's sermon book).
5. Boyer and Nissenbaum, 172 (quoting Parris's sermon book).
6. Boyer and Nissenbaum, 135–136.
7. Chadwick Hansen, *Witchcraft at Salem* (New York: George Braziller, 1969), 10.
8. In October 1691, a new slate had been elected as members of the village committee, the
entity that made decisions on issues confronting the village's population. The new men on
this committee (Joseph Porter, Joseph Hutchinson, Daniel Andrew, Francis Nurse, and
Joseph Putnam) had all opposed Parris. Once they took power, they made their intention to
investigate the validity of Parris's title to the parsonage clear and they also gave him reason
to doubt he could count on payment of his expected salary. This situation induced paranoia
in the minister that he would undoubtedly have carried over into his home life. The children
in his house, whether or not they knew the specifics of his concerns, must have sensed them.
This may have instigated their symptoms.
9. Mary Beth Norton (*In the Devil's Snare*, 23–24) effectively dismisses the oft-repeated story
that the slave oversaw a group of the girls who met frequently in Parris's home and indulged
in means of foretelling the future. As Norton demonstrates, the tale is not supported by any
contemporary evidence. The only indication of any such occurrence comes from the writing
of John Hale (minister of the town of Beverly in 1692), whose 1702 work *A Modest Inquiry
into the Nature of Witchcraft* (published posthumously) cites an instance in which one of the
afflicted girls used a Venus glass (an egg and a glass) to determine the occupation of her
future husband. The belief was that the shape the egg yolk took would provide the answer
sought. In this case, Hale noted, the yolk took the shape of a coffin which, if his account is

to be believed, did foretell the future because this afflicted girl (whoever she was) died un-married before he completed work on the book. Hale did, however, only mention that case and one other similar one, the latter of which may not have even involved one of the girls afflicted at Salem. Nothing in this account or any other offers any evidence that Tituba taught fortune telling to the girls in Parris's household or anyone else. Another writer, Frances Hill, mentions that legend about Tituba in her travel guide titled *Hunting for Witches: A Visitor's Guide to the Salem Witch Trials*, noting that the Venus glass was an English custom that Tituba would have known nothing about. If any of the afflicted girls used it, they would have learned it from their own families or from neighbors who were also of English back-ground.

CHAPTER TWO: A CRUEL DAY IN APRIL

1. The British Empire did not adopt the Gregorian calendar to replace the Julian calendar until 1752 (placing dates eleven days later than previously), and so one could reasonably say that the actual anniversary of these events of the witchcraft trials is April 30 rather than April 19. This author has followed the practice of historians, who do not generally choose to mod-ernize these dates for the simple reason that the resulting differences between dates cited in published works on history and dates on original documents would be too confusing.

2. Hansen, 65–66. To a large degree, Hansen's thesis about Bishop has been discredited since the 1970s. Indeed, he overplays that card—arguing that particular suspects had practiced their craft for years when all they had done was pronounce a curse on certain specific indi-viduals they had quarreled with. Wilmot Redd of Marblehead (hanged for witchcraft on September 22, 1692) had, according to the testimony of some of her neighbors, pronounced a curse of constipation on a certain Mrs. Simms a few years before. This could very well be true, but Hansen uses that single incident to identify Redd as a longtime practitioner of black magic with the intent to inflict harm on others she disliked in the community (71–72). The evidence for that is just not adequate. Redd may not have even spoken the curse with the intent of actually harming Mrs. Simms—she may only have been expressing a wish for her to experience such symptoms. The hypothesis of Hansen's that does withstand scrutiny in this case is the possibility that Mrs. Simms suffered from constipation as a result of Wilmot Redd's curse—for the simple reason that she believed in the power of the curse. Psychology can affect the function of the bowels and may have in this case, whether the sus-pected witch actually expected her words to have such a result or not.

3. Norton, 81.

4. A pattern is emerging here. Once one member of any family was accused, others in the family were more likely to fall under suspicion. Two husband-and-wife tandems and a pair of sisters are already noted here—a total of six of the first fourteen arrested for witchcraft were immediate family members of other suspects. The pattern continued with the father and stepmother of Abigail Hobbs being arrested shortly after Abigail was.

5. The first was Rachel (Haffield or Hatfield) Clinton of the town of Ipswich who had been suspected of witchcraft a few years earlier—another suspect who fit the pattern of having an existing reputation for witchcraft.

6. "Old boy" was a common way to refer to the devil in that era.

7. Norton, 112–113.

8. Bernard Rosenthal, *Salem Story: Reading the Witch Trials of 1692* (Cambridge: Cambridge University Press, 1993), 41.

9. William Manchester, *A World Lit Only by Fire: The Medieval Mind and the Renaissance, Portrait of an Age* (Boston: Little, Brown, 1992). Manchester was writing about medieval Europe, but "a world lit only by fire" applies just as readily to colonial New England.

10. Giles Corey, who was crushed to death in an effort to force him to enter a plea, also un-

derwent examination on April 19. Although he may be more famous than any of the women examined that day due to the manner of his eventual death (he was crushed to death under stones after refusing to enter a plea of guilty or not guilty), his specific court appearance did not affect the later course of events as much as the aforementioned ones did.

11. Carol F. Karlsen, *The Devil in the Shape of a Woman* (New York: W.W. Norton, 1987), 91.

12. Some sources mistakenly identify John Ballard's brother, Joseph Ballard, as the constable of the South End of Andover at the time of the witch trials. The error is not surprising given that Joseph Ballard had served as constable a few years earlier and he and John both ended up playing major roles in the witchcraft accusations in Andover. The documentation of the arrests and Andover's own town records, however, clearly identify the constable as John Ballard.

13. Diane E. Foulds, *Death in Salem: The Private Lives Behind the 1692 Witch Hunt* (Guilford, CT: Globe Pequot Press, 2010), 55–56.

14. Chadwick Hansen, "Andover Witchcraft and the Causes of the Salem Witchcraft Trials," in Howard Kerr and Charles L. Crow, eds., *The Occult in America: New Historical Perspectives*, 38–57 (Urbana: University of Illinois Press, 1983), 43.

15. These two residents, Thomas Gage and Elias Pickworth, presented evidence against Toothaker, telling of his alleged killing of a witch by his own witchcraft.

CHAPTER THREE: A SHADOW OVER ANDOVER

1. Philip J. Greven's *Four Generations: Population, Land, and Family in Colonial Andover, Massachusetts* (Ithaca, NY, and London: Cornell University Press, 1970) and Elinor Abbot's *Our Company Increases Apace: History, Language, and Social Identity in Early Colonial Andover, Massachusetts* (Dallas, TX: SIL International, 2007) both provide important details about the development of the town in the years leading up to 1692. Greven's work barely mentions the witchcraft accusations and while Abbot does discuss them, they are not the focus of her research. Both books trace the history of the town from its founding in 1646 into the eighteenth century and while Greven's work focuses primarily on economic factors, Abbot's is more cultural in nature. Nonetheless, both stress the importance of the earliest economic hierarchy in Andover.

2. The given name of the elder William Ballard's wife was Grace. Her maiden name has been given as Berwick in countless genealogical sources over the past century, but none of these sources offers documentary proof of that assumption. James Henderson's article "English Origins of John Lovejoy of Andover, Massachusetts" (*New England Historical and Genealogical Register,* February 2009) demonstrates that John Lovejoy arrived in Massachusetts in 1638 on the ship *Confidence* as a servant to John Stevens. Another servant of the Stevens family who arrived at the same time was John's sister, Grace Lovejoy. Grace was an unusual given name in that era, and because William Ballard and John Lovejoy are listed consecutively among the first arrivals in Andover on Faulkner's list, Henderson offers the hypothesis that Ballard's wife Grace was this Grace Lovejoy. While not proven, the connection makes sense. Grace Lovejoy, born in 1620, was a logical age to have been the wife of William Ballard (born about 1617).

3. Abbot, 139–140.

4. Abbot, 141.

5. The committee consisted of Thomas Chandler and Richard Barker (both of them original town proprietors) and five sons of original proprietors—Dudley Bradstreet (son of Simon), John Osgood (son of John), John Frye (son of John), John Stevens (son of John), and John Barker (son of the aforementioned Richard).

6. The involvement of the courts in this case demonstrates that Andover did not always address its own problems internally as Mary Beth Norton stated in her work (Norton, 264).

7. Bethany Groff, *A Brief History of Old Newbury from Settlement to Separation* (Charleston, SC: History Press, 2008), 77–78.

8. Groff, 78–79.

9. Groff, 105–107.

CHAPTER FOUR: PRELUDE TO WITCHCRAFT

1. Willard I. Tyler Brigham, *The Tyler Genealogy: The Descendants of Job Tyler of Andover, Massachusetts, 1619–1700* (Plainfield, NJ: Cornelius B. Tyler and Rollin U. Tyler, 1912), 4 (quoting Andover Records, book 4, page 8).

2. Deposition dated March 7, 1665 (though actually from the 1659 trial), quoted in David D. Hall, ed., *Witch-Hunting in Colonial New England: A Documentary History, 1638–1693* (Boston: Northeastern University Press, 1991, 1999), 124.

3. Records and Files of the Quarterly Court of Essex County, June 1662 (transcription), 403.

4. Ibid., 404.

5. Ibid., (transcription), 404.

6. Ibid., 405 (spelling corrected).

7. Ibid.

8. Ibid., 404.

9. Brigham, 7 (referenced also in Records and Files of the Quarterly Court of Essex County, November 1665 (transcription), 284.

10. Records and Files of the Quarterly Court of Essex County, March 1668 (transcription), 14. It is not clear if Chandler was referring to one of his own sons here or one of Tyler's sons.

11. Ibid.

12. Haverhill Vital Records to 1850, 291.

13. Frank H. Swan, *Richard Swan and Some of His Descendants* (Providence, RI: Akerman-Standard Company, 1927), 8–9. Richard Swan, who arrived from England no later than 1638, was the father of Robert, who had been born about 1626.

14. Records and Files of the Quarterly Court of Essex County, April 1686 (transcription), 601–602.

15. Ibid., 602.

16. Jane Emerson James, *The Haverhill Emersons Revised and Extended* (Lake Winnebago, MO: Jane E. James, 1983), 12.

17. Records and Files of the Quarterly Court of Essex County, May 1676 (transcription), 141.

18. Else L. Hambleton, "Playing the Rogue: Rape and Issues of Consent in Seventeenth-Century Massachusetts" in Merril D. Smith, ed., *Sex Without Consent: Rape and Sexual Coercion in America* (New York: New York University Press, 2001), 30.

19. Marilynne K. Roach, *The Salem Witch Trials: A Day-By-Day Chronicle of a Community Under Siege* (Lanham, MD: Taylor Trade Publishing, 2002), 175.

20. This belief still persists among some in the twenty-first century as evidenced by the infamous claim of Todd Akin of Missouri, who ran for one of the state's United States Senate seats in 2012. In an interview for St. Louis's Fox News station, Akin stated, "If it's a legitimate rape, the female body has ways to try to shut the whole thing down." Akin said this in response to a question about whether or not he supported allowing abortions in cases of women who were impregnated during a rape. He dodged the question by claiming pregnancy was unlikely to result from rape because female bodies could prevent conception in those instances.

21. Deposition of Josiah Gage, Records and Files of the Quarterly Court of Essex County, April 1686 (transcription), 603. Apparently Robert Swan did not always succeed in his efforts to be more neighborly after 1680.
22. Hambleton, 30.
23. Roach, 175.
24. Hambleton, 31–32.
25. Some genealogists have advanced the hypothesis that Ann Foster was the same person as an immigrant named Annis Alcock, who arrived in Boston in 1635 aboard the ship *Abigail*. The evidence, however, is far from convincing.
26. If Andrew Foster was, indeed, one hundred years old at the time of his death, he would have been fifty-five at the time of birth of his oldest son Andrew in 1640. Even if he wasn't quite as old as that, he was probably no younger than forty in 1640.
27. Records and Files of the Quarterly Court of Essex County, September 1680 (transcription), 184.
28. Records and Files of the Quarterly Court of Essex County, March 1683 (transcription), 27.
29. Records and Files of the Quarterly Court of Essex County, November 1685 (transcription), 568.
30. Abbot, 145–146.
31. Andover Old Tax and Record Book, 1670–1716, film image 5644, quoted in Bailey, 202.
32. Ibid., 202–203. The widow Allen is Martha's mother Faith (Ingalls) Allen. The elder Andrew Allen, Martha's father, had died on October 24 of smallpox.
33. Examination, May 31, 1692, in Bernard Rosenthal, ed., *Records of the Salem Witch-Hunt* (New York: Cambridge University Press, 2009), 335–336.
34. Henry A. Hazen, *History of Billerica with a Genealogical Register* (Boston: A. Williams, 1883), 22.
35. Timothy Osgood was actually appointed as constable of the North End in early 1692. Foster had served in that role in 1691 and it may that Osgood refused the job for some reason which resulted in Foster serving in that capacity for a second year.
36. Deposition of Ephraim Foster vs. Samuel Wardwell, September 14, 1692, in Rosenthal, ed., 644–645.
37. Deposition of John Bridges vs. Samuel Wardwell, September 14, 1692, in Rosenthal, ed., 645. John was the father of James. John's wife and two of his daughters were among the accused.
38. Deposition of Thomas Chandler vs. Samuel Wardwell, September 14, 1692, in Rosenthal, ed., 644.
39. Diane Rapaport, *The Naked Quaker: True Crimes and Controversies from the Courts of Colonial New England* (Beverly, MA: Commonwealth Editions, 2007), 73–75.
40. Deposition of Joseph Ballard vs. Samuel Wardwell, September 14, 1692, in Rosenthal, ed., 644–645.

CHAPTER FIVE: RUMORS AND NIGHTMARES

1. Philip J. Greven, Jr., *Four Generations: Population, Land, and Family in Colonial Andover, Massachusetts* (Ithaca, NY: Cornell University Press), 84.
2. William Ballard was the only one of the three Ballard brothers to sign any of the petitions supporting the accused witches.
3. Abbot, 84.
4. Greven, 84–85.
5. Of the previous seven confessors, two were slaves—the aforementioned Tituba and a woman of African descent named Candy. Four were not adults—Dorothy Good, Abigail Hobbs, Mary Warren, and Margaret Jacobs. The only European adult who confessed before

Ann Foster did was Abigail Hobbs's stepmother, Deliverance Hobbs, whose confession was offered just days after Abigail's.

6. Examination, July 15, 1692, in Rosenthal, ed., *Records of the Salem Witch-Hunt* (New York: Cambridge University Press, 2009), 467.

7. Examination, July 16, 1692, in Rosenthal, 467. This was the first mention of Timothy Swan during the 1692 witchcraft episode. He was to become one of the most prominent of Andover's afflicted.

8. Examinations of Mary Lacey, Jr., Mary Lacey, Sr., and Ann Foster, July 21, 1692, in Rosenthal, ed., 472.

9. Warrant for Apprehension of Mary Lacey, Jr., and Officer's return, July 20, 1692, in Rosenthal, 470.

10. Examinations of Ann Foster, Mary Lacey, Sr., and Mary Lacey, Jr., July 21, 1692, in Rosenthal, 471–473.

11. Christopher Osgood had recently married his fourth wife Sarah, his third wife (also named Sarah) having died within the past two years. There is no known reference elsewhere to a dispute between Osgood and Martha Carrier, but they were neighbors and she is known to have had a quarrelsome disposition, so something could have happened.

12. Examinations of Mary Lacey, Jr., Mary Lacey, Sr., and Ann Foster, Andover Examinations Copy, in Rosenthal, ed., 475.

13. Cotton Mather, *The Wonders of the Invisible World* (1692; reprinted Mineola, NY: Dover, 2005), 128.

14. Deposition, May 30, 1692 in Rosenthal, 330.

15. Examination of Mary Lacey, Sr., July 21, 1692, in Rosenthal, ed., 477–478.

CHAPTER SIX: THE ANDOVER WITCH HUNT

1. Letter of Thomas Brattle, FRS, October 8, 1692, reprinted in George Lincoln Burr, *Narratives of the Witchcraft Cases 1648–1706* (New York: C. Scribner's Sons, 1914), 180.

2. Timothy Swan's tombstone in the old cemetery in modern-day North Andover indicates that he died February 2, 1692. This has confused some researchers, but at that time, England and its colonies still observed the Julian calendar, which began the New Year on March 25 rather than January 1. That observation was not universal and written documents often gave alternative years for dates in that range (example February 2, 1692/3) as did some tombstones. Swan's tombstone, however, only gave his death date as 1692, but it becomes 1693 when accounting for the eventual calendar change.

3. A notable example, cited by John Demos in *Entertaining Satan*, involved the death of Henry Stiles of Windsor, Connecticut, in 1651. His death came during militia training exercises when another militiaman, Thomas Allen, accidentally shot him when Allen hit a tree with his musket after cocking it. Allen was convicted of "homicide by misadventure," sentenced to pay a substantial fine, and denied the right to bear arms for a year. Three years later, however, another resident of Windsor, Lydia Gilbert (in whose home Stiles once resided), was convicted of causing Stiles's death by witchcraft and condemned to death by hanging, a sentence that was presumably carried out (though no record of her actual execution is known to exist). The accidental death of Edmund Ingalls was no less vulnerable to a witchcraft accusation than that of Henry Stiles (Demos, 4–5).

4. Charles Burleigh, *The Genealogy and History of the Ingalls Family in America* (1903; reprinted Baltimore: Gateway Press, 1991), 17.

5. Examinations of Mary Lacey, Jr., Mary Lacey, Sr., and Ann Foster, Andover Examinations Copy, in Rosenthal, ed., 475.

6. Examinations of Richard Carrier, Mary Lacey, Jr., Mary Lacey, Sr., and Andrew Carrier, copy, in Rosenthal, ed., 479–480.

7. Ibid., 480. The day after this event, John Procter (who was soon to hang) wrote a letter to five Boston ministers describing how the Carrier brothers had been tied "neck and heels till the blood was ready to come out of their noses," Rosenthal, ed. 486.

8. Examinations of Richard Carrier, Mary Lacey, Jr., Mary Lacey, Sr., and Andrew Carrier, copy, in Rosenthal, ed., 480–481.

9. Ibid., 481–482.

10. Examination of Martha Emerson, July 23, 1692, in Rosenthal, ed., 485.

11. Norton, 240. As previously noted, Norton's primary focus involved connecting the witch-craft trials to the Indian wars.

12. Examination of Mary Toothaker, July 30, 1692, in Rosenthal, ed., 491–492.

13. Norton, 240–241.

14. Benjamin Abbot was a son of Hannah Chandler by her first husband, George Abbot. He was, therefore, also a stepson of Reverend Francis Dane.

CHAPTER SEVEN: LOOK WITH AN EVIL EYE

1. Statement of Francis Dane, Sr. Regarding some of the Andover Accused, January 2, 1693, in Rosenthal, ed., 734–735.

2. Ephraim Davis was a son of Mary Johnson Davis Clark of Haverhill, who had been ar-rested a week earlier. Abraham Foster was a son of the jailed Ann Foster and brother to the elder Mary Lacey.

3. Examination of Elizabeth Johnson, Jr., August 11, 1692, in Rosenthal, ed., 543–544.

4. Examination of Martha Carrier, May 31, 1692, in Rosenthal, ed., 335–336.

5. If Margaret Toothaker ever had been examined, it is hard to imagine that at her tender age, she could have resisted the pressure to confess and implicate others (including her mother and aunt) just as her Carrier cousins did. The possibility that she *was* examined and that the record is lost cannot be discounted.

6. Petition of Abigail Faulkner, Sr., for a Pardon, December 3, 1692, in Rosenthal, ed., 704–705.

7. Examination of Abigail Faulkner, Sr., August 11, 1692, in Rosenthal, ed., 542–543.

8. Andover Old Tax and Record Book, 1670–1716, film image 5650.

9. No examination record is known to survive for twenty-two-year-old Sarah Parker so it is not known if she confessed or not. Faulkner gave what some interpreted as an admission of guilt when examined again during the second phase, but it would be difficult to call it a con-fession.

10. The others were Mary (Foster) Lacey and Mary (Tyler) Post Bridges, both of whom con-fessed.

11. Examination of Elizabeth Johnson, Sr., August 30, 1692, in Rosenthal, ed., 568.

12. Ibid., 568.

13. The elder James Howe was Elizabeth (Dane) Johnson's uncle by marriage since his wife Elizabeth (Dane) Howe was a sister of Johnson's father, Francis Dane. The younger James was, therefore, Elizabeth's first cousin.

14. Examination of Elizabeth Johnson, Sr., August 30, 1692, in Rosenthal, ed., 568–569.

15. Statement of Francis Dane, Sr. Regarding some of the Andover Accused, January 2, 1693, in Rosenthal, ed., 734–735.

16. Examination of Abigail Faulkner, August 30, 1692, in Rosenthal, ed., 542–543.

17. This is the same Benjamin Abbot who had testified against Martha Carrier a month ear-lier.

18. Examination of Stephen Johnson, September 1, 1692, in Rosenthal, ed., 574–575.

CHAPTER EIGHT: THE TOUCH TEST

1. Examination of William Barker, Sr., August 29, 1692, in Rosenthal, ed., 561.
2. Greven, 86–87.
3. Examination of William Barker, Sr., August 29, 1692, in Rosenthal, ed., 561.
4. Ibid., 562.
5. Ibid.
6. Ibid.
7. Examination of Martha Carrier, May 31, 1692, in Rosenthal, ed., 336.
8. Examination of Susanna Martin, May 2, 1692 in Rosenthal, ed., 228.
9. Norton, 264.
10. Declaration of Mary Osgood, Mary Tyler, Deliverance Dane, Abigail Barker, Sarah Wilson, Sr., and Hannah Tyler, undated, in Rosenthal, ed. 737–738.
11. Declaration of Mary Osgood, Mary Tyler, Deliverance Dane, Abigail Barker, Sarah Wilson, Sr., and Hannah Tyler, January 3, 1693, in Rosenthal, ed., 737–738.
12. Robinson, 223.
13. Fragment of examination of Deliverance Dane, September 8, 1692, in Rosenthal, ed., 607.
14. Examination of Mary Osgood, September 8, 1692, in Rosenthal, ed., 608–609.
15. Summary of the Examinations of Dorothy Faulkner, Abigail Faulkner, Jr., Martha Tyler, Johannah Tyler, Sarah Wilson, Jr., & Joseph Draper v. Abigail Faulkner, Sr., September 16, 1692, in Rosenthal, ed., 660.
16. This number also includes Roger Toothaker, who is not numbered among the accused during the Andover phase because he died in jail before it began. A total of seventeen members of the extended Ingalls family were accused in the course of the year.

CHAPTER NINE: THE TRIBULATIONS OF JOB (AND MOSES)

1. Warrant for the Apprehension of Mary Bridges, Sr., and Officer's Return, July 28, 1692, in Rosenthal, ed., 488–489.
2. Examination of Hannah Bromage, July 30, 1692, in Rosenthal, ed., 490.
3. Warrant for the Apprehension of Mary Post, and Officer's Return, August 2, 1692, in Rosenthal, ed., 496.
4. At least one author has cited connections associated with Mary's husband John Bridges. His first wife, Sarah Howe, had been a niece of Francis Dane and therefore a sister-in-law of the already executed Elizabeth Jackson Howe. Also, Bridges's late brother Edmund had been the first husband of Sarah (Towne) Cloyce of Salem Village, who had already languished in jail for several months. Robinson, 303.
5. Robert Calef, *More Wonders of the Invisible World* (originally published 1700), reprinted in George Lincoln Burr, *Narratives of the Witchcraft Cases 1648–1706* (New York: C. Scribner's Sons, 1914), 382.
6. Examination of Rebecca Eames, August 19, 1692, in Rosenthal, ed., 547–548.
7. As with John Bridges's connections by marriage to the Howe and Towne families, at least one author has suggested that the Eames's connections to the Tylers led to their arrests. Robinson, 148–150.
8. It is highly unlikely that any witchcraft suspect from 1692 had more varied connections to other suspects than Sarah Bridges had. Her stepmother, half-sister, and three stepsisters had all been accused. Her late mother, Sarah Howe Bridges, had been a first cousin to Francis Dane's two jailed daughters, and the minister's five accused grandchildren were therefore her second cousins. The executed Elizabeth Jackson Howe was her aunt by marriage because Elizabeth's husband James Howe, Jr., was her mother's brother. Finally, her father's deceased brother Edmund Bridges, Jr., had been the first husband of Sarah Towne (Bridges) Cloyce, who had been in custody on sorcery charges since the spring.

9. Warrant for the Apprehension of William Barker, Sr., Mary Marston, & Mary Barker, and Officer's Return, August 25, 1692, in Rosenthal, ed., 550.

10. Robinson, 145.

11. Robinson, 146.

12. Foulds, 30.

13. Deposition of Martha Sprague vs. Abigail Faulkner, Sr., September 17, 1692, in Rosenthal, ed., 669–670.

14. Hannah Foster's mother was the already jailed Rebecca (Blake) Eames. Rebecca's sister Prudence had been the first wife of Moses Tyler and therefore the mother of Joseph Tyler.

15. Court record of the trial of Hannah Post, in Rosenthal, ed., 780–781. Spelling modernized when needed for clarification.

16. Declaration of Mary Osgood, Mary Tyler, Deliverance Dane, Abigail Barker, Sarah Wilson, Sr., and Hannah Tyler, January 3, 1693 in Rosenthal, ed., 737–738.

17. This was true. Mary (Ayer) Parker's late husband, Nathan Parker, had a brother named Joseph Parker who was also deceased. Joseph's widow's name was also Mary Parker.

18. Examination of Mary Parker, September 2, 1692, in Rosenthal, ed., 578–579.

19. Examination of Sarah Hawkes, September 1, 1692, in Rosenthal, ed., 573–574.

20. Examination of Stephen Johnson, September 1, 1692, in Rosenthal, ed., 574–575.

21. Examination of Samuel Wardwell, September 1, 1692, in Rosenthal, ed., 576.

22. The examination record actually refers to these two suspects as Mary Lilly and Hannah Taylor, but there is no doubt that they are references to Jane Lilly and Mary Taylor of Reading, examined four days later on charges of afflicting Mary (Swain) Marshall, also of Reading. Mary Swain Marshall's husband, Edward Marshall, was a cousin of Sarah Hooper Wardwell. He had died August 3, 1692. On August 8, William Hooper, a brother of Sarah, had also died in Reading. At the examinations of the women accused of bewitching Mary Swain Marshall, insinuations were also made that they were responsible for the deaths of Edward Marshall and William Hooper.

23. Examination of Samuel Wardwell, September 1, 1692, in Rosenthal, ed., 576–577.

24. Examination of Sarah Wardwell, September 1, 1692, in Rosenthal, ed., 577.

25. Ibid.

26. For those unfamiliar with Roman numerals, this monument indicates that Job Tyler was born in 1619, died about 1700, and was the first settler of Andover in 1640. Andover did not come into existence as a town until 1646, but the tradition among Job Tyler's descendants is that he and his family squatted in the area that became Andover as early as 1640. Colonial records of Rhode Island disprove that legend however. Job appeared among a list of inhabitants admitted to Newport, Rhode Island, the year it was formed—1638. An item from a Rhode Island court record indicates that he was still there as late as 1643. A statement from the quarter session court held in Newport on June 7, 1643, contains the following entry: "Job Tyler being accused by two witnesses for slighting the authorities when the serjant came to summon him that he said he cared not a fart/turd for all their warrants, be adjudged to be whipt till his back be bloody." The possibility the Rhode Island records refer to a different Job Tyler cannot be ruled out, but this incident fits with the character of Job Tyler of Andover. Rhode Island Colony Records, 1646–1669, Part 1, Pages 1–198, Rhode Island Archives, p. 28 (housed at the Rhode Island State Archives, Providence, RI). The date ascribed to this volume is not accurate since it does contain documents from years prior to 1646.

CHAPTER TEN: THE RESISTANCE GROWS

1. Thomas Brattle, *Letter of Thomas Brattle, F.R.S.,* October 8, 1692 (reprinted in George Lincoln Burr, *Narratives of the Witchcraft Cases 1648–1706* (New York: C. Scribner's Sons,

1914), 184. The ministers Brattle names here are John Hale of Beverly, Nicholas Noyes of Salem Town, and Samuel Parris of Salem Village.

2. By lumping Barnard in with this group, Stacy Schiff's recent account directly contradicts the statement of this contemporary observer. Stacy Schiff, *The Witches: Salem, 1692* (New York: Little, Brown, 2015), 328.

3. Examination of William Barker, Sr., August 29, 1692, in Rosenthal, ed., 561.

4. Brattle, 180.

5. Placement of the Wardwell Children by the Selectmen of Andover, ca. September 28, 1692, in Rosenthal, ed., 675–676.

6. Recognizance of Dorothy Faulkner and Abigail Faulkner, Jr. by John Osgood, Sr. and Nathaniel Dane, October 6, 1692 in Rosenthal, ed., 682.

7. Recognizance for Mary Lacey, Jr. by Francis Faulkner and John Barker, October 6, 1692, in Rosenthal, ed., 684.

8. Petition of John Osgood, Sr., John Frye, John Marston, et al. for Their Wives and Daughters, October 12, 1692, in Rosenthal, ed., 687–688.

9. Increase Mather, *Cases of Conscience Concerning Evil Spirits Personating Men, Witchcrafts, infallible Proofs of Guilt in Such as Are Accused with That Crime* (Boston: Benjamin Harris, London Coffee-House, 1693), 71.

10. Mather, 66–67.

11. Letter of William Phips to the Privy Council, October 12, 1692, in Rosenthal, ed., 686–687. In this letter, Phips attempted to distance himself from the actions of the court by claiming he had been away fighting for nearly the entire duration of the proceedings of the Court of Oyer and Terminer. In reality, he had not left Boston for the frontier until mid-August.

12, The authenticity of the signatures on this document is in doubt according to Rosenthal's work, which notes that they were primarily written in two different inks with some signed by the same hand (Rosenthal, ed., 691). It is possible that this is a copy of an original petition which no longer exists. Rosenthal notes that parts of it are in the hand of Dudley Bradstreet, who was in hiding with his wife at the time due to allegations of witchcraft against them.

13. Petition of Twenty-six Andover Men Concerning Townspeople Accused of Witchcraft, October 18, 1692, in Rosenthal, ed., 690–691.

14. Examination of Martha Carrier, May 31, 1692, in Rosenthal, ed., 336.

15. Petition of Twenty-six Andover Men Concerning Townspeople Accused of Witchcraft, October 18, 1692, in Rosenthal, ed., 690–691.

16. Examination of Susanna Martin, May 2, 1692, in Rosenthal, ed., 228.

17. Petition of Twenty-six Andover Men Concerning Townspeople Accused of Witchcraft, October 18, 1692, in Rosenthal, ed., 690–691.

18. Recantations of Mary Osgood, Eunice Frye, Deliverance Dane, Abigail Barker, Mary Tyler, Sarah Wilson, Sr., Mary Bridges, Sr., Mary Marston, Sarah Churchill, Hannah Post, and Mary Post, as Reported by Increase Mather, October 19, 1692, in Rosenthal, ed., 693–694. The last three did not recant, but brief statements by them were included in the document.

19. Ibid., 693.

20. Ibid., 693–694.

21. Ibid., 694.

22. Petition of Ten Persons of Ipswich, undated (probably late October 1692) in Rosenthal, ed., 697.

23. Petition of Abigail Faulkner, Sr. for a Pardon, December 3, 1692, in Rosenthal, ed., 704–705.

24. Petition of Rebecca Eames for a Pardon, December 5, 1692 in Rosenthal, ed., 705–706. Hobbs and Lacey were also suspects in jail in addition to acting with the afflicted.

25. Ibid., 706.
26. Petition of John Osgood, Sr. and Seven Other Andover Residents for the Accused, December 6, 1692, in Rosenthal, ed., 707.
27. An Act Against Conjuration, Witchcraft, and Dealing with Evil and Wicked Spirits, December 14, 1692, in Rosenthal, ed., 713.
28. Old style calendar date. This date would be January 2, 1693, by modern calculations with the new year beginning on January 1 rather than March 25.
29. Statement of Francis Dane, Sr. Regarding some of the Andover Accused, January 2, 1693, in Rosenthal, ed., 734–735.
30. Petition for Mary Osgood, Eunice Frye, Deliverance Dane, Sarah Wilson, Sr., and Abigail Barker, January 3, 1693 in Rosenthal, ed., 739.
31. Ibid., 739.

CHAPTER ELEVEN: THE TRIALS RESUME

1. Abigail Dane Faulkner had been convicted but was still alive due to her pregnancy. The other non-confessors from Andover had been hanged.
2. Increase Mather, 59.
3. This was a means of folk magic that involved balancing a sieve on a pair of scissors or shears and seeing whether or not the sieve turned. Moses Haggett's wife was Joanna Johnson, the sister of Rebecca's late husband Timothy Johnson.
4. Calef, 382.
5. Ibid., 382.
6. Cotton Mather, *A Further Account of the Tryals of the New-England Witches, Sent in a Letter From Thence, to a Gentleman in London, 1693,* reprinted in *On Witchcraft* (Mineola, NY: Dover, 2005), 171.
7. Letter of William Phips to the Earl of Nottingham, February 21, 1693, in Rosenthal, ed., 810.
8. Ibid., 809–811.
9. Ibid., 810–811.

CHAPTER TWELVE: AFTERMATH

1. Greven, 115–116.
2. Abbot, 156.
3. Account book of Thomas Barnard, pages not numbered. Phillips Library, Peabody Essex Museum, Salem, MA. Photocopy at North Andover Historical Society, North Andover, MA.
4. Petition of Ministers from Essex County, July 8, 1703, in Rosenthal, ed., 851.
5. Examination of Mary Lacey, Sr., July 21, 1692, in Rosenthal, ed., 477–478.
6. Petition of Abigail Faulkner, Sr., June 13, 1700, in Rosenthal, ed., 847–848.
7. An Act of Reversing the Attainder of Abigail Faulkner, Sr., et al., May 26, 1703, in Rosenthal, ed., 850.
8. Petition of Ministers from Essex County, July 8, 1703, in Rosenthal, ed., 851.
9. Lydia was a sister of the accused Abigail Wheeler Barker.
10. Petition of Rebecca Eames for Restitution, September 12, 1710, in Rosenthal, ed., 859.
11. Calef, 382.
12. Joseph Parker's sister Hannah was married to Mary Post's uncle, John Tyler. John and Hannah had relocated to Mendon soon after 1692. Moses Tyler, another uncle, lived in nearby Boxford, so it does seem odd that Mary turned to John Barker and Joseph Parker for help rather than to him. They may have offered to assist her since they were seeking compensation for their own accused family members.
13. Those executed, but not included, were Bridget Bishop, Susanna Martin, Alice Parker,

Ann Pudeator, Wilmot Redd, and Margaret Scott.
14. An Act to Reverse the Attainders of George Burroughs et al. for Witchcraft, October 17, 1711, in Rosenthal, ed., 888–889.
15. Ibid., 889.

APPENDICES
1. Because he died before the Andover witch hunt began, Roger Toothaker is not properly regarded as one of its accused witches.
2. John Aslebee was also a brother of Rebecca Aslebee Johnson of Andover and Sarah Aslebee Cole of Lynn, both of whom had been arrested on witchcraft charges. The Aslebees were the children of original Andover proprietor John Aslebee, Sr. and his wife Rebecca Ayer—a sister of the executed Mary Ayer Parker.
3. Abbot, 115.
4. No married woman whose husband did not also sign is known to have signed the petition of January 3, 1693, the only petition from Andover signed by women. A possible exception is the signer named Elizabeth Stevens. This Elizabeth may have been Elizabeth Abbot Stevens, the wife of Nathan Stevens who did not sign. It is equally possible that the Elizabeth Stevens who signed was Nathan's widowed grandmother, also named Elizabeth.
5. Wright's first wife, Susannah Johnson Wright, had been a sister of Stephen Johnson (the deceased husband of the jailed Elizabeth Dane Johnson) and Timothy Johnson (the late husband of the also jailed Rebecca Aslebee Johnson).
6. Petition of John and Joseph Parker for Restitution of Mary Parker, November 7, 1692, in Rosenthal, ed., 700.
7. Deposition of Thomas Chandler vs. Samuel Wardwell.
8. Two other Abbot siblings may have signed this petition. One of the signers was an Elizabeth Stevens. This might be Elizabeth Abbot Stevens, the younger daughter of George and Hannah Chandler Abbot, who had recently married Nathan Stevens. The signer might also, however, have been Nathan's aged grandmother Elizabeth Stevens. There was also a Hannah Chandler who signed the petition, and it is not clear if it was Thomas's wife Hannah Brewer Chandler or their son John's wife, Hannah Abbot Chandler (also a daughter of George and Hannah Chandler Abbot). John Abbot, as previously noted, was married to Sarah Barker, whose family also played a role in the resistance.
9. Deposition of Abigail Martin and John Bridges vs. Samuel Wardwell, September 15, 1692, in Rosenthal, ed., 645.

Bibliography

ARCHIVAL MATERIALS

Account book, Thomas Barnard, 1688-1705. Phillips Library, Peabody Essex Museum, Salem, MA (Photocopy at North Andover Historical Society, North Andover, MA).

Andover Old Tax and Record Book, 1670-1716, Office of the Town Clerk, Andover, MA (Photocopy at North Andover Historical Society, North Andover, MA).

A Book of Records for the North Precinct in the Town of Andover There Being a Division in the Towne By His Excellency the Governor and General Assembly's Order and Appointment, 1708 (Photocopy at North Andover Historical Society, North Andover, MA).

Petition submitted to the General Court by Inhabitants of the South Precinct in Andover requesting permission to be annexed to the North Precinct, 27 October 1709, Massachusetts Archives Collection, Vol. 11.

Records and Files of the Quarterly Court of Essex County, 1636-1686, Vols. I-IX (transcription).

Rosenthal, Bernard, ed. *Records of the Salem Witch-Hunt*. New York: Cambridge University Press, 2009. (This work contains transcriptions of all existing primary source documentation associated directly with the witch hunt of 1692. It is also listed among the printed materials.)

PRINTED MATERIALS

Abbot, Elinor. *Our Company Increases Apace: History, Language, and Social Identity in Colonial Andover, Massachusetts*. Dallas, TX: SIL International, 2007.

Allen, David Grayson. *In English Ways: The Movement of Societies and the Transferal of English Local Law and Custom to Massachusetts Bay in the Seventeenth Century*. New York and London: W.W. Norton, 1982.

Anderson, Robert Charles. *Great Migration: Immigrants to New England, 1634-1635*, Volume V. Boston: New England Historic Genealogical Society, 2010.

Andover, Massachusetts. *Vital Records of Andover Massachusetts to the end of the year 1849*. Topsfield, MA: Topsfield Historical Society, 1912.

Andover, Massachusetts, South Church. *Catalogue of Members From the Formation of the Church, in 1711, to 1859*. Andover, MA: Warren F. Draper, 1859.

Bailey, Sarah Loring. *Historical Sketches of Andover, Comprising the Present Towns of North Andover and Andover*. Boston: Houghton, Mifflin, 1880.

Baker, Emerson W. *A Storm of Witchcraft: The Salem Trials and the American Experience*. New York: Oxford University Press, 2015.

_____, *The Devil of Great Island: Witchcraft & Conflict in Early New England*. New York: Palgrave Macmillan, 2007.

Baker, Emerson W. and John G. Reid. *The New England Knight: Sir William Phips, 1651-1695*. Toronto, Buffalo, London: University of Toronto Press, 1998.

Boyer, Paul and Stephen Nissenbaum. *Salem Possessed: The Social Origins of Witchcraft*. Cambridge, MA, and London: Harvard University Press, 1974.

_____, eds. *Salem-Village Witchcraft: A Documentary Record of Local Conflict in Colonial New England*. Belmont, CA: Wadsworth Publishing, 1972.

Brattle, Thomas. *Letter of Thomas Brattle, F.R.S.,* 8 October 1692. Reprinted in *Narratives of the Witchcraft Cases 1648-1706*. George Lincon Burr, ed. New York: C. Scribner's Sons, 1914.

Breslaw, Elaine G. *Tituba, Reluctant Witch of Salem*. New York and London: New York University Press, 1996.

Brigham, Willard I. Tyler. *The Tyler Genealogy: The Descendants of Job Tyler of Andover, Massachusetts, 1619-1700*. Plainfield, NJ, and Tylerville, CT: Cornelus B. Tyler and Rollin U. Tyler, 1912.

Burleigh, Charles. *The Genealogy and History of the Ingalls Family in America*. Baltimore, MD: Gateway Press, 1991 (reprint of original 1903 publication).

Calef, Robert. *More Wonders of the Invisible World* (originally published 1700). Reprinted in *Narratives of the Witchcraft Cases 1648-1706*. George Lincon Burr, ed. New York: C. Scribner's Sons, 1914.

Demos, John P. *Entertaining Satan: Witchcraft and the Culture of Early New England*. New York: Oxford University Press, 1982.

Foulds, Diane E. *Death in Salem: The Private Lives Behind the 1692 Witch Hunt.* Guilford, CT: Globe Pequot Press, 2010.

Godbeer, Richard. *The Devil's Dominion: Magic and Religion in Early New England.* Cambridge: Cambridge University Press, 1992.

Greven, Philip J., Jr. *Four Generations: Population, Land, and Family in Colonial Andover, Massachusetts.* Ithaca, NY, and London: Cornell University Press, 1970.

Groff, Bethany. *A Brief History of Old Newbury From Settlement to Separation.* Charleston, SC: History Press, 2008.

Hale, John. *A Modest Enquiry Into the Nature of Witchcraft and How Persons Guilty of that Crime may be Convicted: And the means used for their Discovery Discussed, both Negatively and Affirmatively, according to Scripture and Experience.* Boston: Printed by B. Green and J. Allen for Benjamin Eliot under the Town House, 1702.

Hall, David D., ed. *Witch-Hunting in Colonial New England: A Documentary History, 1638-1693.* Boston: Northeastern University Press, 1991, 1999.

Hambleton, Else L. "Playing the Rogue: Rape and Issues of Consent in Seventeenth-Century Massachusetts." In *Sex Without Consent: Rape and Sexual Coercion in America.* Smith, Merril D., ed. New York and London: New York University Press, 2001.

Hansen, Chadwick. *Witchcraft at Salem.* New York: George Braziller, 1969.

————. "Andover Witchcraft and the Causes of the Salem Witchcraft Trials". In *The Occult in America: New Historical Perspectives*, eds. Howard Kerr and Charles L. Crow, 38-57. Urbana and Chicago: University of Illinois Press, 1983.

Haverhill, Massachusetts. *Vital Records of Haverhill Massachusetts to the end of the year 1849.* Topsfield, MA: Topsfield Historical Society, 1911.

Hazen, Henry A. *History of Billerica With a Genealogical Register.* Boston: A. Williams and Company, 1883.

Henderson, James. "English Origins of John Lovejoy of Andover, Massachusetts". In *The New England Historical & Genealogical Register* (Vol. 163, January 2009), 27-34. Boston: New England Historic Genealogical Society, 2009.

Hill, Frances, ed. *The Salem Witch Trials Reader.* Boston: Da Capo Press, 2000.

Hoffer, Peter Charles. *The Salem Witchcraft Trials: A Legal History.* Lawrence: University Press of Kansas, 1997.

James, Jane Emerson. *The Haverhill Emersons Revised and Extended.* Lake Winnebago, MO: Jane E. James, 1983.

Karlsen, Carol F. *The Devil in the Shape of a Woman.* New York: W.W. Norton, 1987.

Mather, Cotton. *A Further Account of the Tryals of the New-England Witches, Sent in a Letter From Thence, to a Gentleman in London, 1693,* reprinted in *On Witchcraft.* Mineola, NY: Dover Publications, 2005.

_____. *The Wonders of the Invisible World.* Mineola, NY: Dover Publications, 2005, reprint of work first published 1692.

Mather, Increase. *Cases of Conscience Concerning Evil Spirits Personating Men, Witchcrafts, infallible Proofs of Guilt in Such as Are Accused with That Crime.* Boston: Benjamin Harris, London Coffee-House, 1693.

Norton, Mary Beth. *In the Devil's Snare: The Salem Witchcraft Crisis of 1692.* New York: Alfred A. Knopf, 2002.

Rapaport, Diane. *The Naked Quaker: True Crimes and Controversies from the Courts of Colonial New England.* Beverly, MA: Commonwealth Editions, 2007.

Ray, Benjamin C. "The Geography of Witchcraft Accusations in 1692 in Salem Village," *William and Mary Quarterly: A Magazine of Early American History and Culture* (Vol. LXV, Number 3, July 2008), 449-478.

_____. *Satan & Salem: The Witch-Hunt Crisis of 1692.* Charlottesville and London: University of Virginia Press, 2015.

Reis, Elizabeth. *Damned Women: Sinners and Witches in Puritan New England.* Ithaca, NY, and London: Cornell University Press, 1997.

Roach, Marilynne K. *The Salem Witch Trials: A Day-By-Day Chronicle of a Community Under Siege.* Lanham, MD: Taylor Trade Publishing, 2002.

_____, *Six Women of Salem: The Untold Story of the Accused and Their Accusers in the Salem Witch Trials.* Boston: Da Capo Press, 2013.

Robinson, Enders A. *Salem Witchcraft and Hawthorne's House of the Seven Gables.* Bowie, MD: Heritage Books, 1992.

_____, *The Devil Discovered: Salem Witchcraft 1692.* New York: Hippocrene Books, 1991.

_____, *Andover Witchcraft Genealogy, Volume 1, "Salem Witchcraft" Series.* Goose Pond Press, 2013.

Rosenthal, Bernard, ed. *Records of the Salem Witch-Hunt.* New York: Cambridge University Press, 2009.

_____. *Salem Story: Reading the Witch Trials of 1692.* Cambridge: Cambridge University Press, 1993.

Schiff, Stacy. *The Witches: Salem, 1692.* New York, Boston, and London: Little, Brown, 2015.

Silverman, Kenneth. *The Life and Times of Cotton Mather.* New York: Harper & Row, 1984.

Starkey, Marion L. *The Devil in Massachusetts: A Modern Enquiry into the Salem Witch Trials.* New York: Alfred A. Knopf, 1949.

Swan, Frank H. *Richard Swan and Some of His Descendants.* Providence, RI: Akerman-Standard, 1927.

Ulrich, Laurel Thatcher. *Good Wives: Image and Reality in the Lives of Women in Northern New England, 1650-1750.* New York: Vintage Books, 1980

Upham, Charles W. *Salem Witchcraft.* Boston: Wiggin and Lunt, 1867.

Weisman, Richard. *Witchcraft, Magic, and Religion in 17th-Century Massachusetts.* Amherst: University of Massachusetts Press, 1984.

INTERNET MATERIALS

Ray, Benjamin, ed., *Salem Witch Trials: Documentary Archive and Transcription Project* (Charlottesville: University of Virginia – host) http://salem.lib.virginia.edu/home.html

Acknowledgments

I WANT TO EXTEND my appreciation to a few people who played important roles in helping to make this work a reality.

First of all, I want to thank Carol Majahad and Inga Larson of the North Andover Historical Society for their invaluable assistance with my research —both when I was on site and through email. Their support of this project from the time I first told them about it has been invaluable.

I also want to thank the staff of the Andover Historical Society. I was there on Saturdays when students were generally working in the reading room and unfortunately, I never came to know any of their names, but I appreciate their assistance.

My former colleague, Daniel Linke, now Archivist at Princeton University, helped me obtain information from their collections and I must express my appreciation for his efforts. We began our careers working on the same project at the Western Reserve Historical Society in Cleveland many years ago.

I attended lectures by scholars Emerson Baker and Margo Burns, both of whom offered valuable insight and encouraged me. In addition, Margo provided useful information on maps of the area.

Enders Robinson's earlier work on the witch hunt in Andover provided much consolidated material on the events in Andover during the witch hunt. Although I ultimately disagreed with some of the conclusions he reached, his publications made my work far easier by pointing me to issues that called for further investigation. For that, I am grateful.

My cousin David Dinwiddie and his wife Shirley gave me a copy of Bernard Rosenthal's edited *Records of the Salem Witch Hunt*, the most comprehensive compilation in existence of the documents associated with the witch trials of 1692. This was a few months after their visit to the New England states, during which time I gave them a tour of the town of Salem.

Their interest helped to inspire me to pursue my research further and I saw a void in the scholarship on the event that needed to be filled.

I also want to thank Cassandra Michael who accompanied me on a few of my early trips to Salem and Andover and who took most of the photographs that appear in this volume. Cass is a direct descendant of no fewer than four residents of Andover who were accused of witchcraft in 1692, some of whom were undoubtedly arrested by my own ancestor John Ballard (the constable of Andover's South End).

Two of my former teachers should be mentioned. One is William Beezley, who was a history professor at North Carolina State University during my time in graduate school there. He taught the class I took on the writing of history and my topic was the 1692 witch hunt. I must also thank one of my high school English teachers, Dan Wolber, with whom I have reconnected in the past few years. He was the one who first gave me confidence in my ability as a writer.

I also want to thank Bruce H. Franklin of Westholme Publishing and Noreen O'Connor-Abel for their work in editing this manuscript into the final form.

Finally, I must thank my sister Jacqueline Hite Bell, who first told me a bit about the story of the witchcraft trails when we were children. She was the one who first sparked my interest in the subject.

Index

Abbot, Benjamin, 30-31, 38, 96, 103, 115, 179-181, 189, 214, 227, 242-244, 249, 260n14, 261n17

Abbot, Dorcas Graves, 189

Abbot, George, 38, 42, 59, 178, 180, 189, 214, 221, 241-242, 246, 260n14, 265n8

Abbot, John, 38, 120, 143, 151, 179, 189, 227-228, 265n8

Abbot, Sarah Barker, 189

Abbot, Sarah (Farnum), 31, 38, 97, 111, 189, 214, 242, 249

Abbot, William, 178, 242

Allen, Andrew, 30, 57-59, 72, 84, 89-90, 93-94, 201, 211, 258n32

Allen, Elizabeth Richardson, 59

Allen, Faith (Ingalls), 30, 57, 60, 89-90, 99-100, 201, 211, 223

Allen, John, 26, 58, 233

Allen, Mercy Peters, 59

Allen, Thomas, 59

Andover Village Center in 1692, list of villagers, 40-41

Andover (village in 1692), list of households accused of witchcraft and, 38-39

Andrew, Daniel, 5, 254n8

Andros, Edmund, ix, 36, 121

Aslebee, John, 40, 120, 151, 208, 225, 235, 265n2

Aslebee, Rebecca, 234

Atkinson, Sarah, 26

Babson, Ebenezer, 198

Bagley, Orlando, 26

Ballard, Eleanor, 235

Ballard, Elizabeth (Phelps), 38, 65, 70-71, 83, 85-88, 90, 94, 102, 179, 184, 214, 235, 242-243, 250, 252

Ballard, Grace, 69-70, 235, 252

Ballard, Jeremiah, 184

Ballard, John, xv-xvi, 30, 36, 38, 65, 67-70, 83, 86, 91, 112, 119, 128, 142, 151-152, 179-180, 185, 189, 220, 229-231, 235, 252, 256n12

Ballard, Joseph, xv-xvi, 65, 68-71, 73-74, 83, 86-87, 91, 102-103, 128, 148, 184, 189, 195, 214, 229-230, 250, 252, 256n12

Ballard, Jr., Joseph, 184, 207

Ballard, Jr., William, 67

Ballard, Rebecca (Hooper), 68, 151, 230

Ballard, Rebecca Johnson, 184, 189

Ballard, Rebecca Rea, 184

Ballard, Sherebiah, 68, 185

Ballard, Uriah, 69

Ballard, William, 36, 38, 47, 65-69, 73, 214, 220, 229-231, 252, 256n2, 258n2

Barker, Abigail (Wheeler), 119, 153, 158, 167, 172, 191, 194, 199, 203, 216, 227, 249, 264n9

Barker, Ebenezer, 153, 191, 194, 199, 227

Barker, Joanna, 143

Barker, Joanne, 226
Barker, John, 38, 152, 174, 178, 194,
    196, 199, 227, 247, 256n5, 265n12
Barker, Jr., William, 173, 183, 194, 199
Barker, Mary, 116, 131, 166, 173, 177,
    183, 199-200, 227-228, 242
Barker, Richard, 45, 68, 116-117, 143,
    199-200, 226-227, 241, 256n5
Barker, Sarah, 143, 265n8
Barker, Sr., William, 38, 116-118, 131,
    149, 173, 194, 200, 227
Barnard, Elizabeth Price, 239-240
Barnard, Francis, 43
Barnard, Hannah, 192, 226
Barnard, John, 192
Barnard, Robert, 43, 224
Barnard, Stephen, 43, 192, 224
Barnard, Thomas, xvii, 40, 42-43, 109,
    119-120, 148-149, 155-156, 169,
    182, 189-193, 197, 220, 224, 227,
    239
Bishop, Bridget, 15-16, 21, 23, 77, 80,
    104-105
Bishop, Edward, 16
Bixby, Daniel, 87, 187, 215
Bixby, Hannah (Chandler), 38, 87, 124,
    129, 187, 189, 215, 242-244
Blanchard, Jonathan, 238
Blanchard, Samuel, 179, 238
Bly, John, 16
Bly, William, 16
Boyer, Paul, xi, xiv, 35-37, 253-254n3
Bradbury, Mary, 26, 28-30
Bradbury, Mary (Perkins), 26, 28-30
Bradstreet, Anne Dudley, 121
Bradstreet, Ann Wood, 120-121, 240
Bradstreet, Dudley, 40, 68, 97, 102, 119-
    121, 129, 143, 148, 152, 167, 169,
    178, 220-221, 240-241, 256n5,
    263n12
Bradstreet, Mercy, 64
Bradstreet, Simon, 35, 46, 64, 121, 220,
    240, 256n5
Brattle, Thomas, 84, 148-150, 157-160,
    198, 263n1
Bridges, James, 61, 64
Bridges, John, 127, 131, 146, 152-153,
    158, 174, 200-201, 210, 215, 231

Bridges, Jr., Mary, 200
Bridges, Mary (Tyler), 40, 94, 153, 177
Bridges, Mary Tyler (Post), 128, 131,
    133, 145, 158, 200, 210, 215, 231
Bridges, Sarah, 131, 136, 145-146, 172-
    173, 183, 186, 189, 194, 200-201,
    262n8
Bromage, Edward, 201
Bromage, Hannah, 94, 104, 128-129,
    174, 201
Burroughs, George, 19-20, 72, 75, 84-85,
    95, 98, 103-104, 154, 253n1

Calef, Robert, 4-5, 130, 175, 196, 210
Carr, George, 28
Carr, James, 28
Carr, Richard, 28
Carr, William, 28
Carrier, Andrew, 85, 90, 92, 201
Carrier, Jr., Thomas, 184, 186
Carrier, Martha Allen, 30-31, 36-37, 57-
    60, 72, 81, 84, 90, 93-97, 100-101,
    106-107, 109, 111, 155, 174, 201-
    202, 223, 259n11
Carrier, Richard, 31, 59, 85, 90-93, 98,
    103, 109, 111, 173, 186-187, 202,
    260n7
Carrier, Sarah, 97, 99, 102-103, 105,
    121, 151-152, 182, 187, 202, 234
Carrier, Thomas, 30, 57, 59-60, 97-99,
    101-102, 109, 121, 152, 182-184,
    187, 194, 201-202, 224, 234
Casco Bay, 18-20, 227
Case, Mary, 195, 203
Cases of Conscience Concerning Evil Spirits
    Personating Men, 153
Chandler, Annis, 241
Chandler, Bridget Henchman (Richard-
    son), 97, 215, 243
Chandler, Hannah, 241
Chandler, Hannah Brewer, 243, 250
Chandler, John, 120, 178, 189, 243
Chandler, Joseph, 187
Chandler, Jr., Thomas, 189, 233, 242
Chandler, Mary Peters, 189
Chandler, Phebe, 38, 97, 186-187, 215,
    242, 244

Chandler, Thomas, 38, 42, 46-49, 62, 87-88, 127, 129, 132, 141, 186, 189, 215, 233, 236, 241-244, 250, 256n5, 265n8

Chandler, William, 38, 42, 88, 97, 186, 215, 221, 233, 241-243

Checkley, Anthony, 96, 176

Chubb, Priscilla, 18

Churchill, Sarah, 12, 134-135, 140, 158, 263n18

Clark, Mary Johnson (Davis), 104, 129, 202, 234, 251-252, 260n2

Cloyce, Sarah (Towne), 18, 21, 73, 174, 262n8

Cole, Ann, 2

Cole, John, 2

Cole, Sarah Aslebee, 150, 235-236, 265n2

Colson, Mary Dustin, 202-203

Confidence, 36

Corey, Giles, 12, 17-18, 73, 175, 196, 255-256n10

Corey, Martha, 5-7, 12, 17-18, 22, 73, 175

Corwin, Jonathan, 3-4, 7-8, 19, 22, 104, 115

Court of Assize and General Goale Delivery, 164

Court of Oyer and Terminer, 16, 21, 81, 104, 120, 123-125, 136, 148, 153-154, 164, 176, 198, 263n11

Crosby, Anthony, 28

The Crucible (Miller), 15, 22

Cry Innocent, 16

Dane, Deliverance (Haseltine), 40, 119, 122, 153, 158, 167-168, 194, 203, 223

Dane, Elizabeth Ingalls, 99-100, 203-204

Dane, Francis, 38, 40, 43-44, 60, 89, 100-101, 106, 108-109, 112, 115, 118-120, 122, 125, 130, 149, 151, 155-156, 166-169, 180, 182, 184, 189-190, 192, 197, 201, 203-204, 207, 214-215, 220-223, 225, 234, 239-243, 260n14, 261n4, 262n8

Dane, Hannah Chandler (Abbot), 221, 243

Dane, Hannah Poor, 184, 223

Dane, John, 43, 215, 221, 241

Dane, Jr., Francis, 38, 184, 189

Dane, Mary, 184, 241-242

Dane, Nathaniel, 151, 153, 156, 194, 203

Danforth, Thomas, 164

Davis, Ephraim, 103, 202, 234, 260n2

Demos, John P., 1, 259n3

Dodd, Sarah, 29

Draper, Joseph, 123-124, 203, 246

Dustin, Hannah, 51

Eames, Daniel, 103, 111, 113, 130, 177, 203, 218, 228, 249, 252

Eames, Lydia Wheeler, 195

Eames, Rebecca (Blake), 38, 87, 111, 124, 130, 154, 160-161, 176, 195-196, 203, 216, 248

Earl of Nottingham, 176

Eastman, Roger, 28

Eastman, Sarah, 28

Elatson, Jonathan, 164

Emerson, Elizabeth, 51-53, 93, 204, 218

Emerson, John, 158

Emerson, Joseph, 53, 93, 204

Emerson, Martha Toothaker, 53, 81, 85, 90, 94, 103, 145, 173, 204

Emerson, Michael, 50-51

Emerson, Robert, 50-52

Endicott, Zerubbabel, 28

Entertaining Satan: Witchcraft and the Culture of Early New England (Demos), 1, 259n3

Essex County Court, 51

Essex County, ix-xi, xv-xvi, 3, 19, 21, 24, 33, 35, 44-45, 48-49, 51, 55, 61-62, 70, 122, 138, 146, 151, 164-165, 197, 253n1, 258n21

Esty, Mary Towne, 73, 163, 174, 193-194

Farmington, 2

Farnum, Alice, 111, 216-217, 248-249

Farnum, John, 64, 97, 215-216, 249

Farnum, Jr., Ralph 97, 111, 189, 216-217, 249

Farnum, Mary, 252

Farnum, Samuel, 216, 228, 252
Farnum, Sarah Sterling, 189
Farrington, Edward, 38, 173, 204, 246
Farrington, Elizabeth Knight, 244
Faulkner, Abigail (Dane), 40, 106-108,
    110, 123, 134, 151-152, 159, 174,
    176, 183, 190, 204-205, 223-224,
    242, 264n1
Faulkner, Betty, 190
Faulkner, Dorothy, 123, 151, 174, 183,
    186, 193, 205
Faulkner, Edmund, 35-36
Faulkner, Elizabeth, 190
Faulkner, Francis, 106, 152, 174, 183,
    192, 194, 205, 223-224, 233, 247
Faulkner, Jr., Abigail, 204
Faulkner, Mary, 192, 224
First Church of Boston, 62
Five Mile Pond, 122, 130-131
Floyd, John, 103
Foster, Abraham, 103, 194, 245, 247-
    248, 260n2
Foster, Andrew, 55, 57, 97-98, 205, 216,
    247, 258n26
Foster, Ann, xv, 55-57, 71-74, 76, 78-82,
    84, 86-87, 95, 97, 108-109, 117,
    124, 144, 154, 161-162, 174, 195,
    198, 205, 208, 216, 247, 251,
    258n25, 259n5, 260n2
Foster, Ephraim, 61-62, 74, 80, 104, 11-
    112, 119, 128, 135-136, 139-149,
    142, 146, 165, 172, 180-181, 196,
    216, 248
Foster, Esther, 245
Foster, Hannah Eames, 54-57, 62, 64,
    135, 161, 181, 216, 247, 262n14
Foster, Jr., Ephraim, 181
Foster, Rose, 113, 115, 117, 124, 132,
    135-136, 139, 161, 172, 188, 216-
    217, 244
Foster, Sarah, 245
Foulds, Diane, 132
Friend, Richard, 137-139, 218
Frye, Eunice Potter, 40, 150, 153, 158,
    175, 177, 205, 236-237
Frye, James, 75, 103, 179, 184, 225, 237
Frye, John, 40, 68, 150, 153, 162-163,
    174-175, 205, 236, 256n5

Frye, Jr., John, 174-175, 236
Frye, Mary, 151
Frye, Samuel, 120, 151, 165, 181, 236
Frye, Sr., John, 236

Gale, Ambrose, 29
Gallows Hill, 108
Gedney, Bartholomew, 115
Godfrey, Joanne, 45
Godfrey, John, 45-48, 50, 61, 70, 88-89,
    128, 132, 139, 141, 221, 250
Good, Dorothy, 17, 108, 259n5
Goodhue, William, 42
Good, Sarah (Solart), 2, 4, 6, 8, 17, 98,
    237
Graves, Dorcas, 244
Graves, Mark, 244
Gray, Samuel, 77-78
Great Migration, x, 88, 99, 125
Green, Joseph, 191, 193
Green, Mary, 94, 159, 163, 205-206
Green, Peter, 159, 163, 205
Greensmith, Rebecca, 4, 13
Greven, Philip, 53, 256n1

Haggett, Moses, 172, 264n3
Hale, John, 240
Hansen, Chadwick, 10, 16, 23
Harvard, 43, 148-149, 220
Hathorne, John, 3-4, 7-9, 14, 19, 22, 76,
    98, 104, 107, 109, 114-115
Hawkes, Sarah (Hooper), 66, 182
Hawkes, Sarah (Hooper), 63, 65-66, 142,
    145, 173, 182, 206, 213, 228
Herrick, George, 21
Higginson, John, 115
Hoar, Dorcas, 125, 154, 176
Hobbs, Abigail, 15, 17-21, 23, 25, 73,
    81, 105, 108, 125, 153-154, 160,
    163, 176, 253n1, 255n4, 259n5
Hobbs, Deliverance, 18, 73, 79, 81,
    259n5
Hobbs, William, 18, 73, 163
Holt, Hannah (Allen), 59, 100-101
Holt, Henry, 38, 165, 178, 189, 230
Holt, James, 30, 58-59, 97, 100, 230
Holt, Jr., James, 59
Holt, Nicholas, 237

Holt, Oliver, 230
Holt, Samuel, 38, 58, 97, 100, 223, 230
Holt, Sarah Gerry, 237
Hooper, Rebecca, 65, 185, 230
Hooper, William, 63, 185, 229, 231, 262n22
Houlton, Joseph, 29
Howard, John, 135, 206
Howe, Elizabeth (Jackson), 60, 95, 113, 135, 224, 261n4, 262n8
Howe, James, 60, 113, 260n13, 262n8
Hoyt, Naomi, 252
Hubbard, Elizabeth, 2, 10, 21, 23, 59
Hutchins, Frances, 163, 206

Indian, John, 22
Ingalls, Ann, 88-90, 93, 99-100, 106, 125, 223
Ingalls, Edmund, 88-89, 93, 99, 106, 125, 223, 259n3
Ingalls, Francis, 59
Ingalls, Henry, 38, 59, 89, 223, 225
Ingalls, John, 89
Ingalls, Jr., Henry, 89
Ingalls, Mary Osgood, 59
Ingalls, Samuel, 38, 89

Jackson, Jr., John, 146, 173, 206
Jackson, Sr., John, 135, 145, 173, 206-207
Jacobs, George, 5, 12, 98, 134-135
James, 234
Jewett, Joseph, 129
Johnson, Abigail, 112, 136, 151, 207
Johnson, Elizabeth Dane, 59, 136, 142, 172, 207-208, 234, 265n5
Johnson, Elizabeth, xvi, 101-103, 105-107, 110-111, 113-114, 121, 130, 132, 166, 173, 175, 196-197, 207, 210, 234, 242
Johnson, Francis, 38, 152, 182, 194, 206, 234
Johnson, John, 194, 233-235
Johnson, Jr., Elizabeth, 109, 196, 207
Johnson, Jr., Rebecca, 207
Johnson, Jr., Thomas, 235
Johnson, Mary Holt, 234
Johnson, Mary Lovejoy, 184

Johnson, Rebecca Aslebee, 40, 150, 172-173, 206-207, 209, 234-236, 265n2, 265n5
Johnson, Sarah Hawkes, 194
Johnson, Sr., Thomas, 235
Johnson, Stephen, 59, 101, 115, 142, 151, 166, 173, 207-208, 234, 265n5
Johnson, Susan, 233-234
Johnson, Susannah, 184, 202, 265n5
Johnson, Thomas, 234
Johnson, William, 184, 235, 252

Kelly, Elizabeth, 2
Kemp, Samuel, 187, 247
Kemp, Zerubbabel, 187, 195, 208
Kimball, John, 26
King Charles I, 60
King Philip's War, ix-xi, 49, 127, 200, 212, 219, 250, 252
Kingsbury, Joseph, 163

Lacey, Jr., Mary, 208
Lacey, Lawrence, 57, 73, 102-103, 144, 195, 208, 247
Lacey, Mary (Foster), xv, 57, 73-75, 80-81, 84, 90-91, 93-94, 98, 103, 109, 111, 115, 124, 128, 141, 144, 146, 152, 160, 174, 176, 187, 195, 208, 247-248, 260n2
Lamson, Thomas, 187, 204
Lewis, Mercy, 11, 13, 20, 253
Lilly, Jane, 143, 208-209, 229, 262n22
Lincoln, Abraham, 211
Lovejoy, Grace, 36, 214, 220, 251-252, 256n2
Lovejoy, John, 36, 59, 68, 214, 226, 235, 238, 251-252, 256n2
Lovejoy, Mary Osgood, 252
Lovejoy, Sarah, 235
Lovejoy, William, 189, 252
Lovett, Daniel, 49, 212
Lovett, James, 49
Lovett, Mary, 49

Marble, Joseph, 165, 174, 192, 224
Marks, Roger, 59
Marks, Sarah Holt, 59
Marshall, Mary Swain, 217, 229, 262n22

Marston, John, 153, 162, 195, 209, 225

Marston, Mary (Osgood), 38, 131, 153, 157-158, 162, 172, 185, 194, 209, 225-226, 252

Martin, Abigail, 64, 111-113, 117, 132, 135-136, 157, 188, 217, 244-245, 249

Martin, George, 25

Martin, Mary Pindar, 246

Martin, Samuel, 40, 111, 131-132, 135-136, 157, 178, 217, 227, 244-245, 248-249

Martin, Solomon, 111, 216, 246

Martin, Susanna, 25-26, 28-29, 78, 118, 156

Martin, Thomas, 28

Massachusetts Bay, x-xi, 1, 5, 10, 15, 20, 36, 50, 63, 68, 77, 88, 98, 110, 117, 125, 149, 153, 183, 198, 202, 206, 215-216, 221, 234, 238, 241

Mather, Cotton, 5, 37, 43, 75, 98, 132, 175, 220

Mather, Increase, 6, 153-154, 157-160, 172, 198

Matthews, Hugh, 52

Maverick, Rebecca Wheelwright, 28

Merrill, Hannah, 43, 220

Merrimack River, xi, 44

Miller, Arthur, 15

More Wonders of the Invisible World (Calef), 5

Native Americans, x-xi, xv, 3, 11, 19, 22, 31, 33, 44, 49, 51, 56, 95, 154, 190, 198, 211, 213, 233, 248

Nichols, Elizabeth, 18-19

Nichols, John, 163

Nichols, Lydia, 18-19

Nissenbaum, Stephen, xi, xiv, 35-37, 253-254n3

Norton, Mary Beth, x-xi, 17, 19, 95, 118, 253n1, 254n9

Noyes, Nicholas, 191, 240

Nurse, Francis, 12, 193, 254n8

Nurse, John, 193

Nurse, Rebecca, 5-7, 12, 18, 71, 73, 76, 79, 93, 163, 174, 183, 193-194, 205, 237

Nurse, Samuel, 193

Oliver, Thomas, 16

Osborne, Dorothy, 2

Osborne, Sarah (Warren) (Prince), 2, 4, 6, 237

Osborne, William, 2

Osgood, Abigail, 226

Osgood, Christopher, 75, 153, 157, 162, 165, 178, 185-186, 188-189, 194, 209, 225-227, 251, 259n11

Osgood, Ezekiel, 185

Osgood, Hooker, 156, 192, 224

Osgood, John, 36, 38, 40, 68, 122, 150-153, 156-157, 162, 174, 178-179, 185, 188, 195, 209, 223-225, 240, 251-252

Osgood, Mary (Clements), 40, 119, 122, 146, 150-151, 153, 156, 173, 184, 195, 209, 225-226, 235-236, 241, 249

Parker, Hannah, 232, 236

Parker, John, 193

Parker, Joseph, 44, 193-196, 235-236, 265n12

Parker, Mary Ayer, 40, 110, 124-125, 128, 141, 193, 196, 208-209, 213, 216, 232, 235, 249, 265n2

Parker, Nathan, 44, 46-47, 128, 141, 209, 217, 235-236, 262n17

Parker, Sarah, 209, 260n9

Parker, Thomas, 44

Parris, Betty, 2

Parris, Samuel, xi, xiv-xv, 3, 5-6, 9-10, 12, 14, 17, 20, 42, 117, 149, 190-191, 240, 254n3

Patriots' Day, 15

Peach, Bernard, 78

Peters, Andrew, 178-179, 181, 233

Peters, Elizabeth, 232

Peters, John, 233

Peters, Mercy, 232-233

Peters, Samuel, 233

Peters, William, 233

Phelps, Edward, 250

Phelps, Elizabeth, 250

Phelps, Elizabeth Adams, 250

Phelps, John, 250
Phelps, Samuel, 38, 86, 102, 179, 184, 250
Phelps, Sarah, 86-87, 102, 107, 113, 124, 129, 179, 184, 188, 217, 242-244, 250-251
Phelps, Sarah Chandler, 243, 250
Phillips, Samuel, 189, 191
Phips, William, 16, 121, 125, 136, 162, 164, 176-177, 182, 192, 263n11
Pitman, Charity, 29
Poor, Daniel, 59, 151, 225, 249
Poor, John, 59
Poor, Mary, 59
Poor, Mehitabel Osgood, 151
Post, Hannah, 131, 136-137, 145-146, 158, 210, 263n18
Post, Mary, 129-131, 158, 173, 196, 210, 265n12
Post, Richard, 48-49, 127, 131, 200, 210
Post, Susannah, 131, 136, 145-146, 177, 210
Preston, John, 183, 237
Preston, Jr., Samuel, 183, 201
Preston, Rebecca Nurse, 193
Preston, Roger, 237
Preston, Samuel, 38, 97, 183, 201, 217
Preston, Sarah Bridges, 189, 194
Pritchard, Hannah, 251
Pritchard, William, 251
Privy Council, 154-155, 263n11
Procter, Elizabeth (Bassett), 13, 18, 21, 73, 81, 124, 175-176, 193
Procter, John, 12-13, 18, 21-22, 73, 81, 98, 124, 134-135, 260n7
Pudeator, Ann, 197
Putnam, Ann, 2, 11-12, 20, 23, 26, 59, 102, 107, 124, 128-129, 134
Putnam, Ann (Carr), 11
Putnam, Edward, 17, 88, 98
Putnam, Joseph, 7, 10, 254n8
Putnam, Jr., John, 19
Putnam, Thomas, 2, 5-7, 10-13, 17, 19, 25-26, 88, 97, 102, 129, 134

Quakers, 62-63
Quarterly Court of Essex County, 55

Redd, Wilmot, 29-30
Richards, John, 164
Richardson, Bridget Henchman, 242
Robinson, Enders, 120, 132, 139
Robinson, Joseph, 223
Robinson, Phebe Dane, 38, 193, 223
Rogers, John, 97
Rosenthal, Bernard, 23
Russe, John, 245
Russell, James, 185
Russell, Mary Marshall, 38, 185, 189, 229-230
Russell, Robert, 185
Russell, Thomas, 185
Russe, Margaret, 245
Russ, John, 187, 189

Sadie, Elizabeth Peters, 234
Sadie, John, 38, 152, 210, 232-234, 248
Sadie, Samuel, 232
Safford, John, 188, 217
Salem Story: Reading the Witch Trials of 1692 (Rosenthal), 23
Salem Witchcraft and Hawthorne's House of the Seven Gables (Robinson), 132
Salter, Henry, 110, 146, 172-173, 210-211, 246
Sanders, James, 159, 163
Sargent, Jr., William, 25
Sargent, Mary, 26
Sargent, Thomas, 25
Sargent, William, 25
Scots Charitable Association, 55
Sessions, Elizabeth, 186-187, 202
Sewall, Samuel, 164
Shawsheen River, 68, 93, 98, 115, 131, 143
Sheldon, Susannah, 59
smallpox, 30-32, 58-60, 75, 78, 90, 101, 201, 207, 230, 233-234, 248, 258
Smith, James, 29
Sprague, Jr., Phineas, 138
Sprague, Martha, xvi, 35, 111-113, 115, 117, 124, 131-145, 161, 175, 182-185, 187-188, 217-219, 231, 236, 244-245
Sprague, Phineas, 133, 138, 219

Sprague, Sarah, 133-134
Sprague, Sarah (Hasey), 133, 217, 219
Stacy, William, 77-78
Stevens, Benjamin, 178
Stevens, Ephraim, 178, 192, 218, 228,
    242-243
Stevens, John, 36, 49, 151, 199, 218,
    226-228, 241, 251, 256n2
Stevens, Nathan, 178, 228, 265n4
Stevens, Ruth Poor, 151
Stone, Hannah (Foster), 55-56, 245, 247
Stone, Hugh, 54-56
Stone, John, 55, 73, 245, 247
Stone, Samuel, 43
Stone, Simon, 56
Stoughton, William, 164, 171
Superior Court of Judicature and Court
    of Assize, 137
Swain, Jeremiah, 218
Swan, Dorothy, 137
Swan, Elizabeth, 137
Swan, Elizabeth (Acie), 50, 218
Swan, John, 218, 251
Swan, Jr., Robert, 53
Swan, Robert, 50-53, 86, 137, 218, 251,
    257n13, 258n21
Swan, Ruth, 137
Swan, Samuel, 251
Swan, Sarah, 137
Swan, Timothy, 50-54, 56, 71-72, 74, 79,
    81, 86-87, 91-95, 113, 128-130,
    139, 174, 177, 204, 218, 251,
    259n7, 259n2
Swift, Jane, 197

Tarbell, John, 193
Taylor, Mary, 143, 146, 211, 262n22
Tituba, 3-9, 11, 13-14, 17, 20-22, 71,
    76, 107, 237, 255n9, 259n5
Toothaker, Allen, 30-31, 95-96, 218-219
Toothaker, Margaret, 90, 106, 211,
    260n5
Toothaker, Martha, 53, 81, 90, 103, 173,
    204
Toothaker, Mary (Allen), 30, 53, 57, 90,
    93, 95-96, 99-100, 108, 176, 204,
    211, 218

Toothaker, Roger, 30-31, 53, 90, 93, 99,
    101, 106, 204, 211, 218, 223,
    261n16, 265n1
Towne, Joseph, 163
Tyler, Hannah, 49, 167, 172, 211
Tyler, Hannah Parker, 232
Tyler, Hopestill, 127, 140-141, 153, 158,
    172, 174, 211-212, 231-232, 236
Tyler, Joanna, 123, 140, 174, 212
Tyler, Job, 45-49, 70, 127-129, 132, 140,
    146-147, 186, 229, 231-232, 241,
    243, 262-263n26
Tyler, John, 128, 132, 232, 236, 265n12
Tyler, Jonathan, 186-187, 215
Tyler, Joseph, 135-139, 141-142, 145,
    161, 182-183, 187, 218, 236, 245,
    262n14
Tyler, Martha, 123, 137, 140, 174, 212
Tyler, Mary, 46-47, 119, 128, 130-131,
    133, 135, 140, 145-146, 153, 158,
    167, 173, 200, 210, 215, 229, 231,
    263n18
Tyler, Mary (Lovett), 119, 140, 158, 172,
    211-212, 215, 231
Tyler, Moses, 46-47, 111, 115, 122, 128,
    130-137, 139-142, 145, 147, 161,
    186, 189, 204, 218-219, 227, 231,
    236, 244, 262n14, 265n12
Tyler, Prudence, 48, 130, 133, 161, 204,
    219, 262n14

Wabanaki Confederacy, 3, 19, 95-96
Wade, Elizabeth, 64
Wade, Jonathan, 64
Wade, Nathaniel, 64
Wakely, James, 2
Walcott, Deliverance, 11
Walcott, John, 29
Walcott, Jonathan, 11, 17, 25, 29, 134
Walcott, Mary, 11, 59, 102, 107, 124,
    129, 134
Wardwell, Eliakim, 62-63, 144, 151
Wardwell, Elihu, 64
Wardwell, Elizabeth, 151, 212
Wardwell, Jr., Samuel, 151, 193, 195
Wardwell, Lydia (Perkins), 62-63
Wardwell, Mercy, 66, 173, 182, 186,
    195, 212, 228

Wardwell, Rebecca, 144, 185

Wardwell, Samuel, xvii, 61-70, 83, 124,
    142-144, 146, 150-151, 161, 181-
    182, 185-186, 191, 193, 195, 198,
    206, 212-213, 215, 227-229, 231,
    242, 258n37

Wardwell, Sarah Hooper (Hawkes), 182,
    228-229

Wardwell, Sarah (Hooper), xvi, 65, 142-
    143, 150, 173, 175, 180, 185, 192-
    193, 212, 220, 260n22

Wardwell, Thomas, 63

Wardwell, William, 151, 192

Warren, Mary, 12, 15, 17, 21-24, 70, 74,
    81, 91, 93, 107, 124, 134-135, 140,
    244, 259n5

Webster, John, 51

Webster, Mary, 50-51

Wethersfield, 2

Wilder, Laura Ingalls, 89

Wilford, Ruth, 213

Wilkins, Bray, 85

Wilkins, Daniel, 85

Willard, John, 85, 98

Williams, Abigail, xi, 2, 11, 20, 23

Williams, Robert, 43

Wilson, Joseph, 225, 252

Wilson, Jr., Sarah, 213

Wilson, Sarah, 123, 158, 167-168, 183,
    186

Wilson, Sarah (Lord), 38, 119, 153, 213,
    225-226

Winthrop, John, 33

Winthrop, Waitstill, 164

Witchcraft at Salem (Hansen), 10

Witch Hollow Farm, 134

Wonders of the Invisible World (Mather), 5

Woodbridge, John, 44

Woodman, Edward, 44

Wright, John, 182, 192, 212

Wright, Mercy Wardwell, 195

Wright, Walter, 38, 58, 152, 182, 210,
    232-234